Sexual Divisions:

PATTERNS AND PROCESSES

1992

Sexual Divisions:

PATTERNS AND PROCESSES

Edited by
MARY EVANS
and
CLARE UNGERSON

LIVERPOOL
UNIVERSITY
LIBRARY

FIAT LVX

TAVISTOCK PUBLICATIONS
London and New York

First published in 1983 by
Tavistock Publications Ltd
11 New Fetter Lane,
London EC4P 4EE

Published in the USA by
Tavistock Publications
in association with Methuen, Inc.
733 Third Avenue, New York, NY 10017

Typeset in Great Britain by
Scarborough Typesetting Services
and printed by
J. W. Arrowsmith Ltd., Bristol

*British Library Cataloguing in Publication
Data*
Sexual divisions.
  1. Sex differences—Congresses
  I. Evans, Mary   II. Ungerson, Clare
  305.3   BF692.2
ISBN 0–422–78440–0

*Library of Congress Cataloging in
Publication Data*
  Sexual divisions. "Collection of papers
derives from a conference . . . held at the
University of Kent in April 1980" – Pref.
  1. Women – Great Britain – Social
conditions – Congresses. 2. Women –
Employment – Great Britain – Social
aspects – Congresses. 3. Sex
discrimination in education – Great
Britain – Congresses. 4. Sex
discrimination – Great Britain –
Congresses. 5. Housing – Great Britain
– Congresses. 6. Mental illness – Great
Britain – Congresses. 7. Domestic
relations – Great Britain – Congresses.
I. Evans, Mary, 1936–
II. Ungerson, Clare.
HQ1597.S45 1983   305.4'0941
82–19524
ISBN 0–422–78440–0 (pbk.)

Contents

List of contributors

TESSA BLACKSTONE
Institute of Education, University of London

IRENE BRUEGEL
National Children's Bureau, London

JOAN BUSFIELD
Department of Sociology, University of Essex

BERNARD CORRY
Department of Economics, Queen Mary College, University of London

MARY EVANS
Darwin College, University of Kent at Canterbury

ELIZABETH LEBAS
Graduate School of the Architectural Association, London

MARJORIE MAYO
Haringey Women's Employment Project, London

LINDA McDOWELL
Faculty of Social Sciences, The Open University

JIM NUGENT
Department of Economics, Queen Mary College, University of London

TERESA PERKINS
Department of Sociology, University of Warwick

DAVID SAUNDERS
Department of Economics, Queen Mary College, University of London

JENNY SHAW
Department of Sociology, University of Sussex

CAROL SMART
Addiction Research Unit, Institute of Psychiatry

ERIKA SZYSZCZAK
Rutherford College, University of Kent at Canterbury

CLARE UNGERSON
Keynes College, University of Kent at Canterbury

JENNIE WILLIAMS
Department of Psychology, University of Exeter

Preface

This collection of papers derives from a conference on the institutionalization of sex differences held at the University of Kent in April 1980,
and funded by the SSRC. The conference brought together a number of
researchers – most, but not all, avowedly 'feminist' – all of whom were
engaged in the study of contemporary British social institutions and for
whom the insights derived from consideration of sex and gender had
generated a new impetus to their research. The aim of the conference
was to develop research initiatives, particularly of an interdisciplinary
nature, and to explore the ways in which feminist research can, and
must, be taken on board by the major social science disciplines.

Not all the papers given at the conference are reproduced here, but an
attempt has been made to convey its nature by including the comments
on individual papers made by the discussants at the time. These
comments occasionally indicate a considerable degree of controversy
about both the appropriate concepts and the methodologies available in a
gender-based social science. We consider this inevitable in a relatively
new research area and also see it as a sign of healthy growth and change.
Certainly, the opportunity for authors and discussants to work closely
together to develop their contributions here has promoted friendship
and academic collaboration. Indeed, despite its divided format, this book
seems to have laid the foundation for future solidarity.

We wish to thank the SSRC for funding the conference, and also our
conference secretary, Mrs Siegfried Wright, for typing the papers and
making the wheels run smoothly. Many people contributed to the
conference whose names are not attached to papers here; in particular

Jan Pahl, Thea Sinclair, Ann Marie Wolpe, and Steve Box each chaired one of the sessions and helped us develop the themes of the conference. Above all, the editors are grateful to all the contributors who, due to the format of the book, necessarily had a protracted period of post-conference discussion but nevertheless produced their work in concert at the end, despite the birth of two babies during the process.

Clare Ungerson
Canterbury 1982

Introduction

MARY EVANS

The emergence and sustained growth in the last fifteen years of a tradition of academic feminism have made it increasingly difficult for those working in any academic discipline to continue to assume that the male can be equated with the 'normal' state of human life and that women are some kind of deviant 'other'. The invisibility of women in a great deal of traditional scholarship has been challenged by feminists who have demonstrated that women's contribution to the maintenance and reproduction of the social order is of the utmost significance. Thus it has been shown that the sexual division of labour, with the resultant responsibility that women are deemed to hold for child-care and domestic work, is of fundamental importance in the social relations of all societies. While all societies distinguish between male and female work and, as Margaret Mead (1949) pointed out a generation ago, generally assign greater status to the work done by men, whatever its nature, it is in the most complex, industrialized societies where these distinctions are the most developed and reinforced, and enforced, by the formal institutional structures of these societies. The papers collected in this volume explore various institutional contexts in which the subordination of women is maintained and reproduced. But while the universal subordination of women and their limited appearance in traditional scholarship are central a priori assumptions of these essays, the major issues that are explored here are rather more complex, for while all feminists would accept that women are universally subordinate to men, the degree and means of this subordination are matters of debate. The papers therefore examine specific social institutions in order to illuminate those social processes that both assume and maintain female subordination.

A cursory glance at the majority of social institutions in the industrialized capitalist West (for example, law, the family, the educational system, the trade union movement) demonstrates that they reproduce sexual inequality and the sexual division of labour. In this way they act as ideological state apparatuses in the Althusserian sense, functioning to reproduce the social relations of production (see Althusser 1971; Barrett 1980). The institution in question, be it the law or the education system, takes for granted that the primary social role of women is that of wife and mother. But what also becomes apparent from a study of social institutions, whether repressive or ideological, is that the process through which an ideology of women's 'natural' role is implemented is frequently complex and contradictory. Thus while these papers do not reject the view that women are subordinate and that this subordination is articulated and reproduced in institutional contexts, they all point out that within these contexts a dominant view of women does not necessarily also imply a set of practices or policies that are invariably and only committed to the interests of men rather than women. Two examples may illustrate this point.

First, the idea that women's 'natural' role is that of wife and mother is accompanied by the corollary that women are physically weaker than men and need protection against male sexual violence and the worst conditions of wage labour. Equally, the law of most industrial Western societies demands that women fulfilling their 'natural' functions as wives and mothers should be guaranteed economic support by their husbands. As numerous studies have pointed out, the effectiveness of this protection is far from complete, yet it nevertheless remains the case that at least in law women are seen as in need of specific protection. Thus, despite the fact that the majority of adult women in Great Britain are both wage labourers and wives and mothers, women are still seen as living almost exclusively in the cage of domestic life, a cage that the state sees as the natural habitat of women. While the state explicitly endorses (for example, through its taxation policy) the view that women are primarily wives and mothers, it is also arguably far less interventionist in the lives of women than it is of men. As Mary McIntosh (1978) has pointed out, the full weight of the repressive and punitive apparatus of the state is far more likely to be brought to bear on men than women. Hence in both its written, legal codes and in its formal practices (such as the different attitudes of the police to male and female deviants), the state differentiates sharply between men and women.

But although the state distinguishes both formally and informally between men and women, its view of human beings is more complicated than that of a single dichotomy between male and female. Of the other crucial distinctions that are commonly made between people, differences of social class are by far the most significant. However, the issue of class differences between women is one that raises numerous problems for feminist social scientists, not the least of which is the question of whether or not all women can be said to share a common social class. The question is not the subject of systematic examination in any of the papers included here, but it is nevertheless of such importance that no discussion of the social position of women would be complete without at least some reference to the main arguments.

Essentially, the problem concerns the relative importance of sex and class in the determination of an individual's life chances. No one would deny that both factors have considerable significance; what is at stake is the emphasis that is to be placed on each. For some feminists the position of all women within the division of labour in the family is such that sex, rather than class, is the crucial determinant of social and economic status. It is argued that the domestic role of women ensures that all women, regardless of the relative wealth or poverty in which they fulfil their domestic roles, belong to a single, united class. Other feminists assert that although the great majority of women have domestic responsibilities and share a common, and hitherto inescapable, association with child-care and domestic work, the conditions in which women fulfil these commitments and interact with social institutions outside their immediate family, are vastly different and are determined by their position in the class structure.

However, to say that the social class of women is determined by 'their' position in the class structure is, for feminist social scientists, an intensely problematic description. The first issue that we confront is not specifically feminist, but is familiar to all social scientists. Should we assume a person's class position to be their position in the occupational structure (or, more precisely, their socio-economic status as defined by occupation), or do we mean by class position an individual's relationship to the ownership of the means of production? If the latter description is used and men and women are studied in terms of the extent to which they own productive capital, it is found, at least in the case of Britain, that there are few significant differences between the sexes: the ownership of productive capital is concentrated between approximately equal numbers of men and women (Stark 1977), although the numbers of either sex who own any significant amount of productive capital are extremely small, and for the majority of the population it is wage labour that provides the means of material existence. However, in the case of wage labour, unlike that of the ownership of productive capital, the differences between the sexes are marked. The majority of women enter the labour market with few marketable skills and are concentrated in badly paid, low-status jobs.

It has been traditionally assumed by social scientists that a woman's position within the hierarchy of occupational status and reward is not determined solely by her own occupation, but is also affected by the occupation of her husband or father.[1] Consider, for example, a woman who works as a catering assistant and is married to a man who is a trained and qualified electrician. The woman's own job would place her in the Registrar General's social class IV (semi-skilled manual workers), while classification through her husband's job would place her, with him, in social class III (b) (skilled manual workers). Quite apart from the somewhat dubious significance of having a superior position within the classification of the occupational structure, it could be argued that the woman enjoys, through her husband's occupation, access to the rewards of skilled employment.

The assumption that the primary determinant of a woman's socioeconomic status is the occupation of her husband or father is not one that many feminists would accept uncritically. First, it would be pointed out that women's access to the resources and rewards of their husbands' occupations is far from automatic. The allocation of resources within the household does not always function according to the most stringent rules of equality and distributive justice (see Pahl 1980). Hence, we cannot assume that women always enjoy an absolutely equal share in the resources at the disposal of their husbands or fathers, although both contemporary and historical evidence suggests that poverty and misery are often distributed equally between men and women. Second, it is false to assume that all households are supported by a male wage labourer.[2] Few households now conform to the pattern of a male wage earner with an economically dependent wife and children. Increasingly large numbers of married women are employed, and the number of households with no male wage earner has risen considerably in the last fifteen years. Yet despite these changes, the British state still assumes that all women are, or will be, economically supported by men throughout their lives and that wage labour will be entirely secondary and peripheral to the major social role of women, that of wife and mother. We therefore have a situation in which both the ideological and the repressive apparatuses of the state continue to operate on assumptions about women's social role, their class position, and their relationship to men, that are manifestly in contradiction with reality.

The crucial role that an individual's occupation plays in determining his or her life chances makes it no accident that two of the six essays in this collection are concerned with women and wage labour. Teresa Perkins discusses a major feature of the employment pattern of women, namely that employment for large numbers of women is part-time. Traditionally, it was widely assumed that this situation arose from choice, because women had no economic need for full-time employment and, unlike men, could choose to work only those hours that suited them. Like other assumptions about 'choice' in the capitalist market, this view has now been widely criticized and, in the context of a particular group of women in Coventry, Perkins demonstrates that a belief in women's 'choice' of part-time work is entirely fallacious. Women do not choose to work part-time; part-time work is the only way in which married women, and especially married women with children, can reconcile their domestic responsibilities with their economic needs. Even so, the reconciliation is very far from being a perfect compromise between equally matched partners. The unwritten law of exclusive female responsibility for child-care and the maintenance of the household guarantees that women can only sell their labour power on grossly unequal terms. As Perkins points out, rates of pay, as distinct from total earnings, for part-time work are lower than for full-time work, and job security and fringe benefits are minimal.

A model of the labour market that suggests that the sexes enter employment on equal terms is one that no feminist could accept. Indeed, most would see the situation as quite the reverse, namely that women enter the labour market under the tacit, yet crippling, assumption that their wage labour has a secondary importance to their domestic labour. This view has been so widespread and so influential (and, it must be added, still remains the prevalent assumption about women's employment of many individuals and institutions) that it has been generally impossible for the majority of economists to perceive female unemployment as a feature of the labour market. In the paper by Corry, Nugent, and Saunders, the authors argue that female unemployment has been consistently underestimated or ignored by labour economists, who have been incapable of seeing that women's unemployment is as significant as men's.

The implications of this kind of conceptual blindness about women's wage labour are developed by Irene Bruegel in her remarks on this paper. While accepting that in the case of Corry's, Nugent's, and Saunders's work there is a recognition of women's unemployment, Bruegel goes on to suggest that among labour economists in general the model of the labour market that is used is too narrow (and too much based on the assumption of male experience of employment constituting the norm) to be of much use in the discussion of women's participation in wage labour. Thus the constraints on the participation by women in paid work, and both the formal and informal discrimination against female employees, are generally not part of the discussion of labour economists since the questions are considered irrelevant to the understanding of the labour market as they see it. Indeed, the whole concept of 'employment' is founded on the assumption that paid employment, and participation in the labour market, are the definitive form of work and economic activity in industrial society. Unwaged work cannot be understood within the context of this model because it attracts no financial reward. Yet one of feminism's major contributions to the understanding of the social world has been to show that women's unpaid domestic work (work that takes place outside the labour market) plays a major role in the maintenance of a male paid labour force. We do not need to enter the talmudic intricacies of the debate about the contribution (or otherwise) of domestic labour to the accumulation of surplus value to acknowledge that the responsibilities that women customarily undertake within the home (the care of children, dependent relatives, and male wage labourers) are of crucial importance in the maintenance and reproduction of social life.

Since one of the traditional concerns of sociologists has been the study of the process of socialization, it is hardly surprising that feminist sociologists should also have taken a more than passing interest in the means by which women learn that their primary social role is to be wives and mothers. Peer groups, the mass media, the family, and schools have all been shown to play their part in creating a belief in the normality of the proper place of women being the home. Yet too often the complexity of the process through which women are socialized into their primarily domestic role has been obscured by somewhat simple accounts of the part that various social institutions play in the socialization of girls. These accounts, while rightly stressing the end product of the process of female socialization, tend to imply that a monolithic model of appropriate female behaviour exists, and that this is implemented in a consistent and coherent way by various social institutions. Thus, for example, it would be suggested that schools assume the domestic future of their female pupils and explicitly encourage the development of appropriate female skills and behaviour. As Jenny Shaw argues, the reality of the situation is that although 'schools certainly encourage girls to view marriage and motherhood as important in ways that they do not for boys, these biases are insufficient to explain the form or the direction that the sexual divisions take' (see pp. 100–01).

Therefore, sexual inequalities in educational achievement are not the result of any deliberate policy on the part of a school or the educational system, but of subtle, complex, and implicit assumptions about the appropriate behaviour of boys and girls. In particular, Shaw suggests that 'the models of learning that are used in school lead to distinctions, or differences, that are not inherently sexist or gender based, though they come to be associated with divisions that are' (see p. 98). She points out that subjects that are traditionally thought of as 'boys'' subjects (such as the sciences or mathematics) are those that are taught in such a way as to encourage the development of deductive and systematic thought. 'Girls'' subjects, on the other hand, are those in which creativity and originality are praised and where a more fragmented approach to learning is discernible. Schools are not, therefore, deliberately forcing boys and girls into particular social roles so much as implicitly encouraging in each sex the behaviour and thought processes appropriate for the adult lives of men and women.

The school is far from being the only social institution that can be accused of basing its practices on redundant and narrow sex-role stereotypes. In her paper on women and mental illness, Joan Busfield discusses the complex ways in which common-sense views of women, and their appropriate behaviour, are understood and articulated by doctors and psychiatrists. Busfield begins by pointing out that: 'Women have . . . higher rates of admission to and residence in psychiatric beds; they have higher consultation and episode rates for conditions diagnosed as mental disorders by general practitioners, and, according to field studies, they quite often have higher rates of psychiatric symptomatology than men' (see p. 112). It is tempting to explain this by pointing out that women's social situation is more likely to induce mental stress than is men's. As George Brown and Tirril Harris (1978) have pointed out, women's domestic responsibilities within the nuclear family, together with their associated isolation and dependence, are major contributory factors in the onset of depression in women.

Yet while few feminists would deny that domestic life in the nuclear family as it is presently constituted is often unsatisfactory for women, Busfield argues that it is dangerous to conclude that the apparently higher rates of diagnosis and treatment of mental illness in women are the result of any single explanatory factor. First, as she points out, 'the female predominance among patients with diagnosed mental disorders is not as all pervasive as it seems at first sight' (see p. 112). Second, a crucial factor involved here are assumptions of the diagnostic process that mentally 'disturbed' men and women encounter: who decides what constitutes mental 'illness', and how is the application of the label of mentally 'ill' complicated by the common-sense understanding of appropriate male and female behaviour? In her discussion of definitions of hysteria, Busfield suggests that numerous difficulties exist in distinguishing between the pathological and the normal. As she points out, the description of the hysterical personality in a standard psychiatric textbook is a stereotypically chauvinist description of women by men.

This example suggests that men, or at least those men who write medical textbooks and hence exercise the power of institutionalized knowledge, unquestionably accept some of the general assumptions of Western culture about the proper behaviour and personality traits of men and women. Mentally healthy ('normal') women are expected to be economically dependent on men, but they are not expected to become depressed or over-dependent as a result of this state. We might conclude that the material reality of the lives of many women is supposed to have nothing to do with psychological health or happiness. So strong, and so limited, is the ideology of femininity in our culture that normal female existence − the hearth and home − is expected to furnish all that life might have to offer.

Contemporary feminism has more than amply demonstrated that this is not the case. One of the major arguments of the Women's Movement has been that the division of labour within marriage places a considerable mental and physical burden on women. The domestic responsibilities that women are expected to assume for husbands, children, or dependent relatives have a central, and determining, place in their lives, limiting the opportunities they have for independent action. While this argument has now been well documented, and the isolation and constraints of the life of the housewife vividly described, one particular area of the condition of domestic life remains relatively unexplored, namely the sexual division of space. Linda McDowell's paper explores some of the assumptions that determine, and have determined, the decisions made by town planners and architects in organizing urban space. As she writes, the patriarchal structures of Western capitalism not only influence social relations between men and women but are embodied in the structure of the urban system and are given concrete expression in the built form of cities. One of the features of urban life that emerges from the paper is the spatial separation in cities of industrial societies between wage labour and unpaid domestic labour. Men, it is assumed, will go out to work, while women will stay at home to maintain the domestic space and care for dependants.

The physical segregation and separation of the worlds of men and women that is a consequence of patriarchal assumptions about their respective roles is, as much in industrial capitalism as elsewhere, a feature of that universal distinction between the public male world and the private female world that has been frequently remarked upon by anthropologists. Two aspects of this distinction are significant here. First, in industrial societies it has been predominantly the public world that has been the object of study by social scientists. As we have already seen in the case of economists' perception of the labour market, social scientists in general have largely ignored or overlooked the relationship of those social processes of the private world (in which women are involved) to those of the public world. Other, similar, instances can be suggested that demonstrate the problems that arise when a language and a form of analysis designed principally to study men is used to study women. Thus in their work on power, anthropologists (and to a great extent sociologists as well) have generally examined formal, institutionalized social power and paid little attention to those areas of social life and social relations in which women exercise a degree of power – for example, in the selection of marriage partners, the control of social behaviour in a community, and in the organization and distribution of resources within the household. Equating power with government ignores the informal power of women and assumes that all social power is about the control of public institutions.

While it is important to acknowledge the activities of women in the private domestic world, it would be wrong to imply that female private power is equal to male public power. The exercise of public institutional power and control is virtually exclusively male and is arguably much greater and far more socially significant than that exercised by women in the domestic world. Yet when women become political leaders, as in the case of Mrs Thatcher, it is interesting to note the way in which the traditional values that women are supposed to represent (caring, concern for others, and preoccupation with the minutae of daily life) can easily be turned to political advantage. Jeremy Seabrook and Trevor Blackwell (1982) have argued that Mrs Thatcher has been able to turn the strength of homely but powerful metaphors about the family and domestic life to her own advantage:

> 'This domestic imagery is well known; it is all about "not getting any-thing for nothing", work "not only as a necessity but a virtue", it is the nation as "an extended family", a family which has to "go through hard times" and "postpone cherished ambitions".'
>
> (Seabrook and Blackwell 1982: 7)

What we see here, therefore, is a woman using traditional ideology about women and their concerns to de-politicize public life. Real conflicts within social life become family squabbles that only the all-loving mother can settle since only she knows what is in the interests of family members. An 'iron lady', who commits a country to war or reduces social security benefits can by the very fact of her sex be presented – apparently credibly to many people – as a warm, compassionate, human being who speaks in hushed and patient tones of her real concern for human life.

Mrs Thatcher is, however, an exceptional case in the history of political life and in general it is men who have ruled, and rule. The over-whelming evidence of the public institutional power of men has led many feminists to argue that all the institutions of the state serve the interests of men rather than women. The problems of this view – a generalized assumption of the dominance of sex, rather than class, interests in the organization and functioning of the capitalist state – are discussed by Carol Smart in her paper on English law in the 1950s. She points out that however tempting it is for feminists to assume that the state is organized solely in the interests of men, there are two major problems that challenge this view. First, while the capitalist state is not always, or simply, the 'ruling committee of the bourgeoisie', it is funda-mentally responsible for the continuation of a certain system not merely of sexual domination, but also of class relations. Many socialists and Marxists now widely acknowledge that this does not always take the form of the direct repression of working-class interests. It is accepted that the relationship between the actions of the state and class politics is complex and varied. Indeed, in the case of the relationship between the development of English law and the general interests of the working class, it has been argued, most notably by E. P. Thompson, that: 'The forms and rhetoric of law acquire a distinct identity which may, on occasion, inhibit power and afford some protection to the powerless' (Thompson 1977: 266). Second, while there is a strong case for arguing that the capitalist state is organized in such a way as to ensure the continuation of class and property relations, it is much more difficult to demonstrate that the state is solely, and inevitably, concerned with the interests of men rather than women.

Carol Smart argues that these qualifications should guard us against a too rapid assertion that the law and its practitioners always act in the interests of men rather than women. She writes: 'the outcome of rape trials and the "unwillingness" of law to protect women against domestic violence has led to a situation in which the law as a whole is implicitly taken to be an instrument of patriarchal oppression. . . . But the idea that the law simply serves the interests of men against those of women and that legislation and legal practice is constantly guided by these principles does not stand up to closer examination' (see p. 182). In her study she goes on to suggest a number of reasons why an assumption of the law as an instrument of patriarchal power is untenable. First, the courts were remarkably eager to enforce the husband's marital duty to maintain his wife or ex-wife. Second, although many courts were often particularly harsh in their interpretation of women's rights on divorce, particularly their property rights, they were increasingly likely to grant the custody of children to wives rather than husbands. Inevitably, this merely reflected and reinforced the existing sexual division of labour, but what it also did was to establish a firm, and legally recognized, relationship between those who bear, and those who care for, children.

As Smart stresses, English law 'saw' women in the 1950s as essentially wives and mothers. The duty of the law was therefore interpreted by its practitioners as one of sustaining a particular family form in which women were economically dependent on men and had the sole responsibility for caring for children. So limited was the law's view of women that any deviation from their given role as angel in the house, whether by adultery or homosexuality, was immediately punished in divorce cases by the loss of those fragile rights that women possessed. Lord Denning put the case particularly clearly when he remarked, in 1950, that 'the morality of the race depends on the morality of the womenfolk' (see p. 190). Yet the different moral standards that Western culture demands of men and women has the effect, in certain circumstances, of protecting women from the consequences of their actions. For example, it is now widely noted that female deviants are dealt with less harshly than male.

So great is the belief in female dependence and moral childishness that women who commit crimes are frequently perceived as misguided rather than bad (see Millman 1975).

The less severe punishments that women deviants receive is one of the few examples that can be cited when general assumptions about femininity and appropriate female behaviour favour women. In general, as these papers suggest, the social construction of the category of women works to their disadvantage in that they are less able than men to acquire the occupational skills and power that allow a measure of personal autonomy and power in social bargaining. But it would be wrong to assume from this that the needs that receive priority in social organization and institutional structures are quite simply and straightforwardly those of all men. It may well be the case that some men benefit from some of the institutional arrangements of industrial capitalism, but it is premature to conclude that those benefits extend to all men, and no women. To borrow a phrase from Carol Smart: 'is male interest an homogeneous concept that is so easily identified?' (see p. 181). As the papers in this collection suggest, the perception of women by the state and its institutional structures is largely uniform and yet significant differences *are* demonstrable in the social condition of women, differences that are related to their own (or their husband's or father's) position within the class structure of industrial capitalism.

The worst excesses of that class structure have for decades been the target of working-class organizations. Women, men, and male politicians have struggled to improve the conditions of working-class life. Yet the very successes of some of the campaigns of organized labour − for the family wage, and improvements in working-class housing, for example − were in part based on the effective manipulation of the ideology that states that women's natural, and only, social role was that of wife and mother, economically dependent on a man. 'Homes fit for heroes' and social security from 'cradle to grave' were slogans that invoked visions of the deservedly rewarded working man going home to his loving, faithful, and dependent wife. Indeed, it could be argued that the more the state tried to improve the condition of the family, the more it imprisoned women, and particularly working-class women, within it. By invoking a model of the ideal nuclear family (a male wage earner with dependent wife and children) it forced working-class women to identify more firmly with male and household interests. In terms of the long-term development of class solidarity and cohesion this might be regarded as one of the positive results of the patriarchal assumptions of the capitalist state, but as far as working-class women themselves were concerned it left them in a situation of having to conduct all their social bargaining through men, with little recourse to those privileges of education or financial independence enjoyed by middle-class women. While some middle-class women have benefited from such reforms as the educational innovations of Butler and Robbins and are often, although by no means always, in a position to benefit from assumptions about their 'natural' social role, working-class women have gained relatively little from institutionalized social reform. Hence, by virtue of their access to certain forms of scarce social and material resources middle-class women may be able either to mitigate or take advantage of the consequences of sexual stratification. But no such option exists for working-class women. For them, the institutionalized ideology of female dependence is without alleviation or mitigation.

Notes

1 Most explicitly stated by Frank Parkin: 'Although women today share certain status attributes in common, simply by virtue of their sex, their claims over resources are not primarily determined by their own occupation but, more commonly, by that of their fathers or husbands' (Parkin 1971: 15).
2 The disappearance of the 'traditional' family has been documented by Hilary Land (1975).

References

Althusser, L. (1971) *Lenin and Philosophy and Other Essays*. London: New Left Books.
Barrett, M. (1980) *Women's Oppression Today*. London: Verso.
Brown, G. and Harris, T. (1978) *The Social Origins of Depression*. London: Tavistock.
Land, H. (1975) The Myth of the Male Breadwinner. *New Society* 9 October: 71–3.
McIntosh, M. (1978) The State and the Oppression of Women. In A. Kuhn and A. M. Wolpe (eds) *Feminism and Materialism*. London: Routledge & Kegan Paul.
Mead, M. (1949) *Male and Female*. New York: William Morris.
Millman, M. (1975) She Did it All for Love: A Feminist View of the Sociology of Deviance. In M. Millman and R. Kanter (eds) *Another Voice: Feminist Perspectives on Social Life and Social Science*. New York: Doubleday.
Pahl, J. (1980) Patterns of Money Management in Marriage. *Journal of Social Policy* **9** (3): 313–35.
Parkin, F. (1971) *Class Inequality and Political Order*. London: MacGibbon and Kee.

Seabrook, J. and Blackwell, T. (1982) Suffering Thatcher for the Sake of her Visions. *The Guardian* 3 May: 7.
Stark, T. (1977) The Distribution of Income in Eight Countries. Background paper to Report 5 to the Royal Commission on the Distribution of Income and Wealth. Cmnd 6999. London: HMSO.
Thompson, E. P. (1977) *Whigs and Hunters*. Harmondsworth: Penguin.

1

A new form of employment: a case study of women's part-time work in Coventry

TERESA PERKINS

In this paper I discuss some of the work carried out during the first stage of a project on women's part-time employment in Coventry.[1] It is not, therefore, a general overview of the topic of part-time employment, but rather a discussion of ongoing research in which I describe the statistical evidence about employment in a particular town, and discuss some of the explanations that might be offered to account for this evidence. I attempt to highlight the research process and draw attention to both the difficulties of, and the possibilities for, feminist research at this level. I then focus more specifically on part-time employment and the inter-pretation of employment statistics related to part-time employment in order to draw out the ways in which the concept of part-time employ-ment is problematic, and to discuss the implications for theories of women's work in general, and for our research in particular.

The project focused on the determinants of women's part-time employment in a particular local labour market. Part-time employment has expanded rapidly over the last fifteen years. It is almost entirely a female form of employment, and is becoming increasingly the *typical* form of female employment. The first stage of the project was the collec-tion, analysis, and evaluation of national and local statistics on women's employment. The second stage involved interviewing employers and trade unionists in various sectors (bread and confectionery, machine tools, electrical engineering, hospitals, social services, education, and food distribution) to discover the conditions under which women part-timers are drawn into, and expelled from, the labour force, the types of jobs they are drawn into, the relationship between their employment and the form of the labour process, the availability of training, and other aspects of their terms and conditions of employment. We also had discussions with women in part-time employment about their experience of employment. It was originally planned that the third phase of the project would consist of interviews with part-timers to discover their job histories but the constraints of time meant that this part of the project had to be dropped. The discussions we had with part-timers tended to focus on their current employment to provide us with a better understanding of this situation, rather than on the way it fits into their personal history. Finally, we looked at the legislative and institutional context of part-time employment in order to consider the problems of, and possibilities for, change.

In the initial stages of a research project there are a variety of general questions that need refining. Researchers bring to a project presuppositions and theoretical frameworks that inform the questions they find relevant. They will have been influenced by other explanations that have been given about the topic. This project was set up by Veronica Beechey in the belief that the phenomenon of women's part-time employment had been insufficiently studied. The subject has tended either to be ignored or to be incorporated, uncritically, into existing theories about women's employment.[2] This lack raised questions about the availability and adequacy of the sort of evidence that is, or could be, used to support or refute existing explanations of the growth of part-time employment. There were also more specific questions relating, for example, to the main characteristics of the local labour market, the structure of local industry, and the weight that should be attached to such features. As this is not primarily a theoretical paper, I can sketch only very generally the ways in which I felt existing explanations of women's work were unsatisfactory in order to provide a context for the way I approached the statistical analysis.

In considering the sorts of explanations of women's work that are most commonly given, it seemed that the theoretical explanations tended to be abstract and highly selective in their use of empirical evidence, frequently leaving out of their accounts discussion of a large proportion of women workers. On the other hand, the more empirically grounded analyses are more comprehensive but mainly descriptive; theoretically they rarely go beyond identifying discrimination (in some form) as the sole explanatory variable needed to account for the pattern of female employment. Consequently, both approaches tend to provide oversimplistic accounts of women's work because they identify differences between men's and women's employment as the only feature of women's employment that requires or merits explanation. They adopt a monolithic view of women's employment based on this difference. It is perhaps worth noting that the analysis of male employment never starts from, nor even takes into account, this difference.

The theoretical arguments that we felt contributed most to our understanding of women's employment have adopted a Marxist perspective, and it is from this perspective that we would expect more adequate explanations to be developed. So far, the most influential contribution that Marxists have made to the analysis of female waged labour has been through the application of Marx's reserve army of labour thesis (see Bruegel 1979; Marx 1961). It has been argued that, because of their particular location in the family, women are particularly available as a disposable source of labour power and can be drawn into, and thrown out of, the labour force relatively easily in response to capital's crises and varying needs for labour. There is evidence that women are used in this way, and to that extent it can be said to be a useful way of understanding women's position in the labour market. But this thesis is not sufficiently developed to allow an analysis of different forms of employment, and the recent emphasis on women as the reserve army of labour has not only distorted the thesis but, in emphasizing only this aspect, has also had the effect of theoretically marginalizing women's work, once again encouraging a monolithic view that cannot embrace the variety of ways in which women's labour is used. One problem of the way in which the thesis has been applied is the tendency to conflate the characteristics of an occupation with the characteristics of the occupant. In fact, there have been relatively few attempts to demonstrate (as opposed to assert) the validity of the thesis; more seriously from our point of view we found that there has been little discussion of the sort of evidence that is needed to support it. One attempt to test the thesis was made by Irene Bruegel (1979) in a useful article that starts with a clear and succinct appraisal of the debate. Bruegel goes on to argue (and attempts to show by statistical analysis) that women do fit into one version of the reserve army model and that 'it is part-time women workers . . . who conform most closely to the model of women as a disposable reserve army' (Bruegel 1979: 18). Despite her awareness of the problems of the debate, Bruegel does not seem to me to give enough consideration to the suitability of the evidence she uses to support her argument, and especially to the problems raised by introducing the phenomenon of part-time work into the analysis. Although she comments that 'in certain areas of work, their [part timers'] numbers are still increasing rapidly', and notes that part-time women workers 'form an increasing proportion of women workers' (Bruegel 1979: 18), there is no room in her analysis for consideration of these observations. One is left with the impression that *all* part-timers are used in the way that, undoubtedly, *some* are.

NB . Not all PTs disadvan.

While it is essential that explanations of women's employment do attempt to account for, and highlight, women's difference from and/or (enforced) inferiority to men in the labour market, and the relationship between this and their domestic situation, this cannot be our only concern. Nor should it always be our starting point. (The problem is not, of course, confined to the analysis of work but affects all feminist research. How can we avoid the trap of theoretically marginalizing women and thereby lending support to their ideological marginalization?) It seems important that we do not encourage the view that the only thing that is interesting about women's work is how it differs from male employment – which we will have to construct in a similarly general-ized category in order to make comparisons. We can start by recognizing that there is a common denominator, an abstract way in which male and female labour is similar, namely that both provide labour power that is organized and controlled, and used in a variety of ways. If we assume that in the abstract both sexes are equally useful as labour power then we must ask under what circumstances and for what reasons this is not realized in practice. In order to understand why women's labour takes a particular form at a particular place and time we have to study the way in which its use has been determined by a variety of processes, some of which may be sex-specific, rather than explaining, tautologically, the form taken by female employment as a consequence of its being female. The question 'Why is this the form taken by labour in this instance?' needs to be asked in place of the explanation 'This form exists because the labour is supplied by women'. They are, of course, sometimes two sides of the same coin. In practice, however, it means that the point at which we accept an explanation as adequate is different. We do not assume that part-time labour exists solely because the jobs are filled by women with children. While that explanation may have validity at a certain level, we must bear in mind that the existence of women's full-time employment (either in similar or in different jobs) may invalidate that explanation at another level. We need to look, therefore, at the way in which a particular use of part-time labour fits into the labour process and the overall organization of the division of labour.

I am suggesting that we need to move towards developing explanations of women's work that include an account of its complexity and variety as well as its specificity. We need to show also that these explanations are a necessary part of *any* adequate account of the organization of the division of labour in capitalist society and are not relevant only to the analysis of women's participation.

From a research point of view, the object of the initial stage of the project was to see how helpful the statistics could be in illuminating and refining questions concerning the determinants of women's part-time employment. It also served an important 'mapping-out' function, indicating in broad terms the sectors in which women are, or are not, employed part-time, and allowing us to identify the ways in which national patterns were reflected locally. The assessment of existing explanations, and our own research objectives, gave rise to the following questions, which inform the rest of the paper:

1 In what ways does Coventry's industrial structure affect women's employment? How important are local traditions and characteristics for understanding the current employment situation in Coventry?

2 How has the amount and distribution of women's employment, especially their part-time employment, changed since the mid-1960s? How varied is the use of part-time labour?

3 It has often been suggested that there is a trend to increased female participation in the labour force that is taken to be an irreversible social change. This implies that the trend is an independent variable reflecting an ever-increasing *supply* of female labour (at least until such time as all women are economically active). Was this the case, or was it a dependent one, reflecting a demand for female labour? Or were some other factors involved?

4 Politicians, civil servants, and some theorists have attached much importance to the correlation between the increase in women's economic activity and the expansion of the service sector, and have argued that this correlation has explanatory status. How should we interpret this correlation?

5 How can statistics on part-time employment be compared to statistics on full-time employment?

6 Why does Great Britain have such a high proportion of part-time workers compared to other Western countries? (This question is not one that can be answered within our project, but rather serves to remind one of the possible influence of national characteristics,

such as legislative arrangements, the specific organization of the labour movement, or differences in national mores.)

Before moving on to the discussion of the statistics relating to employment in Coventry, some cautionary remarks about statistics need to be made. Employment statistics generally leave much to be desired, and those relating to female employment are notoriously inadequate (see EOC 1980; Hurstfield 1978; Oakley 1979). Perhaps the first point to be made is that women's position in the labour force, and their position in the family itself, have an impact on the reliability and/or validity of statistics. For example, there are proportionately many more women than men among the low-paid; since some statistics count only employees who are paying tax, and are therefore earning a certain amount, this leads to an underestimate of the number of women who are working; some statistics count only employees and exclude the self-employed or casual worker; and statistics on part-time employment are even more subject to these sources of bias. Similarly, unemployment statistics are particularly affected by women's position in the family, and by the preponderance of part-time work done by women. Unemployment statistics are based on those who are registered as wholly unemployed rather than those who are looking for work or who have lost their jobs. Whereas the vast majority of men who are not in employment will be registered as unemployed, this is not the case for women. Many women may not be eligible for unemployment benefit, or may be eligible only for a short time, and are then both less likely than men to register as unemployed when they lose their jobs, and less likely to stay on the register for a long period if and when they do register. Furthermore, women who are looking for part-time employment are more likely to have opted out of the insurance scheme, or to have earned too little to pay insurance stamps, and therefore they probably will not register at all. Thus, the extent of female unemployment is always underestimated in the statistics, and the extent of long-term female unemployment is even less likely to be accurate.

While this underestimation of long-term female unemployment partly reflects the differences in social security arrangements and so on, it also reflects the differences between men's and women's experience of unemployment and domestic life. The woman who is unable to get a job after a few months may simply 'disappear' back into the home and will be omitted from employment statistics altogether (she will cease to be 'economically active'). It is probably as difficult for a married woman to remain 'unemployed' as it is for a man without a job not to be classified as 'unemployed'. The woman who continues to sign on even when she receives no tangible benefits from doing so must be rare indeed. A man, of course, will generally only be able to receive benefit (unemployment or supplementary) if he does sign on and remains available for work.

While allowances can be made for such sources of bias – for example, by comparing official statistical series to special surveys designed to assess the extent of the bias – the allowances have to assume a constant and unchanging relationship between 'visible' and 'invisible' unemployment. This may be a false assumption that conceals precisely those changing relationships in which we are most interested. A variety of factors is likely to affect the ratio between registered (visible) and unregistered (invisible) unemployed women – for example, the rate of male unemployment, demand for female labour, and cost of living rises.

One way of checking unemployment statistics if we are interested in how many people have lost jobs recently is to compare the numbers in employment in different industries from month to month, or year to year. While this cannot tell us about those women who have rejoined the labour market, it can give us some idea of the numbers who have lost jobs and who may not be registering. Between 1971 and 1978 an annual census of employment was conducted by the Government. Employers were asked to state how many male full-time, male part-time, female full-time, and female part-time employees they had in their employment in one particular week of the year. While this information was undoubtedly important, it was still inadequate. For example, small employers were only asked to complete returns every three years, and it may well be that female part-timers are more highly represented in those small establishments. As the census was not carried out in 1979, nor in 1980, information about how women's employment was affected as the recession deepened was severely restricted. As anyone who has looked through government statistics will have noticed, most of them are collected in such a way as to render women's employment less visible and more unitary. Many statistical tables relate only to men in full-time employment; even more refer only to full-timers and ignore part-timers. There is no information about part-timers' overtime or short-time (indeed the concepts seem to be rarely used in relation to part-timers); and occupational statistics about typically male occupations are considerably more comprehensive than those about female occupations. These examples are by no means exhaustive and are chosen simply to illustrate the problems that beset those engaged in research into women's work.

Although such problems become even more severe when one is using statistics over a long time period, the importance of the statistics as a source of information also increases. There is, after all, no other way of obtaining an overall picture of employment and its changing patterns in a particular town, country, or historical period. So, while such inadequacies are undoubtedly serious, we did not feel that we should dismiss the value of a statistical analysis, but rather be especially cautious and sensitive in our use of them.

Coventry

Coventry is said to have been the fastest growing town in Britain, for the first half of the century at least. By 1951 the population was more than three and a half times the population in 1901. Between 1927 and 1951 the population virtually doubled. Seventy-one per cent of this increase was due to *migration into* the city rather than to natural increase.[4] It is the only town of its size, and one of the few in the country to have a larger male than female population. This has been true at least since 1951, and probably was before that. Since 1951 Coventry has had a higher proportion of married women, with a greater tendency for them to marry young, a higher proportion of young children, and a lower proportion of old people. Since 1951 the numbers coming into the city have declined, and for most of the 1950s migration and natural increase contributed in almost equal parts to the total growth of the city. More recently, natural increase contributed more than migration, and it appears that in recent years there has been a net migration out of the city. The importance and causes of migration into a city, and its effects on the operation of a local labour market, are clearly factors that have to be borne in mind, especially when considering questions of labour supply.

One way of measuring women's participation in the labour force is by the rate of economic activity. The 'activity rate' of a particular group (say women) refers to the proportion of that group (usually within a particular age range) who are either in employment or are unemployed but seeking employment. These activity rates are usually calculated from the census of the population conducted every ten years.[5] It is the increase in these rates, and particularly in the married women's economic activity rate, that has been so marked during this century and which is taken to represent a fundamental social change.

For a long time, activity rates have been higher for both men and women in the West Midlands than they are nationally. For women they have been the highest in the country. Although both regional and national female activity rates have been increasing, the gap between them seems to be narrowing. In *Table 1* the activity rates for Great Britain and Coventry are compared. The activity rates for Coventry are considerably higher than the national rates, but the patterns are the same, with an overall increase in female rates, and a decline, since 1931, of male rates. It is important to note that there has been a major change in the distribution of married and single women's activity rates since 1931, with an acceleration of married women's rates since 1961. This change in distribution reflects various demographic, legal, and social changes.[6] While Coventry's high female activity rate might lead one to assume that women form a larger proportion of the total labour force than they do nationally, this is not the case. This surprising feature is explained partly by the demographic peculiarities mentioned above – for example, the higher than average proportion of men and of young people in the population. Since 1971 the increase in women's economic activity has continued, and it is estimated now that more than half Britain's married women are economically active. (Figures comparable to the 1971 census are not yet available.)

Table 1 *Economic activity rates, and women as a percentage of the work-force, 1911–71: Great Britain and Coventry*

	Males All	Females All	Married	Single (Divorced and Separated)	Women as % of labour force GB	Coventry
1911	83.8	32.5	8.7	53.8	29.7	
1921	87.1	32.3	8.7	53.8	29.5	
1931	90.5	34.2	10.0	60.2	29.7	
1941			no census			
1951	87.6 (93.7)	34.7 (37.1)	21.7	55.0	30.8	28.5
1961	86.0	37.4 (41.8)	29.7	30.6	32.5	38.8
1966	84.0	42.4 (46.4)	32.1 (42.3)	49.2 (55.5)		34.67
1971	81.4	42.7 (46.4)	42.2 (45.1)	43.7 (49.1)	36.5	35.6

Source: Census of Population. Figures in brackets refer to Coventry.

INDUSTRIAL STRUCTURE

Even when compared to other towns in the 'manufacturing Midlands', Coventry is a city whose industrial structure is more than typically dominated by manufacture. Furthermore, analysis of regional employment

Figure 1 Analysis of employment by sector, June 1975

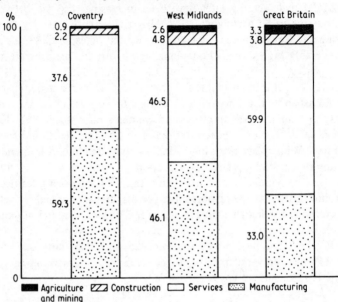

Source: Census of Employment.

statistics shows that Coventry's manufacturing industry is less diversified than other towns'. Nearly all Coventry's manufacturing employment is concentrated in metal-based manufacturing, a large proportion of which is in the car industry. This emphasis on manufacturing, and the extreme concentration within manufacturing on one or two major industries, has been a characteristic of Coventry since the nineteenth century and has been a source of both its strength and its vulnerability. It partly explains Coventry's relatively long periods of high employment and high wages as well as its periodic crises, and the way in which national crises have had specific (although not always bad) effects on the city.[7] We are witnessing the effects of one such periodic crisis at the moment with the collapse of the UK car industry and the effects of the recession on engineering. This has led to a much larger and more rapid increase in the rate of unemployment, which is now about 2 per cent higher than the national rate.

The relative importance of manufacturing to Coventry's industrial structure is illustrated in *Figure 1*, and in *Table 2* we can see how this employment is distributed among different sectors and how it is reflected

Table 2 Proportion of men and women in different sectors of the economy: Coventry, West Midlands, and Great Britain 1975

Employment as a percentage of total employment

	Coventry			West Midlands			Great Britain		
	Males %	Females %	Total %	Males %	Females %	Total %	Males %	Females %	Total %
Agriculture	0.2	0.2	0.2	0.2	0.2	0.2	2.2	1.1	1.7
Mining	0.9	0.04	0.7	0.3	0.0	0.2	2.5	0.2	1.6
Manufacturing									
Metal-based	67.3 ⎱73.4	26.7 ⎱31.2	53.8 ⎱59.3	50.3 ⎱60	25.9 ⎱34.5	41.1 ⎱50.4	22.8 ⎱39.0	9.1 ⎱24.3	17.3 ⎱33.1
Non-metal-based	6.1	4.5	5.5	9.7	8.6	9.3	16.2	15.2	15.8
Construction	2.9	0.7	2.2	6.6	1.3	4.6	8.9	1.1	5.7
Services									
Gas, electricity, and water	0.8	0.4	0.7	1.5	0.9	1.3	2.1	0.7	1.5
Transportation and distribution	7.4 ⎱22.4	17.3 ⎱68.2	10.7 ⎱37.5	13.5 ⎱32.9	17.6 ⎱64.1	15.0 ⎱44.6	18.3 ⎱47.4	19.6 ⎱73.3	18.9 ⎱57.9
Other services	6.3	21.4	11.1	8.6	19.1	12.5	13.1	22.3	16.8
Public administration, education, and health	7.8	29.1	15.0	9.3	26.5	15.8	13.9	30.7	10.7
Total	100	100	100	100	100	100	100	100	100

Source: Department of Employment.

in the sexual distribution of employment in Coventry, the West Midlands, and Great Britain. Comparing the figures for females employed in metal-based manufacture, it is clear that in both Coventry and the West Midlands a considerably higher proportion of women work in these sectors (26.7 per cent for Coventry compared to 9.1 per cent for Great Britain). However, if we take manufacturing as a whole, the difference is not nearly so great: in fact, although a higher proportion (7 per cent) of women are employed in manufacturing in Coventry compared to Great Britain, there is a lower proportion than in the West Midlands. For men, however, the pattern is rather different and the variation between Coventry, the West Midlands, and Great Britain is considerably greater. Almost three-quarters (73 per cent) of Coventry's male employees were employed in manufacturing, compared to 59 per cent of the West Midlands', and 39 per cent in Great Britain. More than two-thirds of Coventry's men were employed in metal-based manufacture. Conversely, only 22.4 per cent of Coventry's employed men were employed in the services compared to 47.4 per cent of Great Britain's.

In general terms, the pattern that emerges is one of considerable divergence from the national average for male employees, particularly in Coventry. For women, the divergence from the national pattern is less marked. The proportion of women in Coventry employed in various sectors is quite similar to the proportion in Great Britain as a whole. So the dominance of manufacturing over Coventry's employment structure and its small service sector was hardly reflected in the pattern of female employment; even in Coventry, with nearly three-quarters of the men in manufacturing, women's work was overwhelmingly and disproportionately in the services.

One way of explaining this would be to argue that the services are 'women's work', and this would be consistent with the claim that it is the expansion of the service sector (with jobs suited to women) that accounts for the increase in female economic activity. This argument points to the fact that the expansion of the service sector over the past fifty years, and particularly since the Second World War, has occurred at the same time as the increase in women's economic activity. However, the nature of the relationship between high female activity rates and the expansion of the service sector is not as unproblematic as this suggests. As discussed above, within the country as a whole, the West Midlands, characterized by a heavy concentration in manufacturing rather than services, is also the region with the highest female activity rate. Within that region, Solihull, which has the highest proportion (63 per cent) of employment in the services, has the lowest female activity rate, and Sandwell, which has the lowest proportion (30 per cent) of service employment, has the highest female activity rate. There is, then, no simple relationship between the size of the service sector and women's economic activity rate. That relationship only exists over time, and not at any particular time. If we accept the explanation that the increase in women's economic activity is a consequence of the expansion of the service sector with jobs suited to women, then, by implication, we also accept the assertion that previously there were no such jobs and, by inference, that manufacturing is not 'women's work'. Although there are probably few analysts who would argue this position to extremes, it seems to have achieved the status of a 'common sense' assumption that does not require investigation. When one is faced with such an overwhelmingly strong female presence in the service sector it is easy to understand why it may *seem* that the explanation for this presence must have something to do with some inherent ('feminine') characteristic of the sort of work that distinguishes this sector from others.

One of the beliefs (or prejudices) with which I approached the analysis of statistics was that the emphasis on the relationship between women's increased activity rate and the expansion of the service sector led to (or arose from) the following analytical weaknesses: (i) ignoring the substantial involvement of women in other sectors of the economy; (ii) *exaggerating* the *increase* in women's participation in the labour force – or perhaps, more accurately, understating the extent to which women *have always* provided a substantial amount of labour; and (iii) ignoring the class composition of working women as a significant variable. I will return briefly to the last point later on, since it concerns more general problems of conceptualizing women's work. It is the first two points that inform the next part of the discussion.

Women in manufacturing

The discovery that Coventry's manufacturing industry had little effect on the pattern of women's employment in 1976 was surprising and seemed to undermine my preconception that women were substantially involved in manufacturing. This preconception was based partly on local knowledge and partly on my assumption that the high female economic activity rate in Coventry, and other manufacturing areas, was a reflection of women's involvement in manufacturing industry. The next stage in the analysis involved assessing the extent to which that preconception had some validity, at least as far as statistics could reveal.

In Coventry, as elsewhere, the service sector has expanded considerably since the War, but the rate of increase has rarely matched the national increase. Indeed, for a city of its size Coventry has one of the smallest service sectors in the country.[8] In so far as it has expanded in Coventry, the service sector has relied heavily on women's participation. Furthermore, it has had an immense impact on the distribution of women's employment in Coventry. Between 1951 and 1971 there was a complete reversal of the proportions of women who were employed in manufacturing and those employed in services. In 1951, 60 per cent of Coventry's employed women were in manufacturing; by 1971, 61.7 per cent of them were in the services, and this trend has continued. The first question, then, is how much of this shift has been accomplished by an increase in the numbers of women, that is women being drawn into the labour force in order to work in the services (and this is the implication behind the arguments discussed above), and how much has been accomplished by a *shift* from manufacturing to the services?

Between 1951 and 1961 there was an increase of 3,453 women in manufacturing, and an increase of 5,273 in the services.[9] Between 1961 and 1971 a very different pattern emerged. The number of women in manufacturing declined by 6,799, while the number in the services increased by 13,994. The trend continued between 1971 and 1976 with an increase in the services of 6,860 and a decline in manufacturing of 5,255. Between 1961 and 1976, then, there was a 40 per cent decline in the number of women in manufacturing. In other words, 12,054 women had either been sacked or had voluntarily left their jobs in manufacturing and had not been replaced by other women. So the actual increase in the *total* number of employed women between 1961 and 1976 was only 8,800, an increase of 16 per cent. *Figure 2* shows the distribution of female employment between 1951 and 1976, and the proportion of women employed in each sector that employed more than 1 per cent of Coventry's women workers from 1971 to 1976. The decline in the importance of the three main manufacturing industries (engineering, vehicles, and textiles) was dramatic after 1961. The picture would be even more dramatic today.

The first point to emphasize is that there has been a numerical as well as a proportional shift of women workers from manufacturing to the services. However, we cannot tell what has caused this, nor whether the same women were involved. A number of questions need to be answered in order for us to understand what lies behind this shift and what, as a consequence, we may argue about the nature of women's involvement in

Figure 2 Sectors employing more than 1 per cent of Coventry's female work-force: 1951, 1961, 1971, 1976

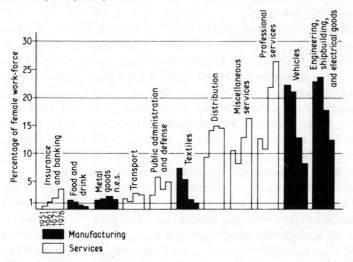

Source: Department of Employment.

the service sector. For example, did women who were dismissed from their jobs in manufacturing then find jobs in the services, or did they give up their jobs in manufacturing (for family reasons) and were then not replaced by other women? In either case, did the demand for female labour in manufacturing decline, was it that the jobs that women were doing disappeared, or was there a general decline in the demand for labour? Alternatively, was the shift to the services voluntary – did women leave in order to take up or look for jobs in the services? If so, what factors influenced that decision – higher wages, more attractive jobs, better conditions, shorter hours, or more flexible hours? Did the shift from manufacturing represent a change in occupations, or was it merely a question of changing employers but remaining, for example, a typist or a cleaner? If women left voluntarily, where did employers turn to fill the vacancies? Did they recruit white male labour from outside Coventry or immigrant labour from within? If the vacancies were not filled, was the lost labour power replaced by increasing productivity, or by increasing male overtime? Most of these questions cannot be answered by statistical analysis but require instead detailed historical and ethnographic research. However, it is important to point up these sorts of questions in order to illustrate that the processes underlying women's involvement in the services are complex and problematic, and involve consideration of more than simplistic assumptions about 'women's work'.

Despite the above reservation, statistics can be useful. *Table 3*, taken from the population censuses for 1961, 1966, and 1971, suggests that (assuming for the moment that the same women were involved) for many women what was involved was not merely a change of employer but also a change of occupation. Moreover, trends within manufacturing were not the same. Textiles declined throughout the period, and the numbers of *both* male and female weavers declined. In electrical engineering there was a rise in the number of women employed between 1961 and 1966, followed by a larger decline between 1966 and 1971. For men, however, there was no change in male assemblers, and only a very small overall decline. In engineering there was the same pattern of increase between 1961 and 1966 and decline between 1966 and 1971. But whereas the numbers of female machine tool operators declined by thirty-three (330), the numbers of male machine tool operators increased between 1966 and 1971 by twenty-five (250).[10] None of this evidence is conclusive of course. Since these are occupational statistics, they can tell us neither whether the same employers nor even the same indstry were involved. However, our field-work has provided us with more information on this. For example, in the machine tool industry we found that in two firms there had been women machine tool operators in the 1960s, virtually all of whom disappeared during this period. This was achieved partly through 'natural' wastage and partly in the first round of redundancies. When the industry recovered, briefly, the women were replaced by men. This seems to have been the result of a complex of factors: partly changes in trade union bargaining power and the introduction of new pay arrangements, and the defence of skills, which, indirectly, had the effect of excluding women because they had not served apprenticeships; and partly the consequence of changes in technology and in products, which brought an end to the jobs on small machine tool production that previously women had done.

The shifts in clerical occupations followed the same pattern of increase between 1961 and 1966 and declined thereafter (except for clerks and cashiers), but we do not know how this was distributed between manufacturing and the services. The decline in typists and secretaries was surprising and interesting. Certainly the figures for clerical workers suggest that we must be cautious about assuming too much stability for these occupations. It is perhaps too easy to forget that female clerical work is

Table 3 Numbers of women in selected occupations in Coventry: 1961, 1966, 1971

Occupational group and most important subdivisions	1961	Direction of change	1966	Direction of change	1971	Change 1966–71	Overall change 1961–71
Electrical engineering	190	+	233	–	167	–66	–23
Assemblers	112	+	144	–	74	–70	–38
Engineering	466	+	556	–	508	–48	42
Machine tool operators	134	+	158	–	125	–33	–9
Textiles	104	–	67	–	38	–29	–66
Weavers	53	–	23	–	18	–5	–35
Clerical workers	1419	+	1650	+	1603	–47	184
Clerks, cashiers	866	+	931	+	983	+52	255
Office machine operators			143	–	138	–5	
Typists, etc.	547	+	568	–	476	–92	–71
Sales workers	658	+	754	–	695	–59	+37
Shop assistants (food)	190	–	152	–		–29	+44
Shop assistants (non-food)	306	+	417	–	540		
Service workers	970	+	1295	+	1356	61	386
Cleaners	327	+	432	–	423	–9	96
Restaurants, waitresses	223	+	332	–	239	–93	16
Professional and technical	409	+	485	+	538	53	129
Nurses	128	+	166	+	189	23	61
Teachers	153	+	183	+	218	35	65
Draughtsmen	48	–	30	–	18	–22	–30

Source: Census of Population 1961, 1966, 1971, County Economic Activity Tables. Ten per cent sample included for interest.

Figure 3(a) Percentage of insured workers unemployed in Coventry as compared with that of Great Britain

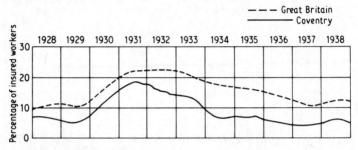

Source: West Midlands Plan.

an important part of the manufacturing sector. Economic crises that affect male engineering workers, for example, will also affect female clerical workers in those firms, although for a variety of reasons this is less likely to be noticed. (Certainly most of the discussion of the effects of the recession on engineering has focused on the unemployment of male engineering workers whereas our research in one firm showed that the decline in female clerical workers had been proportionately greater in the last five years, and had followed a consistently downward trend.)

The decline in male manufacturing employment was less consistent than the decline in female manufacturing employment and if we take the ten-year period between 1961 and 1971 there was virtually no overall decline in Coventry in male manufacturing employment (and there was an increase of 6,652 men employed in the services). The decline for men in manufacturing did not start until the mid-1960s and even then it was not a steady decline. While 1964–68 showed declines in all the major male manufacturing industries (vehicles, engineering, and metal goods n.e.s. (not elsewhere specified)), male employment increased again in 1969–70. In retrospect, 1966 seems to have represented a watershed in Coventry's industrial history. For the first time (at least since the 1920s when the cycle industry collapsed) unemployment equalled the national average. The car industry's decline in the mid-1960s can now be seen to have been the effect of a restructuring of the industry rather than the short-term effect of some political crisis as it had been (after Suez, for example) in the 1950s. Between 1971 and 1976 there was a renewed decline in male manufacturing jobs, and 8,733 jobs were lost (a decline of 9.15 per cent). The 1970s continued to show some variation in male manufacturing employment, but the overall downward trend was

Figure 3(b) Coventry's unemployment rate compared to Great Britain's, 1950–1981

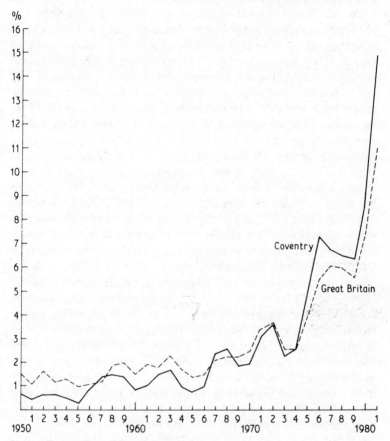

Source: Department of Employment.

unmistakable. The statistics show a decline in male manufacturing employment between 1971 and 1972, an increase in 1972–73, followed by a substantial decline between 1974 and 1976 in all the major industries. Between 1973 and 1976 male employment in the vehicle industry alone declined by 22 per cent (a loss of 9,879 jobs), and has declined even more rapidly since. Between 1975 and 1977 male unemployment was higher than the national average, and since then it has remained close to it, rising above it again during 1981. *Figure 3* shows this is a marked change for Coventry, which for most of this century was a 'boom-town' with high employment and high wages.

The small proportion of women in manufacturing in Coventry is a phenomenon that has arisen over the last fifteen years with the number of women employed in Coventry's manufacturing industries declining rapidly. This contrasts starkly with Coventry's post-war boom period and the increase at that time in women's employment in manufacturing, and should warn us against accepting any simplistic assertions that the increase in women's economic activity is simply a consequence of the expansion of the service sector. There was a substantial shift of women *from* manufacturing *to* the service sector. This did not happen for men, however. It appears that up until 1971, in so far as the labour power of women who left manufacturing was replaced it was replaced by male labour. Since then male employment has also declined. However, this has not as yet had a major impact on their contribution to the service sector. Between 1971 and 1976, despite increasingly high male unemployment, the number of men in the service sector increased by only 2,150 compared to 6,880 women. In this period the trend to increased female employment did continue even in a period of high male unemployment (see question 3 p. 19) and was not simply a consequence of a shortage of male labour. This may suggest that Bruegel is right when she argues that 'the low pay offered to women in the expanding service sectors virtually precludes any wholesale takeover by men, even when unemployment is high' (Bruegel 1979: 19). However, although I feel sure there is an element of truth in this observation, the argument may not be very applicable to a city where there are still so few men in the service sector, and probably over-simplifies the processes involved. It may well be that it is the predominance of part-time work in the service sector rather than low pay *per se* that prevents such a takeover.

PART-TIME EMPLOYMENT

At this point we should raise the question of part-time work and ask whether the increase in female employment may have been a consequence of the increased demand for part-time labour. Did employers prefer part-time labour and therefore employ women? Or did they have to, or want to, employ women (for other reasons) and therefore create part-time jobs in order to attract women in sufficient numbers?

The expansion of part-time work has been particularly rapid in the last fifteen years and has coincided with the decline of manufacturing employment (particularly for women), the expansion of the service sector, and the overall increase in the number of women in employment. The vast majority of part-time work is in the service sector, particularly in the three major service industries – distribution (shops), professional and scientific services (mainly schools and medical services), and miscellaneous services (such as pubs, hairdressers, and so on). In 1976 this sector accounted for 61 per cent of all part-time work in Great Britain, and 73 per cent of all women's part-time work. However, the intense concentration of part-time work in the services should not blind us to the fact that it exists also in the manufacturing sector. In fact between 1950 and 1970 part-time work became an increasingly important form of female labour in manufacturing, increasing from 11.8 per cent of all female manufacturing employment in 1950, to 19.7 per cent in 1970. Only in 1952–53, 1958, and 1967 did the number of part-time women decline as a proportion of women in manufacturing.

In 1961 women's part-time employment in manufacturing appears to have been even more important in Coventry than it was nationally (25.8 per cent compared to 20.2 per cent in Great Britain).[11] But by 1971 it was less important (15.3 per cent compared to 20.1 per cent in Great Britain).[12] This change in the relative importance of women's part-time employment in manufacturing occurred at the same time as the particularly rapid decline of women's employment in manufacturing in Coventry, particularly in the electrical engineering and metal goods industries. While the car industry employed a large number of women, only a small proportion of them were part-timers.

The unavailability of local statistics on part-time employment before 1971 (except in census years) makes any thorough comparison of Coventry with Great Britain impossible. We can note, however, that in the 1960s there appeared to be a greater decline in women's part-time employment in manufacturing in Coventry than there was nationally. This was mainly accounted for by one electrical engineering firm's decision to dismiss a large proportion of their very large part-time female work-force. Research by Colleen Chesterman (1979) showed that this firm adopted a policy of getting rid of groups of part-time women workers first (those on twilight shifts, for example), and before putting into operation the 'last in, first out' policy. This firm's highly organized use of part-time labour in a variety of shift arrangements to meet its requirements in a period of labour shortage illustrates the way in which capital can use part-timers in the way Bruegel describes. But this tells us only about one form of part-time labour, a form that is easily identified

Figure 4 Changes in employment by industry, 1974–77 (percentage change for each group), Great Britain

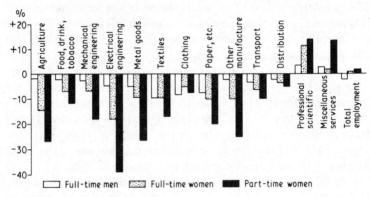

☐ Full-time men   ▨ Full-time women   ■ Part-time women

Source: Bruegel (1979).

and segregated, and which was occupationally specific; all women were doing the same job, which, moreover, was not similarly done by any man.

Before using this information as evidence to support any claim about the special function of women's part-time employment, we need to consider patterns of part-time employment in relation to other forms of employment, and especially women's full-time employment. In her attempt to show that part-timers are used as a particularly disposable form of labour, Bruegel (1979) compared the annual percentage change between 1974 and 1977 in the employment of male and female full-timers and female part-timers in different industries. She was able to show decisively that a much higher proportion of part-time workers lost jobs in declining industries, and gained them in expanding ones, than was the case in either of the other two groups (see *Figure 4*).[13] In *Table 4* we can see a similar pattern in Coventry from 1971–76 as Bruegel showed for Great Britain as a whole between 1974 and 1977. In fact, some declining industries show an increase in part-time employment (paper, printing) while some expanding industries (mechanical) show a decreasing use of part-time labour. These exceptions do not disprove the general thesis that Bruegel wishes to argue, which is that part-timers are used to cope with short-term fluctuations in demand for labour, any more than the other industries necessarily confirm it. It may be that a declining industry takes on part-time labour (or reduces the hours of full-timers so that they become part-timers) in order to save labour costs at a

Table 4 Proportions of part-time women's employment by various measures, 1971 and 1976 in Coventry

Sector	Direction of overall employment change	PT employment as % of all employment in sector 1971	1976	PT employment in sector as % of all PT employment 1971	1976	PT women as % of total work-force in sector 1971	1976	PT women as % of all women in sector 1971	1976	Women in sector as % of all women 1971	1976
Agriculture	−	19.8	25.2	0.3	0.3	11.8	13.8	47.5	48.7	0.2	0.2
Mining	+	1.4	1.6	0.1	1.4	1.4	1.6	47.2	65.6	0.1	0.1
Food, etc.	−	13.2	14.7	0.8	0.6	11.3	13.0	43.1	49.0	0.6	0.5
Coal, etc.	−	2.9	0.2	0.1	0.0	2.4	0.2	36.8	6.7	0.1	0.0
Chemical	−	4.2	2.1	0.0	0.0	3.8	2.1	21.4	11.1	0.1	0.1
Metal manufacture	+	4.3	6.0	0.1	0.2	2.5	4.0	19.0	28.1	0.2	0.2
Mechanical	+	3.0	2.8	2.2	1.8	2.2	2.3	10.2	12.2	6.0	5.4
Instrument engineering	−	1.4	8.9	0.0	0.1	1.4	8.0	3.0	18.0	0.3	0.1
Electrical engineering	−	9.3	2.6	7.3	1.5	9.3	2.6	23.8	8.7	11.8	7.3
Shipbuilding	−	—	—	—	—	—	—	—	—	—	—
Vehicles	−	0.9	0.7	2.6	1.3	0.8	0.6	7.3	6.5	13.1	8.5
Metal goods n.e.s.	−	4.9	5.1	1.2	0.9	4.0	3.8	17.0	16.3	2.6	1.8
Textiles	−	5.7	3.8	1.0	0.5	5.4	3.5	19.5	15.1	2.0	1.3
Leather	+	—	—	—	—	—	—	—	—	—	—
Clothing and footwear	+	3.4	9.0	0.0	0.1	3.4	9.0	3.9	9.3	0.2	0.5
Bricks, etc.	−	7.7	8.2	0.2	0.1	6.3	6.5	30.8	35.8	0.2	0.1
Timber, etc.	−	4.5	8.5	0.2	0.3	3.0	5.8	15.8	26.5	0.3	0.3
Paper, printing, etc.	−	10.1	13.6	0.7	0.7	6.1	9.0	18.1	25.0	0.9	0.8
Other manufacturing		—	—	—	—	—	—	—	—	0.3	1.0
Construction	−	3.3	5.3	0.7	0.9	2.7	3.7	38.5	38.0	0.6	0.7
Gas and electricity	+	6.8	5.7	0.4	0.4	6.5	5.5	27.7	28.5	0.5	0.6
Transport and communication	−	5.3	7.4	1.4	1.4	4.5	5.9	15.1	18.7	2.8	2.7
Distribution trades	+	34.2	39.4	21.4	20.7	29.1	34.4	46.9	54.8	15.2	14.9
Instruction and banking	+	18.2	20.5	2.5	2.9	14.9	15.5	25.7	26.6	3.1	3.8
Professional services	+	37.4	40.1	30.9	32.7	33.4	38.0	47.6	52.6	22.1	26.6
Miscellaneous services	+	44.1	50.3	24.5	28.5	33.0	40.9	54.6	63.1	13.1	16.6
Public administration and defence	+	7.3	12.5	1.9	3.5	6.4	11.4	17.1	28.7	3.8	5.0
Total											
Coventry		12.2	15.1			10.4	13.2	33.1	39.4		
Manufacturing				17.7	8.2						
Services				80.9	90.6						

Source: Census of Employment.

time of decreased demand. In this case we would find an increase in the numbers of part-timers and a *decline* in the numbers of full-timers in a recession.

The problem is further illustrated in *Table 5*, which compares Coventry's two largest manufacturing employers of women (full- and part-time) in 1971. The table shows the annual numerical as well as percentage changes in women's full- and part-time employment in the electrical engineering industry and the vehicle industry. If the change is calculated in terms of a percentage, women part-timers suffered a greater loss of employment in both industries. However, if we look at the actual numbers involved, it was full-time women workers in the vehicle industry who suffered the greatest loss of jobs. On the other hand, in the electrical engineering industry's only year of increased employment, 1973, it was full-timers (women and men) who provided the additional labour while the number of part-time women workers continued to decline. Had it not been for the increase of full-timers in this one year, the overall loss of jobs for full-time women workers between 1971 and 1976 would have been numerically greater than it was for part-timers. Indeed between 1973 and 1976 there was a decline of 1,692 (or 29 per cent) full-time women workers in the industry, compared to a much smaller numerical decline of 630 (61.3 per cent) of part-timers.

While not denying that part-time employment can be, and *is*, used to deal with short-term fluctuations, and that a higher *proportion* of part-time women workers lost their jobs, we cannot yet go on to argue that part-time employment is 'privileged' in that respect. Nor can we yet show that it is always the preferred form of employment for coping with such fluctuations, or that it is always used in the same way. The problem with Bruegel's analysis is that it conflates two separate issues. She does show that as a *group* part-timers have suffered more unemployment, that is, a higher proportion of part-timers have lost their jobs. None of my reservations about her argument should be taken to detract from the importance of this point. However, this is not the same as saying that part-timers are especially useful for capitalism as a particularly disposable form of labour. As we have seen, if we compare the actual number of part-timers losing their jobs to the number of full-timers (rather than comparing proportions), it is not necessarily the case that part-timers appear to be more useful than full-timers to employers needing to dispose of labour. In *Table 5* we can see that in the vehicle industry, disposing of 6.6 per cent of the full-timers was a much more significant contribution to reducing the labour force than getting rid of

Table 5 Annual numerical and percentage changes in full- and part-time women's employment in Coventry 1971–76

		1971–72 Change in nos	% Change	1972–73 Change in nos	% Change	1973–74 Change in nos	% Change	1974–75 Change in nos	% Change	1975–76 Change in nos	% Change	1971–76 Change in nos	% Change
Electrical engineering	FT	−151	−2.8	+556	+10.5	−251	−4.3	−578	−10.3	−863	−17.2	−1287	−23.6
	PT	−275	−16.1	−406	−28.3	−95	−9.3	−88	−9.4	−447	−53	−1311	−76.8
Vehicles	FT	−481	−6.6	−683	−9.9	−324	−13.4	−108	−1.9	−796	−13.9	−2392	−32.7
	PT	−104	−18.1	−72	−18.1	+18	+4.5	−56	−13.4	−19	−5.2	−233	−40.5

Total Numbers

		1971	1976
Electrical engineering	FT	5444	4157
	PT	1708	397
Vehicles	FT	7316	4924
	PT	576	343

Source: Census of Employment.

Table 6 Selected industries' dependence on part-time employment, Great Britain and Coventry 1976

1976 10 largest employers of part-time workers plus 3 important for Coventry		Part-time in 000's	Part-time workers as % of all women in sector	Part-time women as % of all women in sector	All women as % of total employed in sector	Women in sector as % of all women	Employed in sector as % of all employed	Comments
Professional services	GB	1299	36.5	47.3	67.9	27.0	16.1	*Nationally* – the 3 largest
	COV	9.2	40.1	52.6	72.3	26.6	12.3	sectors, largest employers of
Miscellaneous	GB	917.9	40.8	56.9	57.5	14.5	10.2	women, and largest
	COV	8.0	50.3	63.1	64.8	16.5	8.5	employers of part-timers.
Distribution	GB	898	33.6	50.7	55.7	16.6	12.1	
	COV	5.8	39.4	54.8	62.7	14.9	7.9	
Public Administration	GB	192.0	12.1	25.5	37.5	6.6	7.2	
	COV	0.9	12.5	28.7	39.9	5.0	4.2	
Insurance and Banking	GB	191.2	17.6	28.9	50.9	6.2	4.9	
	COV	0.8	20.4	26.6	58.2	3.8	2.1	
Food, drink and tobacco	GB	106.2	15.4	34.9	39.9	3.1	3.1	
	COV	0.2	14.8	48.9	26.7	0.5	0.6	
Transport and Communication	GB	80.0	5.5	21.7	17.5	2.8	6.6	
	COV	0.4	7.4	18.6	31.6	2.7	2.9	
Agriculture	GB	70.8	18.6	42.0	2.6	1.1	1.7	
	COV	0.1	25.2	48.7	28.4	0.9	0.2	

Industry	Area							Notes
Electrical Engineering	GB	61.1	8.4	21.0	36.6	3.0	3.3	(1) Decline from 23.8% 1971
	COV	0.4	2.6(1)	8.7(2)	29.4(3)	7.32(4)	8.3	(2) Decline from 11.8% 1971
Clothing	GB	56.5	15.5	19.2	75.6	3.1	1.6	(3) Decline from 38.8% 1971
	COV	0.03	8.9	9.3	96.2	0.5	0.2	(4) Decline from 9.3% 1971
Textiles	GB	52.8	11.0	21.5	45.1	2.4	2.2	* Lower proportion of part-time women in manufacturing in Coventry Textiles decline 1971–76.
	COV	0.1	3.8	15.1*	23.4	1.3	1.9	
Metal goods (n.e.s.)	GB	44.6	8.6	25.5	28.0	1.6	2.3	† Decline from 13.1% in 1971. Total employed was 35.7% in 1971, but vehicles still largest employer.
	COV	0.2	5.1	16.3*	23.0	1.8	2.6	
Vehicles	GB	13.6	1.9	12.9	12.0	1.0	3.3	
	COV	0.4	0.7	6.5*	9.6	8.5†	3.3	
All others	GB	300.3	—	—	—	11.0	29.3	
	COV	1.6	—	—	—	9.7	25.4	
GB		4284	20.0	40.1	40.6	100	19.0	(1) Increase from 23.5
COV Industries and Services		28.1(1)	15.1(2)	39.4(3)	33.4(4)	100	(5)	(2) Increase from 12.2
								(3) Increase from 33.0
								(4) Increase from 31.4
								(5) Decline in total workforce. Increase only in part-time employment.

Source: Department of Employment.

18.1 per cent of the part-timers. This meant getting rid of 481 full-timers and only 104 part-timers. The reduction in labour costs is, of course, even greater than this suggests as full-timers will be earning more since they work longer hours; similarly the reduction in labour power is greater.

Part of the problem is the level at which one analyses changes in employment. If we are interested in the extent to which women's part-time work serves particular functions for capitalism should we look at aggregate data or only at what happens within individual firms? It could be argued that the statistics on women's employment in Coventry over the last twenty years support the thesis, and this may well prove to have been the case. Recently Coventry has had a particularly severe manu-facturing crisis and the decline in women's part-time employment in the manufacturing sector has been greater in Coventry than it has been nationally; by 1976 Coventry's manufacturing industry was consider-ably less dependent on part-time women workers than was the case nationally. *Table 6* illustrates the use of part-time labour in Coventry's most important manufacturing industries. It shows that part-timers constitute a considerably smaller proportion of the total female work-force in the main manufacturing industries than is the case nationally. It is, however, difficult to argue that this shows that part-timers conform most closely to the disposable reserve army. There is no denying that the expansion in the early 1960s did lead to the introduction of twilight shifts to meet the demand for increased production in some of Coventry's factories. Research has shown that often it was these twilight shifts that were the first to be cut when, in the late 1960s and particularly the 1970s, the demand was made for rationalization and redundancies (see Chesterman 1979). But in some cases this appears to have been as much a response to union demands as to employers' own requirements. The version of the reserve army thesis that stresses the greater dispos-ability of part-timers tends to imply that employers are responsible for the 'disposing'. The effects may be the same (part-timers lose their jobs), but it is important to know the reasons. There has been a tendency to assume that it is always more profitable for employers to get rid of part-timers who generally are not entitled to receive redundancy pay, but there may be conditions in which it is less profitable and still the part-timers are dismissed. Although there is a sense in which getting rid of part-timers first may have served to solve capital's problems by dissipat-ing potential industrial conflict, the implications for political strategy are different. If part-timers are dismissed because of trade union pressure, possibly supported by an ideological credo that part-timers are not 'really' wage-earners, then improving part-timers eligibility for redundancy pay is not likely to affect the issue. *- has this attitude cgd?*

In conclusion to this section on manufacturing I want to make two points. First, my criticism of Bruegel's article primarily concerns the method she uses to illustrate that part-timers perform a particular function for capitalism; I want to emphasize that this only refers to the way in which *some* part-timers are used. But there is also a more general issue at stake. On the whole I think many attempts to apply a Marxist perspective to women's work have adopted too formalistic an approach. That is, they adopt a position whereby in attempting to show the specific exploitation of women they predict specific manifestations of this rather than allowing for a variety of manifestations, a tendency that arises, I suspect, from a fear of being accused of eclecticism. It seems to me that the reserve army of labour thesis does not lead us to expect any *particular* manifestation, but rather that employers, in attempting to achieve the *utmost* flexibility at the least cost, which is what the thesis presupposes, will develop a variety of ways of doing that. The means by which women's labour (or the labour of other groups) is exploited in furtherance of this aim will vary from time to time, and place to place. I think it is possible, for example, that the ways in which employers have used part-time labour over the past twenty years have changed. If, twenty years ago, part-timers were typically used to solve short-term problems (by working twilight shifts, for example), they are now frequently used as a permanent and essential part of the overall organization of labour. Just as employers use overtime and short-time for full-time employees in order to gain flexibility, so they can use part-timers in a similar way. Since part-timers are only paid at the ordinary rate when they work more than their contracted hours, they provide a cheap form of overtime labour. As a permanent part of the labour force part-timers can be seen as experienced workers who are able to fill in for labour lost because of sickness and holidays. This clearly obviates the need for expensive and perhaps unreliable temporary and casual labour.

My second point is that in discussing women's employment in manufacturing we are nowadays talking about the minority of women workers, and we cannot assume that our conclusions about their employment in manufacturing can be applied to their employment in the service sector.

- don't assume my research can be applied to manufacturing. However, the latter is declining.

Part-timers in the services

The low proportion of part-time work in manufacturing is not repeated in the services sector. On the contrary, Coventry's service sector is even more dependent on women's part-time employment than is the case nationally (see *Table 6* cols 2 and 3); and, conversely, women part-timers as a group are much more dependent on the service sector for employment in Coventry. Indeed in 1976, 90 per cent of all women's part-time employment in Coventry was in the service sector compared to 80 per cent nationally. Within the city's service sector part-time work was highly concentrated in the three main service industries – professional and scientific services, distribution, and miscellaneous services. While nationally 61 per cent of all part-time work is found here, in Coventry 81 per cent of it is in these three sectors (and 83 per cent of all women's part-time work compared to 73 per cent nationally).

To give some idea of the place of part-time work in the service sector it may be helpful to look at it in terms of four different measurements. First, how is it distributed within each of the three main service sectors (col. 4)? Second, how dependent are particular service industries on part-time labour – that is, what proportion of the entire work-force (male and female) is part-time (col. 1)? Third, what proportion of all women's work in the industry is part-time (col. 3)? Four, how important is the industry as an employer of part-timers (col. 5)? It is worth recalling that in looking at the part-time employment of women in the three main service sectors we are talking about 20,283 women, or one-third of the entire female labour force in Coventry in 1976. *Table 7* summarizes the information that is discussed below.

In *Table 7* (col. 4) we find that women's part-time work is again concentrated within the three broad industrial groupings designated by SIC (Standard Industrial Classification). Within distribution, 63 per cent of women's part-time work was in non-food retail distribution, and 28 per cent of it in food distribution (col. 4). Within professional services, 68 per cent of it was in education, and 27 per cent in medicine. Within miscellaneous services, 39 per cent of the women part-timers worked in pubs, clubs, and hotels. These industries are highly dependent on women's part-time labour (col. 1); for example, women part-timers form nearly 43 per cent of the entire work-force in both food and non-food distribution, 41 per cent in education, 37 per cent in medicine, and 57 per cent of the entire work-force in pubs.

The third way to measure the importance of women's part-time work is as a proportion of all women's work. Again we find that women's employment in these industries is 'typically' part-time (col. 3). For example, 82 per cent of all women employed in pubs, and 59 per cent of those in non-food distribution, and in education are part-timers. Finally, we can

Table 7 The proportion of women employed part-time in selected service industries by various measures, Coventry 1976

	1 Part-time women as % of total work-force	2 All women as % of total work-force	3 Part-time women as % of all women in sector	4 Part-time women as % of all part-time women in sector	5 Part-time women as % of all part-time women in Coventry
Distribution (SIC XXIII – MLHs 810–832)					
MLH 820 Retail distribution of food and drink	42.6	74.3	57.4	27.6	5.7
MLH 821 Other retail distribution	42.7	72.3	59.0	62.8	13.0
SIC XXIII Total	34.4	62.7	54.9	100.0	20.7
Professional and scientific services (SIC XXV – MLHs 871–879/5)					
MLH 872 Education	41.2	69.5	59.3	68.0	24.2
MLH 874 Medical services	36.6	84.3	43.5	27.4	9.7
SIC XXV Total	38.0	72.3	52.6	100.0	35.5
Miscellaneous services (SIC XXVI – MLHs 881–899/7)					
MLH 886 Public houses	56.6	69.1	82.1	20.0	5.3
MLH 887 Clubs	44.1	55.5	79.3	8.7	2.3
MLH 884 Hotels	41.5	67.5	61.5	10.1	2.7
SIC XXVI Total	40.9	64.8	63.1	100.0	26.5

Source: Department of Employment. Census for Coventry 1976.
Statistics on employment are generally presented on the basis of a classification of different sorts of industries, known as the Standard Industrial Classification (SIC). There are currently twenty-seven broad industrial groupings (see *Table 4*), and within these groupings there are more detailed sub-divisions known as Minimum List Headings (MLH).

see the importance of the different industries as a source of part-time 'opportunities'. Education is the largest employer of women part-timers, employing 24 per cent of all Coventry's part-time women workers, while non-food distribution employed 13 per cent, and pubs 5 per cent.

Although male employment in the services is concentrated in the same areas, it rarely constitutes a large proportion of the total male work-force. Only in pubs and clubs do male part-timers form more than half of the total male work-force (64 per cent and 69 per cent respectively), and even here they contribute much less part-time work than women. In pubs, that ultimate domain of masculinity, men provide only 26 per cent of part-time labour, and 31 per cent of total labour.

While in general terms the distribution, professional services, and miscellaneous services sectors may appear to represent very different sorts of occupations, the differences are not universal, especially for women. For example, a cleaner may be classified as an employee in all three sectors (indeed in all industrial sectors).[14] School dinner ladies will be classified under education (professional services), while waitresses in cafés will be counted in miscellaneous services. A high proportion of women's part-time work in education refers to the non-teaching (*non*-professional) occupations (cleaners, secretaries, dinner ladies). A similar effect will be found in medical services, where the number of part-timers includes cleaners and receptionists as well as nurses and radiographers, for example. On the other hand, virtually all teachers, doctors, and nurses will be counted as employees in the professional services and shop assistants will be included in distribution.

Nonetheless, these three sectors do still contain a variety of part-time work that is subject to different influences, and that has been constituted as part-time in response to different demands. While it may be obvious why there is so much part-time employment in pubs (given their opening hours), it is not obvious why there is so much in distribution with opening hours more often equivalent to a normal working week. Distribution's sensitivity to the general economic climate, and the resulting need to be able rapidly to increase and decrease the work-force, does not seem sufficient to account for the extent of part-time work in this sector. The other factor that is often used to account for the extent of part-time work in distribution, namely a heightened demand at certain times of the day or week, does not a priori provide an explanation. There are other occupations or industries of which this is true – most notably perhaps the teaching profession – but this has not led to their being constituted as part-time occupations (even though so many of women's jobs in the education sector are).

The centrality of part-time work in the service sector brings us back to the question of the extent to which men will be able to find work in the service sector. At the moment, the majority of male part-time employment is either a second job, or a retirement job. With current social security legislation, part-time employment as sole employment is not a realistic option for men (unless their wives are in full-time employment) since it is likely to make them ineligible for certain welfare benefits. The extent to which the service sector (or sections of it) has utilized part-time employment to increase productivity therefore becomes crucial. It may not only be the low pay of women in the service sector that precludes any wholesale take-over by men; it may also be that employers in the service sector find part-time employment more productive, more flexible, and therefore men are excluded from it.

I do not wish to argue that this applies throughout the service sector. I have emphasized the point in order to focus attention on a facet of part-time work that perhaps is insufficiently considered. That is, to look at its permanence rather than its instability, and to see it as a form of employment *demanded* by employers rather than merely *provided* by them in order to get (female) labour. This brings me to the last point I want to make for my statistical analysis.

I have said little about why women take part-time employment and I have avoided addressing myself directly to the question of the extent to which the increase in women's part-time work in the services was a consequence of a shortage of full-time (male or female) labour. The question probably has various answers. Many studies have shown that part-time women workers would increase their hours of work if they could make suitable domestic arrangements. That employers 'chose' to provide part-time jobs rather than lend their support to demands for improved child-care facilities is one factor that must be considered in answering this point. In considering the Coventry statistics, and the greater dependence of the service sector on part-time women workers, the possibility that there was a *shortage* of full-time female or male labour clearly should be investigated. It is not clear, however, that there was such a shortage. Between 1971 and 1976 there was an overall decline in full-time female and male employment. Three thousand seven hundred and thirty-one full-time women workers in manufacturing lost their jobs. However, full-time employment in the service sector increased by only 867, leaving a 'surplus' of 2,864 women full-timers.

At the same time, registered female unemployment increased. (This means women looking for full-time employment; those looking for part-time jobs are not included in the statistics. It seems unlikely then, that there was a shortage of women wanting and or being able to cope with full-time employment.[15] On the contrary, it seems that employers wanted part-time employees. Part-time employment in the service sector increased by 6,013. The overall increase in female employment in this period is an increase in the *number* of women employed, but not necessarily in the amount of hours worked by women. The conventional method of comparing full- and part-time work is to count two part-timers as equivalent to one full-timer. Despite the obvious problems of this method, it will serve to illustrate my point, derived from calculations based on *Table 8*. No increase in the *numbers* of women employed was needed if employers really wanted full-time women. All other things being equal, there would have been a surplus of 564 full-time women. In fact there was an increase of 1,625 women in employment.

These calculations do not take into account the increase in male and female unemployment and the availability of men and women for full-time work. Nor do they allow for any continuation of a trend, for example of more women wanting full-time employment (but not registering as unemployed). What they do suggest is that the expansion of

Table 8   *Number of women in employment in Coventry in 1971–76*

		1971	1976	Change 1971–76
Manufacturing	PT	3542	2018	− 1524
	FT	19589	15858	− 3731
Total				− 5255
Services	PT	16167	22180	+ 6013
	FT	20354	21221	+ 867
Total				+ 6880

Combined Full-time decline   3731−867   = 2864 (available full-time women)
Combined Part-time increase 6013−1524 = 4589 (required labour)
Required Part-time increase expressed as Full-time equivalent

Assuming 2 PT = 1 FT $\dfrac{4589}{2}$ = 2299.5 (required labour)

Difference between available FT women and required labour FT equivalence	2864 −2299.5
Surplus FT women's labour	564.5

Source: Census of Employment.

part-time women's work is not explicable solely or even mainly in terms of labour market factors such as the unavailability of full-time women.

I have suggested throughout this paper that we need to problematize the notion of part-time work both in terms of how we conceive of it theoretically, and how we investigate it empirically, and the conception and the investigation are of course intricately linked. At the level of statistical analysis one general point remains to be made more explicitly. I have not at any point defined part-time work, but left it rather to the reader to use his or her own understanding of the concept.[16] However, I have constantly stressed the importance of defining it in the sense of understanding to what concrete reality the category 'part-time employment' refers, and many of my comments have centred on the lack of clarity. It may be useful to draw out these points.

1 The one thing we can say, categorically, about part-time work is that by definition it is a relational concept. It makes sense only in relation to full-time work. In that respect it is also a very open-ended concept. Full-time work, which is the norm, implies a specific number of hours (usually thirty-seven hours for white collar workers and forty hours for manual workers). Anything more than that is overtime; less than that is short-time. There are no such boundaries for part-time work; its only real boundary is full-time work. Full-time work provides the context within which part-time work is situated, and to that extent we can say that full-time work is dominant.

2 In any given workplace, and indeed in nearly all workplaces, full-time work is typically of a regular pattern (from nine o'clock until five o'clock, five days a week), or it is organized in two or three shifts; even flexitime systems are organized around a substantial core of the day. Part-time work has no typical pattern. Different patterns exist within the same workplace and often within the same sub-section of a workplace. One characteristic of some part-time work is that it is a 'fill-in' for some piece of work that for some reason does not fit neatly into the overall organization of labour that has generally been structured in terms of full-time labour.

These two points have implications for comparisons between full-time and part-time workers since there is no constant basis by which we can compare them. At times we may want to compare them on a one-to-one basis, for example when we want to know whether as a group they suffer more from unemployment; at times we may want to compare them in terms of the amount of labour they provide, at which point a one-to-one comparison that assumes a part-timer to be equivalent to a full-timer is clearly fallacious. One consequence of comparing full- and part-timers on a one-to-one basis has been to overestimate the increase in employment opportunities for women, and to detract attention from the ways in which these opportunities have in some respects contracted, or have become increasingly an opportunity for a limited range of part-time jobs. *PT jobs not to be 'celebrated'*

Conclusion

At the beginning of this paper I identified a number of questions that I was considering when I came to analyse the statistics, and stressed that although such an analysis by itself could not provide a complete answer, it might point up the areas that need to be explained.

Much of the paper was framed in terms of a comparison between national statistics and those on Coventry. In doing this I hoped to be able to highlight two things: first, the extent to which arguments based on national statistics may have encouraged us to focus on correlations between employment trends and led us to assume causal relations, and to provide explanations that cannot in fact account for a local situation. For example, the correlation between the expansion of the service sector and the expansion of women's participation in the labour force seems to have encouraged the identification of the service sector as the domain of 'women's work' and to have ignored the extent to which manufacturing has also been ('traditionally') 'women's work'. This encourages the perception of 'women's work' as a marginal and unitary phenomenon such that the variety of forms it takes, and the different ways in which it is used, are ignored. Second, the obverse of this, any particular local situation, however different it may appear from the national average, will still be influenced by national trends. For example, in considering the extreme concentration of part-time women's work in Coventry, and the (presumed) continued local availability of full-time women, the potential influence of national patterns of employment in the service sector must be considered. For example, how far can any local employer's recruitment policies remain independent of national patterns, whether these are mediated through legislation, government, trade union policy, head office policy, or ideology? The ways in which these factors influenced the constitution of part-time work clearly must be one aspect of our investigation.

While no attempt was made to discuss all the different types of evidence that might be used to support the reserve army of labour thesis, the problems involved in one method (at one level quite acceptable) were discussed, and some alternatives were implied. Two points emerged from this analysis. First, it is misleading to view part-time work as a unitary phenomenon, or to see part-time workers as an identifiable group which is typically used in a particular way by capital. Some part-timers are used in this way but there are other forms of part-time labour that cannot be seen as similarly disposable. On the other hand, it was argued that it may be wrong to expect any single manifestation of the reserve army of labour thesis; we should rather expect to find employers using part-time labour in various ways. While the reserve army of labour thesis is about the labour market it is premised on the argument that capital will organize labour to maximize flexibility and disposability. However, flexibility and disposability can be achieved in various ways. For example, getting rid of overtime, reducing a part-timer's hours of work, putting workers on short-time, may all be ways of disposing of labour and take a different form from making workers redundant such that they appear on the employment statistics. As Marx (1961) noted, all those not in full-time employment are a potential source of additional labour and therefore are members of the reserve army. Thus employers who use part-time labour as an integral part of the normal organization of labour may use their already employed part-timers as their (private) reserve army.

I felt it important to stress these points not least because much of what I have said may initially appear to detract from the general premise that capital is able to, and does, exploit women's labour in a specific way because of their particular location in the family. But that was not the point of my argument. On the contrary, it seems to me that this continues to be the basis on which our labour is exploited. My intention was not to refute this but rather to show that this exploitation takes a variety of forms. I would conclude by suggesting that it is precisely on this basis that we may find a new form of women's work developing, namely the constitution of women's work as *part-time* work rather than merely the constitution of part-time workers as women.

Notes

1 The project was set up by Dr Veronica Beechey at the University of Warwick, and funded by the EOC/SSRC joint panel. I am indebted to Veronica Beechey and Simon Frith for discussions about earlier drafts of this paper,

and to Carole Brigden for help with the compilation of statistics. None of them, of course, is responsible for the views expressed or mistakes made.

2 The two exceptions are both pamphlets. First, Jennifer Hurstfield's (1978) *The Part-Time Trap* is an extremely useful study and essential reading for anyone interested in the subject. Second, Ann Sedley's (1980) *Part-time Workers Need Full-time Rights* is also a very useful brief introduction which is mainly concerned with legislation.

3 In discussing statistics it can be useful to distinguish between their reliability and their validity. Reliability refers to whether the statistics have been collected accurately. For example, if firms are asked to say how many people they employed on a certain date, did they answer the question accurately? Validity refers to whether the mode of gathering the information, and the information gathered (assuming it to be reliable) − for example counting those registered as unemployed − measures what we want it to. Many of the criticisms about unemployment statistics are about their validity as a measure of unemployment (they are much more valid as a measure of male unemployment). The criticisms of statistics on women's part-time employment tend to be of both their validity and of their reliability.

4 Population: 1927 − 129,500; 1951 − 258,211. Increase = 128,711. Increase due to migration = 91,485 (Coventry City Structure Plan 1951).

5 There was no census during the war (1941); in 1966 there was an additional 10 per cent sample census. On changing economic activity rates see Department of Employment Gazette (1974)

6 For example, the decline in the 'single' rate (which includes widowed and divorced) reflects the increase in divorced women, the greater possibility for 'single' parents to support children without working because of the development of the welfare state, the increased participation of younger women in Higher Education, and the raising of the school leaving age.

7 For example, the national crisis of the War. The concentration of the car industry in Coventry led to the city being used as a centre of armament manufacturing before and during the War (and consequently to its being severely bombed). *Figure 3* shows how relatively well protected Coventry has been from the 1930s until the recent recession.

8 This partly reflects social need. The age structure of its population meant that until recently there was rather less demand for services than in other towns of similar size (given the small proportion of the elderly). This is no longer true, and in a time of cuts in public spending the provision of additional services to meet new demand created by an ageing population is clearly problematic for a local authority. It may have implications for their employment policy, and even for their use of part-time labour.

9 It is worth recalling the importance of Coventry in manufacturing during the War. Female employment increased much more during the War than it did nationally and although its post-War decline was also greater, the percentage increase in women's employment over the whole period (1939–48) was 18,106 (63.6 per cent) in Coventry.

10 This table is based on a 10 per cent sample. The numbers thirty-three and twenty-five refer to the difference that can be seen in *Table 3*. However,

because it is only a 10 per cent sample, a decline of thirty-three in the table reflects an actual decline of 330 (that is 33 × 10).

11 Figures calculated from the Census of Population 1961.

12 Figures calculated from Census of Employment 1971. Not comparable with the above.

13 This figure is reproduced from Bruegel's article.

14 Cleaners were the third largest occupational group for women according to Coventry's 1971 population census. Of course statistics relating to numbers of employees do not tell us anything about the *occupations* of those employees. Conversely, statistics about occupations do not tell us anything about the industries in which those people are employed. There are few statistics that give both sorts of information. The census of the population is the only comprehensive source of such statistics.

15 Given the unskilled nature of most women's part-time employment in the services it also seems unlikely that women from manufacturing lacked the appropriate skills.

16 Most of the statistics that have been used define part-time work as any employment (except for teaching) under thirty hours a week (see Hurstfield (1978) and Department of Employment Gazette (1973 and 1979)).

References

Bruegel, I. (1979) Women as a Reserve Army of Labour: A Note on Recent British Experience. *Feminist Review* **3**: 12–23.

Chesterman, C. (1979) 'Women in Part-Time Employment', MA thesis. University of Warwick.

Department of Employment (1973) Part-time Women Workers 1950–1972. *Gazette* November.

—— (1974) Female Activity Rates. *Gazette* January.

—— (1979) Part-time Working in Great Britain. *Gazette* July.

Equal Opportunities Commission (1980) Women and Government Statistics. Research Bulletin **4**.

Hurstfield, J. (1978) *The Part-time Trap*. Low Pay Pamphlet **9**. London.

Hyman, R. and Price, B. (1979) Labour Statistics. In J. Irvine, I. Miles, and J. Evans (eds) *Demystifying Social Statistics*. London: Pluto.

Manley, P. and Sawbridge, D. (1980) Women at Work. *Lloyds Bank Review* January.

Marx, K. (1961) *Capital*, Vol. I. Moscow: Progress.

Oakley, A. and Oakley, R. (1979) Sexism in Official Statistics. In J. Irvine, I. Miles, and J. Evans (eds) *Demystifying Social Statistics*. London: Pluto.

Sedley, A. (1980) *Part-time Workers Need Full-time Rights*. London: NCCL Rights for Women Unit.

2

Rejoinder to Teresa Perkins

MARJORIE MAYO

Teresa Perkins offers her paper as a contribution to the reformulation of the questions to be posed about women's work, its complexity and variety, as well as its specificity.

> 'In order to understand why women's labour takes a particular form at a particular place and time, we have to understand the way in which its use has been determined by a variety of processes rather than explaining, tautologically, the form taken by female employment as a consequence of its being female.' (see p. 18)

The following comments focus some of the possible implications for further analysis and research of pursuing such an approach. At the outset, I should like to acknowledge that the Coventry study has been of considerable influence in planning an ongoing study of women's changing employment and training opportunities in North London (supported by the EEC Social Fund, the Equal Opportunities Commission, and the Greater London Council). It is therefore also in this more specific sense that we are attempting to take up some of the questions raised by the Coventry study.

Perkins's paper starts from the assumption that a Marxist perspective has contributed most to their understanding of women's employment, and that the reserve army of labour thesis has been particularly influential. Yet the reserve army thesis has itself been problematic, and the emphasis that has recently been put upon women as being *the* reserve army has not only distorted the thesis in emphasizing only this aspect of it, but 'has also had the effect of theoretically marginalizing women's work, once again encouraging a monolithic view that cannot embrace the variety of ways in which women's labour is used' (see p. 17).

These reservations about recent uses of the reserve army concept in relation to women's employment are central to the paper's subsequent analysis of the varying uses of female labour in the manufacturing and service sectors in Coventry. They also have crucial longer-term implications for the analysis of the common strands in capital's changing use of male and female labour. Marx himself was not, of course, specifically concerned with women's employment in the development of the reserve army of labour thesis. In fact Marx considered that every labourer belonged to this category during the time when she or he was only partially employed or wholly unemployed. As the process of capital accumulation proceeded over time, there was, Marx argued, a tendency for the industrial reserve army to expand, to suck in more and more sections of labour:

> 'the greater the social wealth, the functioning capital, the extent and energy of its growth and therefore, also the absolute mass of the proletariat, and the productiveness of its labourer, the greater is the industrial reserve army.'   (Marx 1974: 600)

It is not just that women are not specifically considered in Marx's own development of the reserve army thesis (although they are mentioned in passing), it may even be the case that (married) women are decreasingly likely to emerge as the ideal-type of the reserve army of labour as more categories of workers of both sexes are drawn within its ambit. In other words, capital's use of female labour is not ultimately separable from capital's changing use of labour more generally. This is in no sense to deny that women, and particularly married women, do have specific characteristics as workers, or that they can, and do, fulfil the function of an industrial reserve army, the 'latent' category being an especially appropriate means of analysing married women's moves into and out of the labour force (Beechey 1978). Rather, as Perkins argues, the problem arises in moving on to the hypothesis of greater disposability, and the implication that women will be among the first to leave the labour force in periods of recession because of their reserve army status.

In the current recession, feminists' preoccupation with this question hardly needs elaboration, whether as a theoretical problem or in more practical terms within the labour movement. (As Pat Turner, Women's Organizer for the GMWU has commented for example, 'women are still considered (even by male trade unionists) a reliable safety net for an unreliable labour market which we can use when we have need of them and can disregard at other times' (Turner 1980: 9). For Perkins, however, the issue is not whether women have a greater potential for disposal – given women's position in the labour force, their higher turnover rates, and their concentration in more vulnerable and less organized industries and occupations, it is virtually tautologous to argue the greater disposability thesis in these terms – but, whether, and how, employers choose to dispose of female labour in times of recession. In posing this latter question, the paper considers Bruegel's (1979) summary of evidence from, for example, Barron and Norris (1976), Jenness et al (1975), and Daniel and Stilgoe (1978), to support the contention that women do tend to carry a disproportionate risk of being made redundant. The paper also raises questions about the sort of evidence that can be used to investigate this contention.

Despite the limitations of using British unemployment statistics, their inherent tendency to underestimate women's unemployment, and their inconsistency over time, the statistics provide some illustration of the problems. If we look at international patterns of unemployment, it seems clear that there is no simple relationship between the rate of increase of female unemployment and the recession. The British trend, which is for women's unemployment to rise faster than men's, has not, for instance, been uniformly matched by parallel trends across OECD countries. While the rate of female unemployment did rise faster than men's unemployment rate in some countries, the reverse process occurred in others. Over the 1974–75 recession, for example, six countries followed the former trend as compared with ten following the latter.

Overall unemployment figures obscure the fact that it has been predominantly the duration of unemployment, rather than the absolute numbers of those becoming unemployed, that has been increasing in the current recession (Daniel 1981). The duration of unemployment is, therefore, also a relevant factor that should be examined. Women's unemployment has been of shorter duration than men's, although as Corry, Nugent, and Saunders (in this collection) demonstrate, there has been some tendency for differences between male and female unemployment patterns to converge as the recession bites deeper. How can this difference be accommodated within the greater disposability approach? One explanation would be that married women simply give up hope of finding another job and disappear back into the home to perform their functions as domestic labourers so that the mean duration of women's unemployment is distorted by the absence of women registered as 'long-term' unemployed. To some extent it would seem reasonable to suppose that this happens, at least in so far as married women are ineligible for benefits in their own right and therefore lack incentives to continue registering as unemployed (if they bother to register at all).

In our survey of 200 unemployed women and men in North London we found that even a third of the women then actively using the Job Centre to look for work had not formally registered. Although non-eligibility for benefit was by far the most important reason for non-registration, a minority simply did not understand the procedure. However, our own research suggests an alternative explanation, namely that women, especially married women, may be unemployed for shorter periods precisely because of the nature of the jobs that are on offer, vacancies being disproportionately concentrated at the lower-paid end of the service sector (that is, casualized jobs that have traditionally been considered as 'women's work'). This is a view that has been put to us by the managers of local employment exchanges in North London, and is one that calls for further investigation. Superficial examination of Job Centre vacancies in the area would certainly seem to support this view. Even if men did not hold any prejudices against seeking low-paid and typically part-time employment as housekeepers, mothers' helpers, and kitchen and sales assistants (typical of the jobs we found advertised), there are, as Perkins points out, obvious limitations on their doing so if they are the primary earner in the family, and not the least of these is the social security system itself. Married women, on the other hand, are more likely to be faced with having no alternative sources of independent income whatsoever, as they are not entitled to claim any benefit in their own right.

Clearly, the available data on sex differences in the duration of unemployment are fundamentally inadequate and cannot support such a hypothesis. All that is being suggested is that the reserve army of labour thesis, in relation to women's employment and unemployment, is not simply, or even predominantly, a means for theorizing the greater disposability of women workers. Even if any individual woman is more at risk of redundancy and unemployment than a man in an equivalent situation (a distinction which Bruegel (1979) makes to the greater disposability thesis), this still leaves the problems of explaining why, overall, women seem to be unemployed for shorter periods (if indeed they are), and why women's unemployment opportunities, overall, have fared better than men's (more demonstrably the case on the basis of existing Department of Employment data) so that, at least until recently, the balance has been shifting towards women's employment. But can these recent shifts towards women's employment be explained as a 'hiccough' in an otherwise regular downward curve, an exception to the more general trend caused by the concurrent growth of service sector employment? One of the implications of Perkins's paper is that such an approach can lead to precisely the type of marginalization of women's employment that she is seeking to avoid.

However understandable the concern of feminists with the greater disposability issue in a period of recession, disposability is only one aspect of the reserve army of labour thesis. To focus upon disposability is to concentrate upon the distribution of the costs of industrial restructuring in terms of gender, rather than to locate these within the restructuring process itself. And, finally, as Perkins also suggests, emphasizing women's greater disposability could generate misleading predictions about the changing pattern of women's unemployment and employment. But how can these assertions be justified?

If the reserve army thesis is considered in the context in which Marx developed it, it has to be considered in terms of the general law of capitalist accumulation, that is, the fundamental dynamics of capitalist development rather than the specific effects of recession upon any particular category of labour. To summarize, Marx was considering the tendency for the ratio of constant to variable capital to shift over time (for labour to be replaced by more mechanized production methods) as capitalists strive to maintain their profits, especially in periods of recession.

In analysing the specific situation of women, and indeed of other categories of the reserve army of low-paid workers, such as school leavers, it is relevant to consider also that within this general tendency outlined by Marx, there are also specific differences between the strategies adopted by different sections of capital. Successful capital tends to become more capital-intensive, and thus tends to dispose of labour, including the most readily disposable labour as well as the more skilled and organized sections of labour. While women may be disposed of in the rationalization process, they may, alternatively, by that very process of deskilling, even be drawn into the production process. This possibility is, of course, an issue that has long concerned feminists. Olive Schreiner (1978), considered the possibility that the process of technological change may shift the balance between male and female labour.

'That the delicacy of hand, lightness of structure which were fatal when the dominant labour of life was to wield a battle-axe or move a weight, may be no restraint but even an assistance in the intellectual and more delicate mechanical fields of labour.'

(Schreiner 1978: 214–15)

Obvious examples may be found in the potential use for female labour on new technology processes in the printing industry, or in the production of micro-chip equipment. However, it is essential to qualify any such tendency for substitution because of the effects of job segregation, and to distinguish, too, the socially determined aspects of women's supposed suitability for such new technology employment (Elson and Pearson 1981).

Before considering in more detail the questions of how and why female labour may be so attractive to employers and, therefore, relatively in increasing demand in certain sectors, it has been relevant (in our study in North London, at least) to consider also an alternative set of strategies for capital that may, in particular circumstances, nevertheless lead to similar outcomes. So far we have been considering the rationalization process in terms of the changing labour requirements of sectors that are becoming more capital-intensive. Even if the concentration as well as the centralization of capital has been the dominant underlying trend, not every capitalist can, or does, pursue such a strategy at any particular time. On the contrary, when such an option is not available – for example, to the small employer in a relatively low technology industry – alternative strategies have to be pursued, typically involving an increase in the pressure upon labour. The clothing industry in North and East London is an example of precisely such a process, from reorganization of the production process itself by breaking down the tasks performed by each individual worker, to more overt attacks upon the interests of labour – for example, the expansion of self-employment, that is, the use of lump labour (formally self-employed, *de facto* casualized), and the relatively increased use of home-workers. In each case there are both direct and indirect financial benefits for the employer.

Massey (1981), has set out these two fundamentally contrasting strategies for capital, in the face of pressures to improve their profitability: the labour shake-outs that characterize potentially more capital-intensive sectors, contrasted with the increasing exploitation of labour in 'sweated' industries.

It may even be the case that the relative predominance of part-time employment among women in Great Britain, compared with women in the OECD countries, could, in turn, be related to the relatively low wages of the British work-force more generally, and the relative weakness of the British trade union movement (as suggested by Fine and Harris (forthcoming)), and that both these characteristics could also, in turn, be related to the relative predominance of the latter strategy rather than the former, in British industry. Either strategy may involve a relatively increased demand for female labour, so that even in periods of recession the reserve army thesis can involve women in some sectors being drawn into the labour force as part of the same process that is simultaneously pushing women back into the home. Nor is women's attraction as employees simply that they can more readily be disposed of, although that may, of course, be a relevant factor. Married women's readiness to work part-time may be relevant, too. For example, while, overall, part-time married women workers have typically been considered as the most vulnerable category of workers, in certain circumstances – as Perkins's paper considers – they may actually be *more* attractive to employers in a recession, precisely because of their flexibility. So, in the retail industry in Haringey in North London there seems to have been some tendency for certain firms to have preferred part-time women sales assistants because they can be hired for peak periods only, and because it is easier to increase their hours to suit employers' fluctuating requirements than to put full-time workers on short-time.

Women's vulnerability at work has, of course, been more generally the very source of their attraction – they have a lower bargaining power, through their relative lack of training and trade union organization, for example (Barron and Norris 1976). In particular, married women have had the qualification of being prepared to work for less than the value of labour power (Beechey 1978), because of the prevalent assumption that married women are secondary rather than primary earners (whether or not this has any basis in the reality of individual cases of single parents and sole earners); although this characteristic is shared by certain other categories of labour, for example, those school leavers, male as well as female, who are forced by low wages to remain living with their parents. So married women do have particular advantages for employers who want to press down wages, advantages that are more evident in a period of high unemployment and intensified competition for jobs.

This point has not been missed by male trades unionists. For example, pressure for the 'family wage' (Land 1980) has had some rational basis in the fear that married women's labour is of benefit ultimately to capital rather than labour – dragging down wage levels so that eventually two sources of labour power rather than one are required to reproduce the family. This is, of course, to seek to explain, not to justify male defences of the notion of the family wage, rather than the pursuit of an equal opportunities or positive action strategy. Given the proportion of families already dependent on a second wage and the estimated increase in the number of families in poverty if women did not work, the whole issue of the family wage may in practice have little continuing relevance as a contemporary bargaining strategy for the majority of working-class men.

What are the implications of focusing upon the processes by which women are drawn into the labour force, rather than the mechanisms by which they are expelled from it? If both processes are, in fact, reverse sides of the reserve army of labour coin, then is this thesis as useful for predicting the relative expansion of women's employment as well as their expulsion from the labour force? As soon as we move away from the emphasis upon greater disposability, prediction becomes increasingly complex, as the work of Rubery and Tarling (1981) demonstrates. If the key mechanisms are indeed rooted in the accumulation process and more specifically in the different responses of capital to the crisis of falling profitability, then no single pattern is necessarily to be expected in terms of gender differences. Women may be made redundant more readily, and hired more rapidly, as part of the same process; employers may hold on to their cheapest and most vulnerable workers, or they may lay them off. While certain general patterns may be anticipated in particular sectors and industries, understanding them becomes, as Beechey (1978) has argued more generally in relation to the reserve army thesis, a matter for historical analysis, rather than assertion.

This brings the discussion back to Perkins's study of part-time women's employment in Coventry, and the relevance of her analysis of part-time labour in terms of the needs of capital as well as in terms of sex-specific limitations on women's full-time employment. The Coventry example illustrates these changing requirements for labour in a very particular way because of the predominance of manufacturing as contrasted with service industries in the area. Over the past two decades, as this pattern shifted, women's employment shifted from the manufacturing to the service sector (in typically lower paid and less organized jobs) relatively more markedly than did men's employment.

A similar pattern of women being the spearhead of a downward change in local employment opportunities from better paid and better organized manufacturing jobs to inferior service jobs seems to emerge in North

London. There is a pattern of downwards convergence for men, too, as their employment and unemployment situation increasingly resembles that of women. For example, we found some indication that men were being shifted over time (partly via the process of becoming unemployed) away from the better paid manufacturing jobs into more casualized jobs, often at the poorer paid manual end of the service sector. Similarly, while three-quarters of the men had been members of a trade union at some time in their working lives, less than half had been members of a trade union during their last job.

If there does indeed prove to be more systematic evidence to illustrate this downwards convergence, this would be consistent with a view of the reserve army as a key element in a restructuring process that comes, by definition, to affect men's employment in increasingly similar ways to women's. Such an approach would certainly be consistent with Perkins's analysis of women's shifts from manufacturing to the service sector in Coventry in response to capital's increasing need for a relatively cheap and flexible labour force in the expanding service sector, with women's part-time employment increasingly typical of this rather than simply an increasingly disposable category of labour.

This approach has crucial implications, too, in terms of both women's and men's demands for alternative employment policies. For men and women would both ultimately share an interest in a long-term strategy to tackle the relative disadvantages of 'women's work', as part of a joint defence against the spiral of downwards convergence (through the efforts of restructuring, including unemployment itself). This does not imply that men's and women's interests are necessarily identical in the short-term, nor does it deny that male trades unionists (as Perkins illustrates) have in fact defended themselves, on occasions in the past, in ways that have effectively excluded women. The point is rather to emphasize that if men are ultimately affected by the restructuring process in similar ways, then there is no long-term future for women in emphasizing their demands upon men, to share with them the benefits of the alternative economic strategy, since both have more urgently to organize to defend themselves from the increasingly similar impacts of the strategies of different sections of capital.

Finally, in the present context, the issues that Perkins raises about the politics of part-time work may be considered as particularly relevant in the light of conflicting current pressures and demands to improve the status, pay, and organization of part-time workers as part of positive action programmes on the one hand, and for trade unions to remain ambivalent, if not actually hostile to the use of part-timers, on the other. Yet the definitions of full-time work, and of part-time work as a secondary form, could themselves become more evidently problematic if demands for a shorter working week can be increased in the face of continuing high unemployment. The present distinctions between full-time (primary status) and part-time (secondary status) employment could then become more demonstrably a socially determined construct, and, in consequence, so also could the current pattern of the division of labour within the family.

References

Barron, R. and Norris, G. (1976) Sexual Divisions and the Dual Labour Market. In D. Barker and S. Allen (eds) *Dependence and Exploitation in Work and Marriage*. London: Longman.

Beechey, V. (1978) Women & Production: A Critical Analysis of Some Sociological Theories of Women's Work. In A. Kuhn and A. Wolpe (eds) *Feminism and Materialism*. London: Routledge & Kegan Paul.

Bruegel, I. (1979) Women as a Reserve Army of Labour: A Note on Recent British Experience. *Feminist Review* **3**: 12–23.

Daniel, W. (1981) *The Unemployment Flow*. London: Policy Studies Institute.

Daniel, W. and Stilgoe, E. (1978) *The Effects of the Employment Protection Act*. London: Policy Studies Institute.

Elson, D. and Pearson, R. (1981) Nimble Fingers Make Cheap Workers. *Feminist Review* **7**: 87–107.

Jenness, L., Hill, H., Reid, N. M., Lovell, S., and Davenport, S. E. (1975) *Last Hired, First Fired*. New York: Pathfinder.

Land, H. (1980) The Family Wage. *Feminist Review* **6**: 55–57.

Marx, K. (1974) *Capital*, Vol. I. London: Lawrence & Wishart.

Massey, D. (1981) The Geography of Industrial Change. In D. Potter *et al.* (eds) *Society and the Social Sciences*. London: Routledge & Kegan Paul.

Rubery, J. and Tarling, R. (1981) 'Women in the Recession'. Paper prepared for the Socialist Economic Review Conference.

Schreiner, O. (1978) *Women and Labour*. London: Virago. First published 1911.

Turner, P. (1980) In A. Coote and P. Kellner, Hear this Brother. *New Statesman* Report No. 1.

3

Female unemployment in the United Kingdom

BERNARD CORRY, JIM NUGENT,
AND DAVID SAUNDERS

In this paper we seek to explain certain features of the female labour market. (The results in this paper are part of a larger study of female unemployment that the authors are undertaking for the Equal Opportunities Commission.) We are not suggesting that these features are necessarily desirable or unalterable. We do, however, take the stand that if we wish to change existing structures or arrangements, it is essential to have some knowledge of how they work.

Over the last two years (1979–80) the total numbers unemployed in the UK have reached historically unprecedented levels. However, because of the growth in the size of the labour force, the unemployment rate is still much lower than that experienced during the inter-war years, especially the 1930s. The main cause of the increase in the size of the labour force since the Second World War has been the rise in the female participation rate. This change raises questions about the composition of the unemployed, and, in particular, how female unemployment has changed in a period when total unemployment has been rising.

The dramatic rise in the unemployment rate over the last two years is a continuation of a process that dates from about 1966. Prior to this date the unemployment rate in the UK averaged 1.5 per cent of the labour force, and rarely rose above 2 per cent. Since 1966 unemployment has rarely fallen below 2.5 per cent and has shown a strong upward trend, reaching double figures in 1980. This transition from relatively low to high unemployment rates has focused (or perhaps refocused) the attention of economists on two aspects of unemployment. First, a focus on the theory of the absolute level of unemployment and second, on the theory of particular unemployment rates of sub-groups in the labour force. Our concern is primarily with the latter problem in terms of female un-employment.

It has long been recognized that there are theoretical and empirical difficulties in distinguishing factors that affect relative unemployment rates from those that affect the absolute unemployment rate. Changes in the aggregate unemployment rate will rarely if ever be matched by equal proportionate changes in the unemployment rates of particular groups in the labour force. One must therefore be careful when attempting to isolate those factors that are specific to the explanation of particular and general unemployment rates respectively.

In this paper we outline the salient facts about female unemployment, summarize briefly the theory of relative and absolute unemployment rates, look at some empirical evidence relating to female unemployment, and finally draw some tentative conclusions and look at certain policy implications.

Female unemployment

The post-war period exhibits two distinct phases of unemployment. While the sharp upward trend in the general level of unemployment begins around 1966, the break with this trend does not reflect a uniform experience for all groups in the labour force. It is not until 1974 that female unemployment shows a pronounced upward movement, at which point it rises dramatically, more than doubling over the following two years. Prior to 1974 there is practically no trend in female unemploy-ment; it exhibits only a relatively low cyclical amplitude. From 1974 onwards the behaviour of male and female unemployment rates are broadly similar.

More puzzling than the trend behaviour of female unemployment is its relative level. Apart from during the early 1950s, the female un-employment rate is consistently below the male rate. This is particularly puzzling as it seems that in this respect the UK is unique among comparable industrialized market economies. (Our reasons for expecting the reverse relation between male and female unemployment rates are discussed below.) It is worth noting that the differences in male and female unemployment rates in the UK cannot be entirely explained by those methods of recording unemployment used by the Department of Employment. It is well known that unemployment in general, and female unemployment in particular, are under-recorded by the official unemployment statistics. Unemployment in the UK is officially recorded as those who are registered unemployed, and it is usually only those with a financial incentive who will actually do so. (Differences in the propensity to register can be estimated both from census data and from the General Household Survey from 1961 and selected years onwards.) Because of differences in social security arrangements, at least prior to 1977, females generally have less financial incentive to register. However, comparisons of male and female propensities to register do not suggest that all of the differences in registered male and female unemployment can be accounted for simply by differences in incentive to register (see Appendix on data sources).

A further feature of female unemployment is that it has been accompanied by a rising trend of female employment. As expected, rising male unemployment is associated with a decrease in male employment. We should ask if this contrast represent a process of labour substitution, and if so how does this substitution take place? We could analyse several other important features of female unemployment that contrast with the male unemployment experience (for example, duration of unemployment, age, and regional specific unemployment rates), but such an analysis would take us beyond the scope of this paper.

Theoretical considerations

There are three particular issues that are usually raised when distinguishing the factors that affect general and relative unemployment rates: (i) why do relative unemployment rates differ across groups in the labour force?; (ii) how do they behave over the course of the cycle?; and (iii) why do their secular trends converge or diverge? In the context of this paper the problems are: (i) in what ways would we expect female unemployment rates to differ from male unemployment rates?; (ii) what would we expect to happen to female as against male unemployment rates over the cycle?; and (iii) in what ways would we expect trends of male and female unemployment rates to differ?

The theory of differential unemployment rates explains the incidence of unemployment across different labour market groups mainly in terms of supply side characteristics. For a given level of labour demand, different groups of workers have different probabilities of becoming and remaining unemployed. These probabilities are a function of a wide set of inherited and acquired personal characteristics, such as age, health, general and specific human capital investments, geographical mobility, and labour turnover experience. Some of these characteristics are not necessarily differentially distributed by sex, but given the existence of discrimination either within or outside of the labour market, it is argued (Niemi 1974) that females are likely to possess more of those that are positively related to the probability of experiencing unemployment. For example, females will generally acquire less general and specific human capital, and will be less geographically mobile than males.[1] Hence it is predicted that females should exhibit higher unemployment rates than males, and this appears to be true for practically all industrialized market economies except the UK. As far as we know, there has been no specific analysis of this apparent paradox in any of the literature on UK labour markets. Several ideas follow from this. One apparently permanent feature of the female labour market is the phenomenon of occupational crowding, which is often given as an example of labour market segment-ation. The over-representation of females in a comparatively small number of occupations and industries is well documented (Department of Employment 1974). Further, it is argued that females are segregated into those occupations and industries that have historically been less prone to cyclical variations in the level of demand. However, while this argument would explain a lower variance in female than male unemploy-ment, it would not itself explain a lower average rate of female unem-ployment. It might additionally be argued that the growth in the demand for female labour (that is, the growth in demand for the output of female employing industries) has more than compensated for the adverse supply side situation of females. Such an argument is both arbitrary and would be very difficult to establish empirically. Without an investigation based on relevant data it is difficult to see how this particular problem can be resolved.

Much of the empirical work on the cyclical behaviour of relative unemployment rates (Kalachek 1973) stresses that unemployment rates diverge in the downturn of the cycle as those with already relatively high unemployment rates suffer more than proportionately from a decline in the general level of demand for labour. The argument is that either firms lay off those workers in whom they have the lowest investment (Oi 1962), or that because of higher standards of hiring in the downturn those workers already disadvantaged in the labour market are put at an even further disadvantage (Reder 1962). However, since females in the UK have lower unemployment rates than males, the former should show a less than proportionate increase in their unemployment rate when the general level of unemployment increases.

This expected relation between particular and general unemployment rates over the course of the cycle has led to a confusion about the source of the increase in a particular group's unemployment rate. Often so-called 'structural' reasons are given to explain the particular unemployment rate when, in fact, such changes in the observed unemployment are consistent with a decline in the general level of demand. We return to this problem when we examine some simple hypotheses to explain the behaviour of the relative unemployment rate.

When one is attempting to disentangle the effects of a change in the demand for labour on the unemployment rate from those affecting a particular group in the labour force, there is an empirical problem of finding a variable that controls for demand. A conventional approach is to employ the relationship between unemployment and vacancies. This technique, pioneered by Dow and Dicks-Mireaux (1958) and subsequently used in a variety of explanations of the general level of unemployment, has also been used to examine particular unemployment rates (Hughes 1974), but seems never to have been applied specifically to the level of female unemployment. While the theory underlying this predicted relationship is somewhat heuristic, it is nonetheless empirically well founded. Analysis of the unemployment-vacancy (U V) relationship at the aggregate level has been used to test for the effect of changes in unemployment compensation, the propensity to register, and changes in the structure of labour demand on the level of unemployment (Gujarati 1972; Nickell 1979; and Taylor 1972).

There are three aspects of the U V relationship that concern us in the empirical section of this paper. They are: (i) the negative relationship between the two variables, (ii) 'loops' around the relationship, and (iii) secular shifts or twists of the relationship. We expect the relationship between unfilled vacancies and unemployment, both measured as percentages of the labour force, to be negative. The argument is as follows.[2] Consider *Figure 1* where unfilled vacancies are plotted (y axis) against unemployment (x axis). Suppose that we have a homogeneous labour force such that if labour is available vacancies will be filled immediately. In this case we would either observe unemployment or unfilled vacancies but not both simultaneously. Thus if $V > O$ then $U = O$, or if $U > O$ then $V = O$. The U V curve would coincide with the axis. However, if we posit a heterogeneous labour force, then as the demand for labour increases, unemployed workers will be absorbed into employment but unfilled vacancies will occur and will increase as unemployment falls. This effect will occur if the filling of vacancies becomes increasingly difficult as the pool of unemployment falls. If we assume a similar process as the demand for labour falls, then we have a negative relationship between U and V. Moreover, no matter how great the stock of unfilled vacancies, unemployment never completely disappears, and however high unemployment is, vacancies never completely disappear, then the curve will be convex to the origin (see *Figure 1*).

Figure 1 The theoretical relationship between unfilled vacancies and unemployment

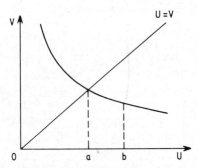

We define equilibrium in the labour market as the position where the demand (D) for labour equals the supply (S). Thus $V = U$ (because $D_L \equiv E + V$: $S_L \equiv E + U$ so $D_L = S_L$ where $V = U$) and in *Figure 1* this is at unemployment level Oa. We may further regard Oa as the non-demand-deficient level of unemployment[3] – basically it will be a combination of search and structural unemployment.[4] (That is, those unemployed having voluntarily left their jobs, and those unemployed because of a mismatch between vacancies and unemployment.)

The cyclical pattern of the demand for labour gives rise to movements around a given UV curve, but the actual time-path of observations may produce clockwise or anti-clockwise loops. This is an important consideration because when we look at these relationships empirically we have to be careful not to confuse these loop effects with actual shifts in the UV curve.

Figures 2 and *3* illustrate anti-clockwise and clockwise loop systems. Anti-clockwise loops show that for any given level of unemployment (Oa in *Figure 2*) there will be two levels of unfilled vacancies: the higher level (ae) when unemployment is falling to the level Oa; and the lower level (af) when it is rising to it. These observations may be generated by expectations effects both on the part of employers and employees.

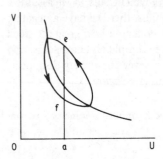

Figure 2 The possibility of anti-clockwise loops around the UV relationship

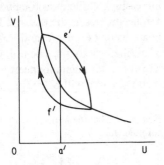

Figure 3 The possibility of clockwise loops around the UV relationship

Employers, observing an increase in demand (falling unemployment) may foresee a recruitment problem and increase their 'official' vacancies for any given level of unemployment. Clockwise loops show the opposite. Vacancies are higher when unemployment is rising to a given level (Oa′ in *Figure 3*) than when it is falling to that level (i.e. a′e′ a′f′). This observation is compatible with a lagged adjustment by employers and employees to changes in the demand for labour. If vacancies are a lagged response to previous levels of the demand for labour, for example.

Figure 4 illustrates an outward shift in the UV curve. How do we interpret such a shift? Ob now becomes the equilibrium level of unemployment (where $D_L = S_L$) and shows that a shift implies a rise in non-demand-deficient unemployment. It is further normally assumed, as we do, that this increase is due to increased structural mis-match. If we assume that observed unemployment is at Oc, then the increase from,

Figure 4 Shifts of the UV curve

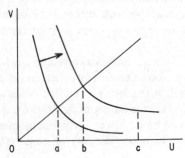

for example, Oa is compounded of a rise in structural unemployment equal to ab plus an increase in demand deficient unemployment equal to bc.

Empirical evidence

All empirical investigations in this field comment on the inadequacy of the data, especially on vacancies, arguing that the estimated U V relationships are most usefully viewed as ordinal indicators of the state of the labour market. This is especially so in the case of U V curves estimated for the female labour market. Nonetheless we feel that our results are not only illustrative but also have interesting policy implications.

While most U V curves are conventionally drawn convex to the origin, we have found that a simple linear specification in natural numbers gives the best results. We used the following form of estimating equation:

$$\%U_t^F = \alpha_0 + \alpha_1 \%V_t^F + \alpha_2 \%U_{t-1}^F + \alpha_3 T + \alpha_4 T^2$$

where: $\%U^F$ is the percentage rate of female unemployment;

$\%V^F$ is the percentage rate of vacancies specificially for females;

T and T^2 are time trends, and t is time (in quarters).

We found that the inclusion of the lagged unemployment rate was the best method of incorporating the effects of the loops observed around the fitted U V curve. The results given below were obtained using OLS (Ordinary Least Squares) on data fitted for the time period 1965(I) to 1975(IV).

Dependent Variable	Constant	$\%V_t^F$	$\%U_{t-1}^F$	T	T^2
$\%U_t^F$	1.14	−0.55	0.63	−0.022	0.0005

$R^2 = 0.96 \ DW = 1.23$

All estimated coefficients were found to be significant at the 95 per cent level.

The results are typical of those found in many other regressions run either over longer time periods, or for selected sub-periods. In no case can we detect any significant shift in the U V relationship for females. Whatever the causes of the changes in the male labour market in the post-1967 period, they do not appear to have affected the female labour market to any great extent over the period examined. The restriction of the estimated relationship to the period prior to 1975 (IV) is the result of legislative changes that came into effect in 1975, making it illegal to advertise separate male and female vacancies. Hence for the post-1975 period we have no way of directly observing female employment vacancy relations.

However, it could be argued that the female labour market in the period since 1975 has undergone significant changes. As we see from the registered unemployment data, female unemployment, at least as regards trends, begins to behave very much like male unemployment from 1974 onwards. Further, the legislation designed to produce equal opportunities for females might itself have produced direct effects on the level of female unemployment that could operate in a variety of ways. For example, to the extent that females and males are treated equally under social security legislation, the propensity for females to register might have increased, and there is some evidence to support this (see Appendix on data sources). Again, to the extent that equal pay legislation raises female labour costs relative to male costs, the demand for female labour may have been reduced. Any of these effects would produce an outward shift of the UV curve for females.

Since direct observation of female vacancies is no longer possible, we have adopted the following procedure in an attempt to evaluate the above arguments. We start from the assumption that the legislation on equal opportunities and equal pay have no effect on the female labour market. Hence the share of female and male vacancies in total vacancies should not have changed. We then calculate the population of female vacancies in total vacancies by estimating an equation of the form:

$$V^F = \beta_0 = \beta_1 V^T + \beta_2 T$$

The equation that gave the best results was one in which the square of time was used to pick up the trend. The fitted equation, using OLS for the period 1960(I) to 1974(I), produced the following results:

Dependent Variable	Constant	V^T	T^2
V^F	0.51	0.85	−0.00009

$R^2 = 0.88$ $DW = 1.44$

All estimated coefficients were significant at the 95 per cent level.

This equation was then used to generate a hypothetical female vacancy series by applying it to the post-1975 observations on total vacancies. This hypothetical series was then used in conjunction with female unemployment to estimate the supposed UV relationship. From this equation we can compare the predicted level of female unemployment rates with those actually observed. If the predicted unemployment rates using this method are close to the actual unemployment rates, then we claim that there has been no significant shift in the female U V relationship. If, on the other hand, the predicted and actual unemployment rates differ significantly, then at least three things may have occurred. First, the equation used to predict female vacancies may simply be an inadequate forecasting equation. Second, perhaps because of legislative changes, the relationship between male and female vacancies may have undergone structural change. Third, the female U V curve has in fact shifted. *Table 1* shows the actual and predicted values of female unemployment for some eighteen quarters in the post-1975 period.

As can be seen, the fitted equations consistently under-predict the actual unemployment rate. We interpret from these results that there have been some changes in the female labour market, but at this stage we cannot tell which of the underlying relationships has changed. We cannot claim that the changes that have occurred are very major ones or that they result from legislative changes affecting the female labour market. Further analysis of the vacancy series is obviously needed, and future investigation using the relationship between employment and vacancies may clarify these issues.

Table 1 *The relationship between actual and predicted female unemployment*

Actual female unemployment Rate (a)	Predicted female unemployment Rate (b)	(a)–(b)
2.93	2.21	0.72
3.12	2.59	0.53
3.33	2.74	0.59
3.48	2.92	0.56
3.60	3.02	0.58
3.82	3.14	0.68
4.00	3.33	0.67
4.11	3.48	0.63
4.07	3.57	0.50
4.07	3.56	0.51
4.05	3.60	0.45
4.01	3.60	0.41
3.92	3.65	0.27
4.00	3.61	0.39
3.91	3.73	0.18
3.92	3.77	0.15
4.04	3.92	0.12
4.50	4.13	0.37

Conclusions

The rise in the level of female unemployment over the last few years cannot be ascribed to features of the labour market peculiar to females. While our empirical analysis has not been able to test very specific hypotheses, there is no strong evidence to suggest that the rise in female unemployment is not due simply to the general fall in the level of aggregate demand. Nor is there any clear evidence that females are worse affected by the current deflation. The paradox of the relation between male and female unemployment has not been resolved. The very fact of segmented labour markets alone would not explain this relationship, but it may explain why females have not been affected by legislative changes in the way usually predicted by neo-classical labour market theory. Because of occupational crowding, there has been little if any substitution of male for female labour. Furthermore, the very occupations in which females are crowded may be the last to feel the full effects of the current policy of severe deflation. We can only guess that this will continue to be the case in the future. Labour market practices and institutions are notoriously slow to change in the U K, and so we doubt whether there will be any significant changes in either the relative levels or the comparative trends in male and female unemployment in the near future.

Appendix

The main source of data on female unemployment is the Department of Employment Gazette. These data, which we term the registered unemployed, are published on a monthly basis for total unemployment, with a finer analysis by age, occupation, and duration, etc. being published on a quarterly basis.

To register as unemployed the individual must be seeking work, and be classified by the local employment office as being 'capable and available for work'. The majority of those who are registered are in receipt of some form of financial assistance, either unemployment benefit and/or supplementary benefit. Those who are not entitled to claim any form of benefit have little incentive to register, and it is thought that a large number of females, particularly married women, fall into this category. Married women entering or re-entering the labour force usually have no contributions to National Insurance in their own right and hence are not entitled to unemployment benefit. Further, until

1977 married women in work could opt to pay a reduced rate of National Insurance contributions but thereby disqualified themselves from entitlement. Since 1977 all new entrants, and some re-entrants, must pay the full rate of social security contributions. This change in National Insurance regulations is likely to encourage women to register, as older married women who previously opted out withdraw from the labour force.

Data on the degree of non-registered unemployment became available in the 1961 census and subsequently in 1966 and 1971. The discrepancy between those who reported themselves out of work in the census returns and those registered as unemployed resulted in a 1972 interdepartmental report on the official unemployment statistics (Department of Employment 1972a). This report suggested several improvements in the presentation and analysis of the statistics on registered unemployed but did not appear to treat unregistered unemployment as a major problem (see Department of Employment 1972b).

In the 1961 census, discounting those who were sick and hence would not appear on the official register, there were 70,000 males and 230,000 females who described themselves as seeking work but not registered as unemployed. (Comparable figures from the 1966 census are 103,000 and 133,000). Perhaps more surprising is the larger number of unregistered females than males. Indeed, it is claimed (Evans 1977) that the rapid rise in registered unemployment in the late 1960s is due to a dramatic increase in the propensity of males to register as unemployed. The registration ratio of males in 1961 was calculated by Evans to be about 0.68 which by 1971 had risen to 0.96. However, for females no such dramatic rise in the registration ratio is observed; indeed, over the years in question it fell (see *Table 1*).

Subsequent analysis of the propensity to register is available on an annual basis from the General Household Survey (Office of Population Censuses and Surveys). The registration ratio for females calculated from the census years 1966 and 1971, and from the General Household Survey for 1972–78 are shown in *Table 2*.

At least up to 1975, there does not appear to be any marked trend. From 1975 onwards the female registration ratio is noticeably higher

Table 2

	1966	1971	1972	1973	1974	1975	1976	1977	1978
All females	0.34	0.33	0.44	0.34	0.30	0.43	0.58	0.61	0.59

than in previous years. Comparing the registration ratio and the unemployment rate, there appears to be a positive correlation between the two. At this stage we are not in a position to explain the time series behaviour of the registration ratio. A more detailed analysis of the personal characteristics of the registered and the non-registered unemployed is required. However, we do know that there are wide regional variations in the propensity to register and this also appears to be positively correlated with unemployment rates. Further, there are, as expected, differences in the propensity of married and single women to register.

The breakdown between the registration ratio of married and single women is only available in the General Household Survey from 1974 onwards. The results of these calculations are shown in *Table 3*.

Table 3

	1974	1975	1976	1977
Married	0.23	0.31	0.37	0.47
Non-married	0.41	0.58	0.79	0.76

As expected, the non-married category has a higher propensity to register than the married category. However, the registration ratio to the non-married category has risen by more than that of the married category, that is by 85 per cent as against 104 per cent.

If the increase in the propensity to register observed since 1976 continues then future 'official' unemployment rates will continue to show rising female unemployment.

Notes

1 This argument predicts strictly that females (particularly married females) would experience relatively more spells of unemployment than males. However, observed unemployment is a function both of the number of spells and of the duration of unemployment. Whether we should expect females to have higher or lower durations than males is not theoretically clear, hence it is possible that even though discrimination may lead to a higher probability of experiencing unemployment, it does not itself predict that females have necessarily higher unemployment rates than males.

2 This relationship may be derived formally from a neo-classical model of the labour market (Hansen 1970). We wish our derivation to be less restrictive than this.

3 Although the level of unemployment (Oa) may be reduced by increasing the overall demand for labour.
4 Given sufficient data it is possible to measure the separate components of non-demand-deficient unemployment (Hughes 1974).

References

Department of Employment (1972a) *Unemployment Statistics*. Cmnd 5157. London: HMSO.
—— (1972b) *Gazette* November.
—— (1974a) Women and Work: A Statistical Survey. *Manpower Paper* **9**. London: HMSO.
—— (1974b) Statistics of Unemployment in the UK. *Gazette* May.
Dow, J. C. R. and Dicks-Mireaux, L. A. (1958) The Excess Demand for Labour: A Study of Conditions in Great Britain 1946–1956. *Oxford Economic Papers* **10**: 1–32.
Evans, A. (1977) Notes on the Changing Relationship between Registered Unemployment and Notified Vacancies: 1961–1966 and 1966–1971. *Economica* **44**: 179–196.
Gujarati, D. (1972) The Behaviour of Unemployment and Unfilled Vacancies: Great Britain 1958–1971. *Economic Journal* **82**: 195–204.
Hansen, B. (1970) Excess Demand, Unemployment, Vacancies and Wages. *Quarterly Journal of Economics* **84**: 1–23.
Hughes, J. J. (1974) The Use of Vacancy Statistics in Classifying and Measuring Structural and Frictional Unemployment in Great Britain 1958. *Bulletin of Economic Research* **26**: 12–23.
Johnston, J. (1972) *Econometric Methods*. New York: McGraw Hill.
Kalachek, E. D. (1973) *Labour Markets and Unemployment*. Hemel Hempstead: Wadsworth.
Lipsey, R. G. (1965) Structural and Deficient Demand Unemployment Reconsidered. In A. M. Ross (ed.) *Employment Policy and the Labour Market*. Berkeley, Calif.: University of California Press.
Niemi, B. (1974) The Female-Male Differential in Unemployment Rates. *Industrial and Labour Relations Review* **27**: 331–50.
Nickell, S. J. (1979) The Effects of Unemployment and Related Benefits on the Duration of Unemployment. *Economic Journal* **89**: 34–49.
Office of Population Censuses and Surveys *Annual General Household Survey*. London: HMSO.
Oi, W. (1962) Labour as a Quasi-fixed Factor. *Journal of Political Economy* **70**: 538–55.
Reder, M. (1962) Wage Differentials: Theory and Measurement. In Gregg-Lewis (ed.) *Aspects of Labour Economics*. Princeton, NJ.: Princeton University Press.
Solow, R. M. (1964) 'The Nature and Sources of Unemployment in the United States'. Wichsell Lectures, Stockholm.
Taylor, J. (1972) The Behaviour of Unemployment and Vacancies: Great Britain 1958–1971: An Alternative View. *Economic Journal* **82**: 352–65.

4

Rejoinder to Bernard Corry, Jim Nugent, and David Saunders[1]

IRENE BRUEGEL

In comparison with other social sciences, economics has remained relatively immune from feminist criticism. Given this it is not altogether surprising that Bernard Corry, Jim Nugent, and David Saunders (hereafter CNS) tackle the question of women's unemployment with an uncritical use of conventional economic theory and procedures, adding on women as a new data set, as it were, rather than rethinking the traditional concepts. While women are no longer completely ignored by economists, this approach can be regarded as equally sexist as its predecessor (see Acker 1980) for it can imply that the traditional theoretical structures, developed largely to explain the position of men in the economy, are sex-neutral, and can be applied without modification to the problems of women.

In discussing the paper I shall take this as the central question, for CNS illustrate very well the limitations of such an 'add-on' approach, particularly in the context of neo-classical economics. Despite the problems that their work throws up, they see no reason to question the value of traditional economic concepts and practices for understanding trends in women's unemployment. I start with a discussion of the theoretical basis of their research, move on to their methodology, and finally look at their results.

The first problem is to decide what questions CNS are attempting to answer. They appear to slip from the question of determining the character of women's unemployment, and particularly women's rising unemployment, to a so-called theory of differential unemployment, considering whether sex is an independent variable in the (un)employment market. This has confusing effects. I will concentrate my comments on their attempt to test a theory of differential unemployment as the more interesting question for feminist analysis.

The theory

In the 1950s, 1960s, and early 1970s, successive British governments operated a range of fiscal and monetary policies to adjust the level of demand in the economy to what were seen to be full employment levels. To do this it became necessary to calculate how much of any given level of unemployment was due to a deficiency in demand (and hence amenable to policies which raised the level of demand) and how much was structural and/or frictional (and hence requiring different policy responses). Structural unemployment is due to a change in the structure of the economy (a long-term decline in particular industries); frictional unemployment is due to the problems of instantaneously matching available workers with available jobs (problems of information, of mobility, etc.). The analysis of the relationship between vacancies and the rate of unemployment was developed in this particular policy context (Bowers 1976).

As CNS describe it, the structural and/or frictional level is taken to be the level of unemployment at which the vacancy rate equals the rate of unemployment, for, by definition, there is then no demand-deficient unemployment. Any excess of unemployment above this level is then demand-deficient unemployment. Conversely, any unemployment rate below this level indicates an excess demand for labour. Changes in the level of unemployment are then analysed in the following way: any rise in unemployment accompanied by a predicted fall in vacancies (predicted from an established UV curve) is attributable to a decline in demand; any rise in unemployment not accompanied by such a fall in vacancies (i.e. if the UV curve has shifted outwards) is identified as an increase in the level of structural and/or frictional unemployment.

CNS apply this procedure to a very different set of questions, those of the differential unemployment between males and females. Their rationale for adopting a UV analysis is to 'control for demand' in explaining the cyclical behaviour of female (registered) unemployment relative to male (registered) unemployment. But it is by no means clear why it should be necessary to control for demand in this particular analysis. If the question posed was how far any given deflation or reflation of the economy could be expected to increase or reduce female registered unemployment, then, following the argument above, it would be necessary to establish how much of any given level of unemployment was susceptible to changes in demand. A U V analysis could be the appropriate way of doing this. But to argue that the relative pattern of male and female unemployment over the cycle can only be satisfactorily explained if the effects of changes in demand are controlled for, is to ignore many of the issues at stake in a theory of *differential* unemployment.

Over the cycle, the relative rates of unemployment between men and women may change both for demand-based and non-demand-related reasons. An overall fall in demand may lead to disproportionate demand-deficient unemployment for either male or female labour and, in addition, differences in the mobility and fluidity of male and female labour may accentuate over the cycle, raising structural and/or frictional unemployment disproportionately for one or other group.

To pose an analysis of the relationship between female unemployment and female vacancies (that is, to control for demand effects) as a theory of differential unemployment is to ignore the first form of differentiation. It is as if CNS see changes in unemployment levels due to changes in demand as sex-neutral, economy-wide factors, and identify only the residual, generally supply-side characteristics as being related to sex. Nowhere do they consider what is an important part of any theory of differential unemployment and any analysis of women as a reserve army of labour, namely how the demand for women's labour fluctuates relative to demand for labour as a whole over the cycle. If the position of women in the economy is as a reserve army, which is brought in at high points of economic activity and discarded as the economy stagnates, this will occur largely through the differential pattern of demand for female labour relative to male labour over the cycle as a whole.

At one point CNS take up this question and appear to argue that a (differential) decline in demand for female labour, whether as a result of the Equal Pay Act (1970) or of the impact of recession on 'women's work', could result in an outward shift of the U V curve for women. But it is difficult to see why it should be the case and therefore that the way to identify differential unemployment is to study changes in the U V relationship over time. Any decline in demand for female labour relative to male labour would be accompanied by a fall in registered vacancies alongside a rise in registered unemployment. Hence it would result in a movement *along* a U V curve. So, it is difficult to see that the analysis of the relationship between female unemployment and female vacancies tells us anything about differential demand-deficient unemployment.

The research design adopted – essentially replicating for women the analysis of the relationship between male unemployment and male vacancies that has so concerned labour economists – is essentially inappropriate to answer the salient questions about female unemployment, namely the differential patterns of male and female experiences of the labour market processes. Adopting a parallel approach that implies that male and female labour markets are completely independent, each operating in its own space, begs all the questions of their interrelationship. It tells us nothing, for example, of how far unemployment levels among men are cushioned by any greater vulnerability of women nor, alternatively, how far the impact of male unemployment on families is mitigated by stability in levels of female employment.

We have here the counterpart of the original sin of ignoring women for now it is the relationship between the experiences of men and women that is ignored. The procedure adopted assumes that the experiences of women are to be explained by the actions of women themselves (it implies a distinct female labour market) and not by the position of women in the overall structure of society in which sexual differentiation is a motivating force.

Methodology

So far I have argued that for theoretical reasons the separate U V analysis of female labour adopted by C N S is not a useful way of analysing differential unemployment between men and women. In addition there are practical problems in undertaking such an analysis even when it is appropriate.

C N S do accept that the official statistics they use seriously underestimate both female unemployment and female vacancies but, except in the Appendix, they ignore the implications of this for their analysis. Thus, even the facts they give on women's unemployment are confined to registered unemployment. For example, if unregistered unemployment is considered, it is by no means clear that 'prior to 1974, there is practically no trend in female unemployment' (see p. 65). Figures from Moore and Rhodes et al. (1978) suggest that the rise in women's unemployment started in 1966 not 1974.

C N S's argument on this point seems to be that if it is possible to make predictions then the inadequacy of the data is a minor issue, and, if policies are to be formulated, then any data is better than no data. Obviously, when one is concerned with change over time, the fact that both registered female unemployment and vacancies are seriously underestimated is not in itself damning. For if changes in the official statistics do reflect changes in the variables under consideration, then they may indeed be adequate indicators for policy purposes. But as soon as one recognizes that the relationships between registered female unemployment and the supply of female labour, and between registered vacancies and the demand for female labour vary unpredictably over the cycle, then the cavalier attitude to the inadequancy of the data becomes clear. It is rather like trying to measure the relationship between heat and length by using a mercury thermometer as the scale of length.

The problem is both statistical and conceptual. As unemployment increases, so the proportion of unemployed women who register may rise as unemployment is concentrated among those women (younger single women) most likely to register. But the proportion may fall as women decide that there is little likelihood of finding a job and that it is no longer worth their registering. As demand for labour falls, so the proportion of vacancies registered may fall, as employers face a buyers' market and recruit with less recourse to the employment office. Thus, because they reflect the priorities and presumptions of government, official statistics are seriously deficient in relation to women (Oakley and Oakley 1979; Hunt 1980) and alternative measures of female unemployment are urgently required.

The analysis of women's unemployment raises serious conceptual problems for any economist attempting to use the conventional categories of demand and supply of labour. An economics developed in an era of a predominantly male labour force can equate the supply of labour with the number of people actually employed plus the unemployed for, apart from some pensioners and some students, the lines of demarcation between being in or out of the labour force are relatively clear. This cannot be true for women, given the definition of married women's primary role as housework. For many people an unemployed married woman is a contradiction in terms. Two unemployed married women, asked how they saw themselves, said:

'I don't class myself as unemployed. I just class myself as looking for a job. . . . I'm a housewife looking for a job, but I don't class myself as unemployed. I think you class yourself as unemployed when you're being paid for being unemployed.'

'No (I don't count myself as unemployed). I think it's because I'm a woman. Men need jobs more than women do.'

(Parry and Green 1981)

There is ample evidence that this is a common sort of response. On becoming unemployed, or on being made redundant, many women simply revert to the status of housewife. This is shown by those few longitudinal studies of the unemployed that do consider women. Daniel's (1974) study found that 20 per cent of the women, compared to 10 per cent of the men, who did start by registering as unemployed in 1973 gave up looking for work within six weeks. A more recent Department of Employment (1977) study found that nearly one-third of unemployed women had given up looking for work six months after first registering.

However, if work does become available, women will often take it without ever defining themselves as 'looking for work', and registering as unemployed:

> 'I wasn't really thinking about working, or at least only vaguely, but when my friend rang me up I suddenly thought I *do* want a job . . . I suppose it's a case of if the temptations there. . . . I sort of gave in to it. I suppose if she'd never said anything about a job going here, I suppose I'd have just stayed at home.'   (Parry and Green 1981)

In his earlier work, Corry (Corry and Roberts 1970) has shown that the level of participation by women in wage labour is highly dependent on the state of the economy. As the economy expands so the supply of women workers rises; as it contracts many women who might otherwise have worked do not begin to think of looking for work. The number of women economically active (employed and unemployed) today is some 500,000–800,000 less than would have been the case had the trends evident at the peak of the cycle continued (Counter Information Services 1981).

Moreover, it is not just the margin between unemployment and economic inactivity (sic) that is blurred for women, but also the margin between employment and economic inactivity. The huge numbers of home workers and part-time workers who earn below the National Insurance limit are not generally considered as employed and so are not seen to be affected by recession. Traditional concepts of employment do not, for example, allow for the possibility of an unemployed childminder.

The concept of a specific female vacancy is also problematic but for different reasons. It implies a rigid division of jobs into male and female categories and, indeed, the statistical series of vacancies by sex ends in 1975 precisely because the Sex Discrimination Act disallows sex categorization. Jobs are indeed categorized by sex at a particular time but the assumption of an unchanging sex categorization of jobs hides one of the issues at stake in understanding the impact of recession on women, namely the degree to which any given categorization is maintained in conditions of recession. There is some evidence that men are now entering the higher paid areas of women's work, such as secretarial work and nursing, in greater numbers than previously.

This set of criticisms implies that CNS are not able to test their theory because the measures they use do not fit the theoretical categories they employ. The supply of female labour power includes not just those women in employment plus the registered unemployed as CNS state; all women of working age form part of a potential supply. Whether they enter the categories of employed or registered unemployed will depend upon a range of factors, including the demand for labour. Similarly, the demand for female labour is not equivalent to the numbers in employment plus registered vacancies, it must also include unregistered vacancies. Moreover, if the decision to employ a woman rather than a man depends to any extent on relative wages, then the demand for *female* labour will be a function of relative wages and hence of relative levels of supply. In econometric terms we have a problem of identification. Any relationship that is established between registered unemployment and registered vacancies could then be spurious in the sense that it bore no relationship at all to the theory. Because women drop out of the labour force as unemployment rises, it is possible for a fall in registered unemployment to accompany a real fall in demand and yet for that not to be registered as a decline in female vacancies. This could be because of extraneous rises in the registration of vacancies or because of a shift in recession towards replacing men by cheaper female labour. In this (admittedly chance) example an apparent relationship between a rise in vacancies and a fall in unemployment would bear no relationship to the theory outlined by CNS.

Leaving aside these objections to the application of UV analysis to women, there are some technical problems with the equation estimated by CNS that seem worth raising.

In presenting their equation of the relationship between (registered) unemployment and (registered) vacancies (Equation 1), CNS imply a defined relationship between 1965 and 1975.

$$1 \quad U_t^f = 1.14 - 0.55 \, V_t^f + 0.63 \, U_{t-1}^f - 0.022T + 0.0005T^2$$
$$R^2 = 0.96 \quad DW = 1.23$$

This equation appears to show that the unemployment rate in one period can be reliably predicted from the vacancy rate in that period and the unemployment rate in the previous period, with some change over time in the relationship. However, one cannot conclude from the high R^2 achieved by CNS with this equation that the methodological problems discussed above can be ignored and that CNS have been able to establish a reliable relationship from which predictions and further analysis are possible.

The problem is that one would always expect a high R^2 – whatever the strength of the relationship between unemployment and vacancies – if a lagged variable such as unemployment in the last period U_{t-1} is included in the regression. The lagged variable also makes the Durbin Watson test for serial correlation unreliable, so that the relationship between unemployment and vacancies, apparently established in Equation 1, could be spurious.

It is not at all clear why unemployment in the previous quarter was used in estimating the UV relationship; it is a very unusual way of dealing with the possibility of loops in the relationship between unemployment and vacancies. Indeed, CNS's own account of loops implies that the relationship between unemployment and vacancies depends on the *point* in the cycle when measurement is made, that is on whether unemployment is rising or falling at the time. Given this account of loops, the unemployment level in the last period does not seem to be the relevant factor to keep constant, rather it is the *direction of change* that needs to be controlled for.

To check on these points four separate regressions were run of the equation:

$$U_t^f = a + bV_t^f$$

using data for Great Britain 1965–76, and dividing the whole period into three, each period relating to one cycle. This follows Evans's (1977) discussion of the procedure for estimating shifts in the UV curve where looping is suspected. When this is done (Equations 2–5) a number of points emerge. First, for the period as a whole the overall level of explanation is lower when the lagged variable and the time trend are excluded: R^2 falls to 0.54. Second, when the time trend and the lagged variable are excluded the DWs no longer look good. Third, in so far as these equations can be relied upon, there is some evidence of an outward shift of the curve after 1971, so that the value of the curve for 1965–76 as an estimating curve for the period after 1975 must remain in question.

2 1965–75 quarterly data
$$U_t^f = 183.4 - 0.91\ V_t^f \qquad R^2 = 0.54\ DW = 0.30$$
$$(11.6)\ (0.12)$$

3 1965 (I)–67 (IV)
$$U_t^f = 151.9 - 0.67\ V_t^f \qquad R^2 = 0.91\ DW = 1.17$$
$$(7.1)\quad (0.65)$$

4 1968 (I)–71 (IV)
$$U_t^f = 148.7 - 0.68\ V_t^f \qquad R^2 = 0.53\ DW = 1.4$$
$$(13.6)\ (0.15)$$

5 1972 (I)–75 (IV)
$$U_t^f = 215.5 - 1.06\ V_t^f \qquad R^2 = 0.73\ DW = 0.47$$
$$(15.5)\ (0.16)$$

The conclusions I want to draw from these points are that CNS have not been able to establish a reliable relationship between unemployment and vacancies for the period before 1975, and, therefore, that their UV analysis cannot help in explaining the post-1975 trends, as their research design requires.

HOW IS THE RISE IN WOMEN'S REGISTERED UNEMPLOYMENT TO BE EXPLAINED?

Even when compared to male unemployment, registered unemployment among women has risen dramatically in the current (since 1976) recession. The actual rise depends very much on the period considered but in the period analysed by CNS (January 1976–June 1980) the rise for women was 84 per cent (214,000) compared to 15 per cent (143,000) for men. (These are UK figures, seasonally adjusted and excluding school leavers.)

In the last section of their paper CNS attempt to explain this rise by investigating how far such a rise can be accounted for by a fall in overall demand. Their results suggest that it cannot be explained in this way (the rise in registered unemployment was greater than that predicted on their vacancy series). However, the conclusion they draw – that there is no strong evidence that the rise is *not* due to demand-deficiency – ignores these very results. If the results tell us anything at all it is that the rise cannot be explained by demand-deficiency alone. I do not think, however, that this conclusion can be drawn from the study given the weakness of the methodology.

As CNS acknowledge, there are a variety of possible explanations for a rise in women's registered unemployment, but the method they employ makes it impossible to choose between them.

1 Registered unemployment might have risen for women because unemployed women have more readily registered. For a variety of reasons the proportion of unemployed women who register rose from 23 per cent in 1975 to 58 per cent in 1978 (General Household Survey 1978). However, this rise does not explain the whole of the greater rise in women's unemployment relative to men's. If unemployed women had registered as readily in 1975 as in 1978, registered unemployment among women would still have risen 29 per cent (82,000) as compared to a rise in male registered unemployment of 25 per cent.

2 Registered unemployment might have risen particularly fast among women because of their concentration in particular industries. As I have argued elsewhere (1979), this is unlikely to be an explanation of the unemployment trends because women are not especially concentrated in industries that are highly vulnerable to recession.

3 Registered unemployment might have risen if within any industry women are selected for redundancy first. This factor certainly explains the decline in some areas of part-time work for women, but the sex segregation of employment restricts the circumstances where employers can select women for redundancy in preference to men.

4 The Equal Pay Act (1970) might well have priced women out of jobs. But the Act's impact on pay should not be exaggerated given the limited circumstances in which it is relevant. Women's pay did rise relative to men's for a period but, at the same time, women's employment continued to expand relative to men's.

5 The greater rise in women's unemployment could be explained by the structural position that women occupy. Like youth, at any given time married women are more likely to be entrants to the labour market and hence subject to a high level of frictional unemployment (Hughes 1974). If cut-backs in demand for labour take place through cut-backs in recruitment in preference to redundancy, unemployment among youth and married women will rise disproportionately.

Unfortunately, CNS's research hardly helps us to decide between the possible explanations for a rise in registered unemployment among women. In part, data deficiencies make it difficult for anyone to make any such choice. However, as I have tried to argue, CNS have compounded the problem by simply 'adding on' women without rethinking economic categories. One hopes, nevertheless, that these criticisms will highlight some of their conceptual inadequacies and that economists like Corry, Nugent, and Saunders will now work towards developing economic concepts and methods that can help to advance our understanding of women's place in the British economy.

Acknowledgements

I would like to thank Thea Sinclair and Nancy Goldstein for their helpful comments on this paper.

Notes

1 At the time of writing this rejoinder, the author was a Senior Lecturer in the Department of Economics at North East London Polytechnic.

References

Acker, J. (1980) Women and Stratification. *Contemporary Sociology* **91**: 25–35.
Bowers, J. K. (1976) Some Notes on Current Unemployment. In G. D. N. Worswick (ed.) *The Concept and Measurement of Involuntary Unemployment.* London: Allen & Unwin.
Bruegel, I. (1979) Women as a Reserve Army. *Feminist Review* **3**: 12–23.
Corry, B. A. and Roberts, J. A. (1970) Activity Rates and Unemployment. The Experience of the United Kingdom 1951–66. *Applied Economics* **2**: 179–201.
Counter Information Services (1981) *Women in the Eighties.* London: CIS.
Daniel, W. W. (1974) *National Survey of the Unemployed.* London: PSI.
Department of Employment (1977) Characteristics of the Unemployed. *Gazette* June: 559–74.
Evans, A. (1977) Notes on the Changing Relationship between Registered Unemployment and Notified Vacancies. *Economica* **34**: 179–96.
Hughes, J. J. (1974) The Use of Vacancy Statistics in Classifying and Measuring Structural and Frictional Unemployment. *Bulletin of Economic Research* May: 12–34.
Hunt, A. (1980) Statistics on Women at Work. *EOC Research Bulletin* **5**: 29–34.
Moore, B., Rhodes, R., Tarling, R., and Wilkinson, F. (1978) A Return to Full Employment? *Cambridge Economic Policy Review* **4**: 22–36.
Oakley, A. and Oakley, R. (1979) Sexism in Official Statistics. In J. Irvine, I. Miles, and J. Evans (eds) *Demystifying Social Statistics.* London: Pluto.
Parry, J. and Green, E. (1981) 'I'm only doing this because of the hours'. Paper to the BSA Sexual Divisions Group.

5

Models of learning and their role in producing educational inequality

JENNY SHAW

Not everything that goes on in schools and that may bear on the process of gender formation can be attributed to the education system. Often schools merely reflect patterns that originate elsewhere and are best understood as interacting with them in ways that may enhance or diminish their effects. Nevertheless, there are some features of schools that are virtually unique and that may be examined for their particular contribution to the marked difference in educational outcomes for boys and girls. The differences are often expressed in terms of examinations entered and passed, entrance into higher and further education, and destination in the labour market. Inevitably, empirical measures such as these, 'hard' though they may be, are not wholly satisfactory for they relate to successively diminishing fractions of the school population and ignore important differences in the subjects and courses followed. While there is no difficulty in showing that at the broadest level there are significant differences in the educational achievement of boys and girls, it seems likely that informal barriers are more powerful in producing these results than those formal ones that remain.[1]

Terms such as 'the hidden curriculum' or 'invisible pedagogies' have earned both popularity and criticism for being too imprecise. They persist because they identify, or summarize, the pressures that *in toto* so often give the impression that gender differences are self-willed, if not exactly 'natural', and hence extremely difficult to combat. At the very least they underline the point that unintended consequences or side-effects are often the most enduring results of social action. Among the specific features of schooling that could be construed as having such effects are the conventions that structure formal learning such as time-tabling and lessons. Though apparently neutral, these organizational devices are superimposed upon various principles that constitute what I want to call 'models of learning'. While not sexist in themselves, they may, when applied, lead to results that are.

To date, some of the discussion of the differential achievement of boys and girls and of the contribution of schooling to sexual inequality, has been confused by the problem of knowing exactly what the central issue is, or was. Is under-achievement a useful concept? Can the under-achievement of girls be usefully analysed separately from the overall fortunes of children from different classes? Is sex stereotyping the basic cause of the inequalities? How far can trends be expected to continue in the same direction so that if gaps between boys' and girls' exam passes continue to narrow, we can safely redirect attention to other issues? Is the sex stereotyping of the curriculum the key process, and can the poorer performance of girls in mathematics and science be remedied by 'action research' with the confidence that this will have a significant effect on the distribution of life chances? In short, how many sources of sexual inequality are there in education, and how many theories should we be looking for in order to explain them?

In the argument that follows I intend to show that a set of apparently separate issues have a common foundation. The disproportionately small number of girls taking mathematics and sciences (other than biology), or doing well in examinations, has often been associated with the overall arts/science stereotyping of subjects. Further, this is linked to the higher number of boys continuing their education and the generally higher number of places offered to students taking science and engineering subjects. To this list of observable sex differences I want to add the higher rate of girls' absence from schools, and I want to go on to suggest that in part all these differences can be accounted for by the existence and operation of two divergent views of the learning process. One view stresses the importance of sequence, continuity, and cumulation; the other devalues such linear conventions in favour of the view that learning is largely independent of the route taken.

Before I expand this argument some reference to the overall theme of this collection might be helpful. Using institutionalization as the vantage point from which to view sex differences highlights some issues that might otherwise be missed. Sex, or rather gender, is itself an institution so in a sense the issue becomes that of sorting out the relationship between institutions.

Accompanying the notion of institutions as the more fixed parts of the social structure is the related view of institutionalization as used by, say, Goffman (1968), Cohen (1972), and Bettelheim (1961). They stress the adjustment that relatively powerless people have to make in order to survive. In their studies of prisons, asylums, and monasteries, for example, a person is described as being 'institutionalized' when he or she has adjusted to living under socially extreme conditions. Often inmates are so cut off from their former lives and sources of identity that, even when allowed to do so, they cannot return to a normal social pattern nor rid themselves of the indelible stain of their period of confinement. Such cases are extreme and although to some extent we all bear the marks of having lived under particular regimes of greater or lesser harshness, and are in varying degrees powerless, it is important not to ignore the differences in the degree of institutionalization or damage and the changes to the self that occur as a result of having lived in or through a particular organization.

Schools, unless they are boarding schools, are not total institutions in Goffman's sense but, along with the family, they come nearer to that model than almost any other institution that most people are likely to experience. Indeed, Rutter et al.'s (1979) study used the title *Fifteen Thousand Hours* in order to emphasize how much time the average child spends in school. While much recent research in education might be taken to suggest that differences in schools and teaching methods have little significant influence on children, such a view has to be highly qualified. The predominant belief among parents, teachers, politicians, and administrators is that schools do have some influence but that this is not always of a positive nature. The direct effects of schooling diminish over time. Nevertheless most research in education is still guided by the belief, or hope, that links may be found between the character of educational systems or practices and features of the wider society, most usually economic ones. In seeking such links, much of this research is, methodologically at least, functionalist; so, too, is this paper. By suggesting that the two models of learning, with their implied consequences for gender differentiation in education, share characteristics that are found to distinguish the pattern of men's and women's lives, it belongs broadly to what is now termed the 'correspondence theory' of education. However, while for comparative purposes an aspect is placed beside broader structural and existential dimensions of adult life, such an alignment should not be mistaken for an adequate explanation of one by the other.

Two models of learning

In recent years the view that learning and education are necessarily rather than contingently related has been severely criticized, although it remains the working assumption of most people directly engaged in teaching. The relationship between learning and education is undoubtedly problematic and has provided the starting point for much criticism of schooling. Despite that, even the harshest critics believe that something is learned in schools even if that turns out to be a form of political socialization rather than the 'skills' and 'knowledge' of official claims. Whatever the ultimate balance between the intended and unintended consequences of the educational process, theories of learning stand in a similar relation to the sociology of education as theories of human nature often do to social and political thought. Except in their most simplified, behaviourist forms, such theories are not, and may never be, testable. Yet they provide many of the axiomatic assumptions that underpin accounts of the educational process as well as serving as a guide to action for those who teach. They are all the more powerful for being implicit rather than explicit and this makes any discussion of them more difficult. The value of these models (as with all ideal types) depends on their capacity to make sense of, or summarize, behaviour, in this instance the actions of those directly involved in teaching and learning in schools.

One aspect of teaching that has been much studied is the extent to which the classroom practice of teachers departs from consciously held ideas and ideals about their role as teachers. Lacey (1977) has documented the speed with which student teachers lose their radical and progressive views once they are established in permanent posts, and Keddie (1971), in a more ethnographic study, has discussed the discrepancy between views that could be aired and heard in the staffroom and teachers' actual behaviour in the classroom. Although teachers might have intended to provide courses that did not discriminate according to class, in fact they were found to order their classrooms according to various common sense conceptions and presuppositions that often contrasted starkly with the pedagogic principles to which, in other contexts, they laid claim. Keddie was mainly concerned to show how teachers activated particular and imputed characteristics of the child's home background and converted them into variables of academic aptitude that they thought were crucial to the learning process. Such a process was hardly visible, so far was it from the stated intentions of the liberally minded liberal studies teachers that she observed, yet its consequences for the children and for the process of teaching were profound. These teachers were not dishonest, rather, as writers from the 1930s to today have stressed, teaching has more to do with straightforward management of a class than with the application of pedagogic principles learned in college or elsewhere (see Waller 1967 and Hargreaves 1977). It is not surprising that social and educational ideals go by the board and that survival on a daily basis takes over. However, under these conditions, other, deeper, principles may reassert themselves. Teachers are not obviously more sexist or concerned to restrict educational opportunities than any other members of the professional classes. Indeed, in terms of their stated views they may well be more progressive if only because their own livelihood increasingly depends upon valuing more education for all. Nevertheless, despite a degree of political consciousness, differentiation and discrimination continue in schools, much of it inadvertent.

In many subjects there are firmly held views on the best order of items that are then taught in sequence. Mathematics, physics, and chemistry illustrate this tendency to a greater degree than subjects such as home economics, geography, biology, or English. Other subjects may, of course, be arranged in a similar manner. For example, few history courses avoid stressing a unilinear view while some courses, for example languages, may display the same linear quality only under particular conditions, such as preparation for examinations. The same teacher will frequently organize an 'O'-level French lesson in quite a different way from a conversational French lesson, although to some extent the subject is the same.

The observation that the differences in the manner of teaching are as important as differences in content is not new and has been discussed in a number of theoretical and practical contexts. Nor has the arbitrariness and traditional quality of these conventions gone unrecognized. However, what is not clear is whether there are any good grounds for continuing with these practices. It is likely that if various forms of educational technology are extensively adopted by schools then the sequential model of learning will be reinforced. In part this depends on whether computers and teaching machines are introduced for all subjects or only for some. Certainly more programs have been written for learning mathematics than for any other subject because, superficially at least, most mathematics teaching in secondary schools resembles programmed learning, particularly the linear non-branching kind. Other subjects present particular problems but computer enthusiasts have no doubts that these can be overcome. The most important problem that has to be resolved is whether there is any cognitive basis to the established patterns of teaching either in terms of the mind or the knowledge that the mind has to absorb, or whether these conventions are purely a matter of social control.

Teachers often say that if their pupils miss a lesson 'they won't be able to follow later on'. Whether this is a prediction or a threat is not clear. Certainly not all missed lessons are treated in the same way and while little practical assistance may be given in 'catching up' (whatever the reason for the absence), it is the excuses offered by the pupil that attract attention and lead to different treatment (punishment). If all learning was incremental and cumulative *and* teaching was organized to take account of this view then *any* absence ought to be equally destructive of that process. It would not matter what subject was being taken nor whether the child was a boy or a girl. Of course such a view depends on how strictly a stimulus-response theory of learning was held to but absences mean interruptions and, according to the pace of the class, these should disrupt the whole enterprise. In fact very few courses or teaching programmes are engineered with such precision and much of what goes on in any classroom can be missed without much loss. As Holt (1977) observed, in a thirty-five-minute period probably only five minutes are used effectively.

Although the learning process can be measured quite reliably, except in partial ways it defies our understanding. Latterly psychologists have noted the erratic aspects of learning, observing that it seems to proceed as much by quantum leaps as by a steady and gradual growth (Jordan 1968). Often a distinction is made between the processes involved in learning skills (which more easily fit the incrementalist or behaviourist model) and those involved in acquiring what we call knowledge or understanding (which are harder to accommodate in that framework). For example, practice does improve one's typing speed but reading the same chapter ten times does not guarantee that after each reading there is even a slight improvement in understanding. Nevertheless, much conventional teaching is organized and justified on a basis that implicitly supports the incremental or linear view of learning. Moreover, this view is widely adopted as an example of good practice even though it is admitted to be difficult to achieve and is frequently departed from. Just as scientific knowledge and the scientific method have been taken as standards of knowledge and knowledge acquisition, so in schools the model of science teaching has come to dominate pedagogic theory. Again, while this view may be widely held it is also widely departed from and it is perhaps from such lapses that another model of learning, possibly only a residual one, can emerge.

The pacing of a subject or a class is clearly a dimension of social control. In most, if not all, instances social order is achieved by stressing sequence even though this may be neither necessary nor intrinsic to the subject being taught. It is extremely difficult to demonstrate that some things are necessarily prior to others although things often seem easier if they are approached in one way rather than another. I am aware that quite soon after picking up a book on linear algebra I would be hurrying back to something more elementary. However, a large number of 'revolutionary' teaching techniques consist of overturning the established ideas of what, say, an eight-year-old can handle in the way of set theory or logic. Subjects such as mathematics, physics, and chemistry are usually seen as the most difficult to learn and it is in teaching these subjects that the linear model is strongest.

Furthermore, boys are generally thought to be more difficult to control than girls even though teachers vary in their abilities to exercise control and will often say that girls are 'just as bad'. What is usually meant is that, on occasion, girls are as bad as boys, not that they routinely cause as much difficulty or disturbance. Routinely, then, so-called 'boys'' subjects may be taught in ways that offer the most opportunities for control. Apparently unrelated to this is another odd but common observation, namely that girls are less willing than boys to tackle what they regard as 'difficult' subjects, for which a variety of explanations have been offered (Kelly 1981). However, as Keddie pointed out, the characteristics of subjects and their conventional organization are sometimes turned around and applied to children as personal characteristics. This process may be reinforced by the exigencies of everyday life so that a teacher's attitude to a child's absence is selective, initially in terms of what has been missed (the lesson) and later in more obviously social terms (the sort of child, girl or boy, clever or dull). In the long run this affects children's self-perceptions and what they regard as conditions that are conducive to learning.

Little has been said about another non-linear model of learning, partly because its existence has to be inferred if teachers are not to be regarded as simply negligent towards some of their pupils. In a research project into secondary school attendance I found that overall more girls than boys were absent from school, and that girls were away from school significantly more often than boys.[2] Unless there is some very obvious explanation such as higher rates of illness for girls than boys at that age, this meant that girls and/or their teachers tolerated a higher rate of interruptions than did boys. Such a difference need not be the result of a simple prejudice that considers the education of boys to be more important than that of girls and that leads both to greater efforts to persuade boys to return to school and to less attention being directed at the absence of girls. It can result from a combination of how the learning process is viewed and which subjects are taken. As schools are increasingly troubled by bad attendance and disaffected and alienated pupils, theories of learning have become more innovative and eclectic. Lessons are broadened and traditional distinctions between work and 'non-work' blurred. Experimentation in the form and content of examinations has taken place specifically to raise the numbers taking examinations, and subjects such as 'learning for life', 'leisure', and 'community service' appear on the curriculum.

Bernstein (1975) has discussed some of the processes behind this movement and central to his argument is the conviction that while changing forms of curriculum organization also mean changing social relationships, these do not always follow the same direction. Bernstein does not explore the implications of his framework for gender differences and his term 'invisible pedagogy' both has a specialized meaning and was coined specifically to describe middle-class teachers in primary schools. Nevertheless, his emphasis on the intimate connections between the content of the curriculum and the way that subjects are taught and their consequences for patterns of social control is both crucial and illuminating. Macdonald (1980) amalgamates Bernstein's concepts of classification and framing to produce a single 'gender code' and considers that this will help us to answer Bernstein's question 'How are the forms of experience, identity and relation evoked, maintained and changed by the formal transmission of educational knowledge and sensitivities?' (1979: 228). The examples that Macdonald chooses demonstrate that for girls, unlike boys, the school may not 'succeed in transmitting gender definitions which can merge easily with prescribed class identities'. Nevertheless 'pupils may still acquire gender identities which prepare them indirectly for their future class positions' (1980: 24).

Bernstein's ideas are perhaps as famous for the controversies that they have provoked as for the ideas themselves. King (1979), one of Bernstein's more able critics, has argued that the notion of invisible pedagogy is more or less unworkable, highly speculative and, at worst, tautological.

Yet King's criticisms are as likely to convince the reader of the inventiveness of the original set of ideas as to dissuade him or her from employing them. The failure to provide empirical evidence and the rather rococo quality of the writing whereby a case is made for seeing a set of arrangements as demonstrating 'weak' classification and 'framing' (two dimensions of power and control, both relating to the strength of boundary demarcation, the first of subjects, the second of the teaching relationship) only to be immediately qualified by the statement that 'behind weak classification is strong classification' are most often cited. However, the case of girls' education might provide a fairly straightforward illustration of exactly the sort of paradox Bernstein was trying to expose. The type of mixed curriculum that girls typically follow – hybrid mixes of arts and sciences which disqualify rather than qualify them for continuing in higher education – fits his idea of weak classification perfectly. 'Weak framing' means that girls' presence or absence from school itself provokes little comment; milder forms of punishment (no corporal punishment, and a 'softer' interpretation of absence as something other than truancy); less and late careers guidance. Yet behind this there are strong classification (a very restricted set of job opportunities for women) and strong framing (much stricter and extensive social control).

These ideas are schematic, as indeed are the two models of learning that are another way of viewing the same phenomenon. However, before setting out the final and speculative part of the argument it is as well to be clear about exactly what is *not* being claimed. First, I am not trying to explain the poorer performance of girls relative to boys by their greater absence from school. Nor can girls' poorer performance in particular subjects, primarily mathematics and science, be explained in this way. Nor do I think that all the variance between girls and boys in terms of measured performance can be accounted for by linear and non-linear models of learning or by any other version of the 'hidden curriculum'; only some variance can be thus explained. For example, this perspective might help us to understand why girls are more intimidated by subjects they think are 'difficult', a concept that serves pupils as a subjective proxy for all those processes that academic investigators seek to identify. It might also explain why researchers like Kelly (1981) could find that although 80 per cent of all pupils agreed that science was interesting, a large number of girls still gave as their reason for not continuing with science the rationale that they did not like it. Kelly adds that while girls were less likely than boys to agree that science was useful for getting a job, and that this was realistic in terms of the traditional job market for girls and boys, nevertheless several of the girls who were planning careers in nursing or catering, where the chemistry they were taking would be useful, did not mention career plans as a reason for taking the subject. Boys, on the other hand, thought chemistry would be useful in their careers even though the careers they were planning were accountancy, banking, law, and town planning. Obviously, it is easy to speculate on why results such as these might be found, and why boys should over-estimate the value of subjects they follow while girls underestimate them. Difficult though it is to prove, this can only make sense by being linked to the processes of self-perception and expectations of the future.

Girls do not do as well as boys in the linear subjects (mathematics and physics). In general their progress through the education system seems to be more easily interrupted and diverted, whatever their level of ability. It has been suggested that 'difficulty' is a euphemism for 'masculine' which is why girls cannot locate themselves within subjects seen as 'male'. I want to amend this argument a little by suggesting that 'difficulty' is another way of describing an approach to learning that is less familiar for girls. To recap, the models of learning that are used in school lead to distinctions, or differences, that are not inherently sexist or gender based, though they come to be associated with divisions that are. It is neither accidental nor irrelevant that the subjects stereotypically thought of as 'boys'' subjects are also the ones arranged in the most linear or sequential manner. These subjects are taught in ways that stress deductive logic, cumulative argument, and the incremental presentation of evidence. The effect of learning subjects in this way may reinforce what Hudson (1966) has called 'convergent thinking', that is, a way of handling ideas that, superficially at least, displays the qualities of being systematic, single-minded, lean, and uni-directional. The arts are conventionally thought to require different intellectual skills. In Hudson's schema those pupils who were good at these skills displayed 'divergent thinking' patterns. They were rewarded, or told that they were making imaginative leaps, subtle distinctions, and associations that were remarkable for their unexpectedness and range.

The research recently collected by Kelly confirms that girls and boys are treated differently within and between lessons and that boys and girls are taught in distinctly different ways. Weinreich-Haste (1981), writing of the image of science, warns that:

'in the education system both sexes are formally expected to develop the skills of objectivity, logical ability, independence of thought and to be ambitious – at least within the context of examination success. Therefore the question is not about innate sex differences, but about the extent to which the image of science coincides with:

1 The kinds of interests and orientations which have developed by the time the individual comes to make the choice between subjects, and

2 The kinds of expectations which the individual has concerning appropriate and desirable characteristics and activities for the self in adult life.' (Weinreich-Haste 1981: 219)

If we turn our attention to adult life, the differences between men and women become sharper. If these differences are described in terms more existential than structural then a distinctly disorganized, episodic, and fragmented quality can be discerned in the lives of most women. This stems mainly from the necessity of combining child-care with work (paid and unpaid) which requires the ability to take on and complete tasks despite many and repeated interruptions. This is something that all mothers, and some fathers, have to learn. Child-care requires a 'split brain' and a parent's attention can never be so devoted to one task that it cannot be detached to cope immediately with whatever crisis or demand the child produces. Thus a tolerance is built up, however reluctantly. This pattern is reinforced at other levels; at work women are expected to be the parent who has to take time off to care for a sick child and pay the financial and social costs of doing so. Often women think themselves lucky to have a job at all, especially as they are likely to be restricted to jobs within a two-mile radius of where they live. As workers they are used to being mistakenly viewed as unreliable and unskilled, and to being paid less as a result. As part-timers and late entrants they are laid off sooner than full-timers (mostly men), and, if married, when they are unemployed they are ineligible for certain benefits. By contrast the lives of men are more predictable, cumulative, and show a greater degree of continuity. This is not true for all men and may be less true in the future than it once was, but in general their experience of and in the labour market is progressive. They can more easily avoid employment in poorly paid, unstable, and seasonal sectors and are more free to travel further to find work that suits them. They are more likely to be employed in sections of the labour market where there is greater job security, where unions are strong, where experience counts and is rewarded, and where the term 'career' is meaningful. Clearly, both these accounts are stereotypical and owe much to the idea that women are, or can be, used as a reserve army of labour, to the theory of dual labour markets, and to the view that family life is not symmetrical. However, in their broad outline, the conditions and features of female paid employment and women's primary responsibility for child-care mark out the major sexual divisions of adult life.

Although too crude in one respect these two stereotypes of adult life are too detailed in another, for the only feature of immediate relevance is the degree of continuity or discontinuity that has been institutionalized. If this can be shown to be characteristic not only of men's and women's experiences in and of the labour market, but also of their schooling, then a little more of the picture suggested by the 'correspondence theory' may be filled in.

Conclusion

Lineality is a culturally specific way of ordering the perceived social world. Although the example used by Dorothy Lee (1959) when she first advanced the argument was rather specialized (the Trobriand Islanders), the distinction she made between cultures that place events situationally rather than temporally is important. Our culture may not 'find all climax abominable' or value only sameness, but, to a degree, both of these perspectives are held and characterize some of the differences between the lives of men and women. Typically, men's lives are viewed and valued as developmental and progressive, and their jobs are described by terms such as 'career' which embody the idea of positive change. Furthermore, Lee's finding that the Trobriander value 'repetition of the known', and 'maintaining the point' (in other words what we would call monotony), would fit very well with a description of most Western housewives and women workers. Lee insists that the 'assumption is not that reality itself is relative, only that it is differently punctuated and categorized, or that different aspects of it are noticed by or presented to the participants of different cultures' (Lee 1959).

In many respects the lives of men and women are unalike and in order to be at all credible correspondence theories need to explain exactly which features of women's adult lives are replicated through schooling. Girls do less well than boys in gaining certificates and places in further education, but not badly enough to explain their inferior position in the labour market. Schools certainly encourage girls to view marriage and motherhood as important in ways that they do not for boys, but these biases are insufficient to explain either the form or the direction that the sexual divisions take (that is, mainly curricular.) What is probably most apparent both to outside observers and to those within the system is how unrelated most schooling is to later life, especially for girls. Of course it is a Gestalt trick to switch from a picture showing two facing profiles to one showing a goblet, but the existing correspondence theories that stress continuities of various sorts work best for boys, while the theories of institutionalization that show how organizations create discontinuities and distinctly fail to equip inmates for life outside fit better for girls. If this is so then a modified version of both theories would show how discontinuity and interruptions are more than a motif of girls' education and women's lives, they are an institutionalized and essential part of them.

Notes

1 For the difficulties involved in removing educational arrangements that are discriminatory, see the report prepared for the Equal Opportunities Commission by Bloomfield and Pratt (1980).
2 The higher rate of absence for girls was statistically significant at the 5 per cent level. Girls were also away from school more than boys overall but this difference was not statistically significant.

References

Bernstein, B. (1975) *Class, Codes and Control*, Vol. 3. London: Routledge & Kegan Paul.
Bettelheim, B. (1961) *The Informed Heart: The Human Condition in Modern Mass Society*. London: Thames & Hudson.
Bloomfield, J. and Pratt, J. (1980) *Guidelines on Secondary School Reorganisation*. Commentary Series 13. Centre for Institutional Studies, North East London Polytechnic.
Bowles, S. and Gintis, H. (1976) *Schooling in Capitalist America*. London: Routledge & Kegan Paul.
Cohen, S. (1972) *Psychological Survival*. Harmondsworth: Penguin.
Goffman, E. (1968) *Asylums*. Harmondsworth: Penguin.
Hargreaves, A. (1977) Progressivism and Pupil Autonomy. *Sociological Review* **25**(3): 585–621.
Holt, J. (1969) *How Children Fail*. Harmondsworth: Penguin.
Hudson, L. (1966) *Convergent Imaginations*. London: Methuen.
Jordan, N. (1968) *Themes in Speculative Psychology*. London: Tavistock.
Keddie, N. (1971) Classroom Knowledge. In M. F. D. Young (ed.) *Knowledge and Control*. London: Collier Macmillan.
Kelly, A. (1981) *The Missing Half*. Manchester: Manchester University Press.
King, R. (1979) The Search for the Invisible Pedagogy. *Sociology* **13**(3): 445–58.

Lacey, C. (1977) *The Socialisation of Teachers*. London: Methuen.

Lee, D. (1959) *Freedom and Culture*. London: Spectrum.

Macdonald, M. (1980) Socio-Cultural Reproduction and Women's Education. In R. Deem (ed.) *Schooling for Women's Work*. London: Routledge & Kegan Paul.

Rutter, M., Maughan, B., Mortimer, P., and Ouston, J. (1979) *Fifteen Thousand Hours: Secondary Schools and their Effects on Children*. London: Open Books.

Shaw, J. 'The Social Context of Non-Attendance amongst Secondary School Children.' SSRC: unpublished.

Waller, W. (1967) *The Sociology of Teaching*. London: John Wiley. First published 1932.

Weinreich-Haste, H. (1981) The Image of Science. In A. Kelly (ed.) *The Missing Half*. Manchester: Manchester University Press.

6

Rejoinder to Jenny Shaw

TESSA BLACKSTONE

Differences in the education of boys and girls is a relatively new area of interest for social scientists. When I first studied this subject in the early 1970s, there was very little literature on which to draw. Practically no research had been done in the UK, and although rather more had been attempted in the USA there were many important questions that remained uninvestigated. Since then there has been a growing interest in this subject, and I welcome Jenny Shaw's paper as an interesting contribution to the debate.

It is important to begin by stating, as indeed does the paper, that it is the informal barriers to girls' educational advancement in certain areas that now require further study. Most of the formal barriers have been removed. There has, in fact, been remarkable progress in this area over the last two decades. One measure of this is the fact that the proportion of women undergraduates has been rising rapidly. In the mid-1960s only 25 per cent of undergraduates were female. In 1982 this figure had reached nearly 40 per cent.

It is an interesting idea to try to link discontinuities in the curriculum (emphasizing the differences between 'girls'' and 'boys'' subjects in this respect) to discontinuities in school attendance, and in turn in adult life. Much of Shaw's argument rests on the claim that there are two modes of learning, one of which is sequential or linear, the other of which is non-linear. The first is associated with 'male' subjects; the second with 'female' subjects. She also implies that there has been an expansion of teaching on a sequential basis that may be important in terms of its impact on boys and girls. However, much of the argument here rests on assertion rather than clear evidence. First, the invention of micro-processors will not necessarily involve more programmed learning on a sequential basis. What it will do is to make micro-computers and video recorders available to every school, and data retrieval systems common-place. However, these do not necessarily imply more sequential learning. A great deal depends on how they are used. Second, Shaw argues that teachers are often heard voicing the opinion that if pupils miss a lesson they will not be able to follow later on. This may well be true, but we are not told that this view is becoming more common than before. Moreover, although it is clearly the case that 'much conventional teaching is organized and justified on a basis that implicitly supports the incremental or linear view of learning' (see p. 94), it is also the case that much teaching is not organized in this way. It is even possible that non-sequential teaching styles are growing at the expense of the sequential.

Not enough evidence is given by Shaw to support her claim that social order is achieved by stressing sequence. In so far as sequence may mean that some pupils can be lost somewhere along the line, and that other pupils find the movement from sequence to sequence too slow and become bored, it may mean that on the contrary such forms of teaching are more likely to generate disorder. Also, the association between linearity and 'male' subjects is not, in my view, as strong as Shaw implies. Traditionally 'female' subjects such as modern languages often put as much emphasis on sequence as do subjects such as mathematics, physics, and chemistry. All this leads to the conclusion that the relation-ship that Shaw postulates between 'boys'' subjects and opportunities for control is not as yet convincing.

Shaw also argues that girls are more exposed to what Bernstein calls 'weak classification' in that they typically follow mixed arts and science subjects. There is, however, little evidence that girls typically take this route, and nor is it true, as the author claims, that mixed 'A' levels dis-qualify girls from higher education. There has been a revolution in the attitudes of universities and polytechnics towards mixed 'A' levels, and many of them now express some preference for entrants who have such qualifications. Moreover, the author does not provide any evidence of girls getting less career guidance than boys and receiving it later.

The very important point is made, however, that girls are less likely than boys to link their educational experience, including choice of subjects, to their future careers. This may partly explain why girls take up or are taken into lower status occupations than their educational attain-ment merits. They sometimes choose careers that demand qualifications below those they have acquired. Presumably this is partly a function of the expectations they have about their adult roles as wives and mothers. As Shaw argues, the differences between men and women become much sharper in adult life than earlier. She points out an interesting difference in the more 'disorganized, episodic, and fragmented quality' of women's lives which stems from the necessity of combining child-care with work. She argues that *if* this difference in the degree of continuity 'can be shown to be characteristic not only of men's and women's experiences in and of the labour market, but also of their schooling, then a little more of the picture suggested by the "correspondence theory" may be filled in' (see p. 100).

Thus Shaw's paper outlines an interesting hypothesis about the way in which gender differences are developed at school and such a hypothesis warrants development and empirical testing. At the same time it is important to bear in mind that differences in achievement between boys and girls at school are relatively small and decreasing over time. It is the case that girls take slightly fewer 'O' levels and CSEs than boys, but their pass rate has been higher. But these differences are very small. What is perhaps remarkable is the degree of similarity between the sexes at this age. It is true that a rather smaller proportion of girls than boys take two or three 'A' levels, but the gap has been narrowing and again there is no evidence that girls do less well than boys in these exams.

In post-school education there are in fact more female than male students in full-time further education. In higher education the participation of women is increasing at a rapid rate so that if the current trend continues the gap between men and women will be eliminated by the end of the 1980s. It is only when we turn to part-time further education that we find there are substantially larger numbers of male than female students. Moreover, UCCA statistics indicate that the number of university places in the arts, social sciences, and education, subjects women tend to study, is substantially greater than the number in the sciences, technology, and agriculture: there were approximately 40,500 acceptances in 1979 in the first group compared with 34,400 acceptances in the second group. Educational opportunities for girls may be greater, and the influence of schooling on adult lives less than Shaw implies. Her interesting argument has not yet been sufficiently developed, and further work is needed to establish her case.

7

Gender, mental illness, and psychiatry

JOAN BUSFIELD

It is frequently argued, on the basis of patient statistics and symptom reports, that mental illness is more common among women than men. By virtue of the various explanations that are offered of it, this observation in turn provides the grounds for further claims about women and their situation in contemporary society. It may be used both to confirm and amplify traditional gender stereotypes. For instance, if one argues that women are by nature more irrational and emotional than men, then the higher incidence of mental illness can come as no surprise. Or it may be claimed that mental illness is a manifestation in an extreme form of women's weakness and frailty, suggesting that women are, in general, more vulnerable to the strains and pressures of everyday life, and, when faced with difficult and demanding situations, are more likely than men to break down and become mentally disturbed. Or, following the assumption that it is the level of strain and stress that people face that determines their chances of mental illness, it may be argued that the higher level of mental illness among women is evidence that their lives are more stressful than men's. This is the type of argument that has been developed by Gove and his colleagues (Gove and Tudor 1972; Gove 1972), who have been foremost in asserting that nowadays more women than men become mentally ill. Gove *et al.* contend that the higher incidence of mental illness among women is due to their position in society, arguing that women's role is 'more frustrating and less rewarding' than men's. Similarly, various feminists (though Gove himself does not fall into this category) suggest that the higher level of mental illness in women is striking evidence of their oppression in contemporary society.

I argue, however, that far from providing good evidence in itself either of women's greater emotional volatility, irrationality, or vulnerability, or of the greater tension and stressfulness of their lives, the data that suggest higher levels of mental illness among women, are primarily a reflection of psychiatry's differential involvement with the problems and difficulties of men and women and, thereby, of the way in which the category 'mental illness' has been constituted. Hence, the only generalizations we can make from patient statistics and symptom reports concern the nature of psychiatric thought and practice; they do not themselves provide a basis for generalizations about the characteristics of men and women or their social situation.

In this paper, I consider first certain features of the notion of mental illness and their implications for the interpretation of patient data. Second, I examine in some detail the gender differentials manifest in patient statistics and symptom surveys, and point to the considerable variation in them. Of particular importance here is the well established association between gender and type of mental illness and this provides a clue to the interpretation of the gender differentials. Therefore, third, I attempt to account for the association between gender and type of mental illness. This is an essential foundation to my fourth concern; to consider how the observed gender differentials in patient statistics can best be interpreted. My focus throughout is primarily on psychiatry in England although, from time to time, I refer to data obtained in the USA.

The concept of mental illness

I want to start with a number of observations concerning the concept of mental illness. First, mental illness, like physical illness, is a generic term given formal content and meaning by psychiatrists not through the specification of certain abstract characteristics, but by means of the delineation of a set of distinct and highly diverse illnesses located within the general category: it is given an extensive rather than an intensive definition.[1] Following the model of infectious illnesses, each mental illness is ideally differentiated and identified in terms of its specific aetiology and distinctive constellation of syndromes. Since, in practice, aetiology may not be clearly established, differentiation is often largely based on symptoms. The range of mental illnesses listed in current classifications includes disorders of thought and intellect, such as senile dementia and schizophrenia, disorders of emotion and mood, such as the various forms of depression and anxiety neurosis, as well as the behaviour or personality disorders, such as alcoholism, sexual deviation, and drug addiction. Attempts to specify common characteristics of these diverse conditions have been conspicuously unsuccessful (see, for example, Kendell 1975a). Their only common features seem to be that, by virtue of their inclusion within the category of mental illness, they are defined both as undesirable and the proper object of medical attention. In that respect the concept of mental illness is both evaluative and prescriptive.[2]

Second, the precise differentiation of particular mental illnesses and their classification vary over time and place, and are a matter of negotiation and debate among professionals. Indeed, it is only possible to generate a single list of mental illnesses or to classify them further by glossing over a number of controversial issues (see Kendell 1975b). Much of this debate is little noticed outside the more academic sectors of the psychiatric profession, apart from the occasional dramatic decision, for example when the American Psychiatric Association decided to no longer regard homosexuality in itself as a mental illness (see Spector 1977). Nevertheless, a number of studies of psychiatric practice have provided evidence not only of the problems (but not impossibility) of securing diagnostic agreement among psychiatrists, but also of the differing interpretations and uses of diagnostic categories by psychiatrists of different theoretical orientation, country, and so on.[3] In the USA, for instance, the category 'schizophrenia' is used more broadly than in this country, whereas the reverse is true for manic depression (Kendell 1975b). Studies also indicate how fashions in the use of diagnostic categories change with theoretical and empirical ideas (Blum 1978). Such work provides clear evidence of the changing and variable nature of the conceptualization of different mental illnesses, and hence of the general category.

Third, the categories and diagnostic descriptions developed by psychiatrists constitute a conceptual framework – a psychiatric discourse – that allows the practical activity of psychiatry to continue and provides individuals and those around them with a way of interpreting their experiences (see Foucault 1971, 1978). Faced with a set of patients and their problems, the psychiatric description of different mental illnesses and the assumptions made about prognosis and suitable treatments represent the cognitive map that psychiatrists have developed to enable them to structure their day-to-day activities. The contours of this map incorporate and organize the vagaries and contingencies of the flow of complaints that, for a range of reasons, have historically been dealt with by psychiatrists. From this point of view the notion of mental illness has been constituted around the problems that have typically faced psychiatrists. It is not, therefore, that a sphere of mental illness exists that is defined independently of the profession's activities over time, but rather that there is a sphere of problems, complaints, disruptions, and disturbances that have, as a result of a number of factors, come to be defined as legitimate objects of psychiatric activity, and, in turn, have been incorporated within the category of mental illness. In other words, we can say that certain types of behaviour and feeling, many already defined as problematic, have been 'medicalized' (using the term only to indicate that they now fall within the province of medicine, and not to suggest that this is necessarily either the consequence of, or an indication of the exercise of medical power)[4] and, by implication, others have not. This is not to deny the material or experiential reality of the phenomena categorized as mental illness, but simply to stress the way in which social judgements and social practices are involved in the constitution of the category.

The concept of mental illness is, therefore, selective, incorporating only certain conditions as undesirable and matters of mental ill-health. The set of neurotic illnesses, for instance, that is usually said to represent exaggerated responses to reality (as opposed to the loss of contact with reality that is held to define psychotic conditions) selects out only certain mental experiences as problematic and the proper province of medical concern.[5] While extremes of hatred or ambition are not in themselves considered symptomatic of sickness, extremes of anxiety and fear are. Of course, it might be said that there are good reasons for this: extreme ambition or hatred appears neither to affect a person's capacity to function in the social environment to any great extent, nor to generate personal suffering and a sense of disease as does, say, depression. In that respect they do not seem to satisfy the first condition of illness, which is that the state should be normally considered undesirable either by oneself or others. But to say this is to beg the question; we categorize only certain extremes of emotion and behaviour as undesirable, and only some that are considered undesirable are then the province of medical activity. The selective nature of the category is entailed both by its evaluative nature and by the fact that not all thought and action that is considered socially undesirable is regarded as a matter of mental ill-health.

Fourth, the boundaries of particular mental illnesses tend to be imprecisely drawn, providing no clear distinction between the presence or absence of illness. There are two reasons for this. On the one hand, the assumption of a qualitative break between the normal and the patho-logical, suggested by the conceptualization of infectious diseases on the basis of germ theory, cannot be readily sustained with many illnesses (Armstrong: unpublished). Often there is an empirical continuity between states of health and sickness in which the identification of clear-cut thresholds of sickness is difficult to achieve. On the other hand, the medical task itself, oriented as it is to the treatment of individuals who seek help, directs attention away from defining the limits of particular illnesses towards distinguishing one from another. Clinical medicine encourages an acceptance of the patient's claim that something is wrong, a search for the source of the problem, and the provision of some remedy (see Parsons 1951 and Freidson 1970). One consequence, shown in a number of studies, is the tendency to presume illness; another is the failure to clarify the precise limits of specific illnesses; and yet another is a tendency to develop categories that will incorporate the residual, vague, and more minor cases (the use of the term 'transient situation dis-turbance' provides a good example) (see Scheff 1963; Rosenhan 1973; and Luker 1978).

Senile dementia illustrates the lack of exact boundaries of mental illness (Armstrong 1981). Because of its known organic basis, the condition might seem to be one that could be clearly delineated and objectively identified. However, there is considerable difficulty in distinguishing the changes symptomatic of senile dementia from those of normal ageing, whether we examine social performance, intellectual deterioration as assessed by psychological tests, or neurological changes. The diagnosis requires evidence of 'a deterioration of previously acquired intellectual abilities of sufficient severity to interfere with social or occupational functioning' (American Psychiatric Association 1978: A10). However, even if we assess the level of functioning with some precision (and judgements of social performance are notoriously difficult to make), this still leaves us with the problem of setting the boundary between normal ageing and senile dementia. Faced with a patient showing some signs of deterioration, it makes sense in the context of medical practice to diagnose senile dementia, but this makes the boundary of illness a matter of the contingencies of an individual's contact with the psychiatrist and not of the level of their symptoms.

It is for these reasons that data on psychiatric morbidity, whether obtained from surveys of patients or from field studies of people living in a particular community, do not provide a sound basis for generalizations about the comparative incidence or prevalence of mental illness among men and women, the working or the middle class, or people from different cultures or historical periods.[6] Not only may the constitution of the category of mental illness differ for the groups that we are attempting to compare, but in practice the boundaries of the particular types of conditions that are embraced within the general term may also vary. And this is no less true of the community surveys of psychiatric morbidity than of studies that rely on patient data (see Mechanic 1970).

Although field studies appear to circumvent many of the problems of patient data, by working with a standard set of diagnostic categories, by training researchers or clinicians in a uniform interpretation of such categories, and by eradicating the contingencies that affect the use of medical services, they do not eliminate all the problems of case identification. On the one hand, some studies still rely on assessments of psychiatric symptomatology in a clinical interview, so that the possibility that the clinicians assessment is systematically affected by the social characteristics of the cases under study is not excluded. On the other hand, even if psychiatric morbidity is assessed in a more standardized way, through the use of rating scales for example, the assessment still depends on statements from the individuals being studied about their feelings, experiences, and actions. Therefore, the possibility of biases in their identification and description of their own feelings is not ruled out. There is also evidence, as I shall argue below, that people's judgements of their own feelings and those of others are affected by social characteristics such as social class, age, and gender.

This does not mean, however, that data from the use of psychiatric services or from field studies are of no interest. While they tell us little about the comparative prevalence or incidence of mental illness, they can tell us much about the contrasting conceptions of mental health and illness for the groups in question, and about the activities of the medical profession. The following section examines, therefore, the gender differentials in patient data and community surveys, with a view to evaluating them in terms of the light they throw on variation and changes in the conception of health for men and women, and on the relation of the medical profession to their problems and difficulties.

Gender differences in patient statistics

It is easy to see why a number of studies have come to the conclusion that mental illness is more common among women than men, for the aggregate picture shows higher patient and symptom rates for women. On the one hand, women predominate in the patient population of those with diagnosed mental disorders, often to a quite striking extent; on the other hand, if questioned, women report more symptoms medically classified as psychiatric. Women have, for instance, higher rates of admission to, and residence in psychiatric beds; they have higher consultation and episode rates for conditions diagnosed as mental disorders by general practitioners, and, according to field studies, they quite often have higher rates of psychiatric symptomatology than men.

However, the female predominance among patients with diagnosed mental disorders is not as pervasive as it seems at first: it varies according to age, marital status, social class, historical period, and diagnosis, as well as the data source.

AGE

There is clear evidence of a variation in the gender differential with age across a range of data, and among children the gender differential is often reversed, with boys having higher patient rates than girls. The figures for admissions to psychiatric beds in England are given in *Table 1* and *Table 2*. They show that beyond fifteen years of age women's admission rates are markedly higher than men's; for ten- to fourteen-year-olds they

Table 1 *Admissions to psychiatric beds in England, average rates per 100,000 population for 1972–76*

Age	All admissions		First admissions		Readmissions	
	Male	Female	Male	Female	Male	Female
0–	15.8	8.2	10.8	5.2	5.2	3.0
10–	36.8	36.6	24.4	24.4	12.8	12.2
15–	182.4	266.4	92.4	137.0	90.2	128.8
20–	417.0	479.6	153.2	192.8	263.8	286.8
25–	471.6	592.4	139.6	194.6	332.0	397.8
35–	468.4	618.2	130.6	166.4	338.0	451.8
45–	427.0	588.4	117.0	145.4	310.0	443.4
55–	348.4	503.6	104.4	128.0	244.2	365.4
65–	382.0	555.4	146.2	175.6	236.0	379.6
75+	647.6	756.2	338.6	363.2	308.6	393.4
All ages	314.8	435.2	105.4	142.8	209.4	292.6

Source: In-patient statistics from the Mental Health Inquiry for England, 1976, Table A1.

are roughly the same, but among those under ten years old, where the admission rates are extremely low, they are higher for boys.

The gender differential in admission rates cannot simply be attributed to a greater tendency for women to be discharged early and then re-admitted (the revolving door phenomenon), for although men do tend to stay longer in hospital when admitted, if we separate our first and sub-sequent admissions, women still have higher first admission rates than men (see *Table 1*), although the differentials are somewhat smaller than for readmissions (see *Table 2*). Significantly, however, men's longer average stay in hospital means that they have higher residence rates than

Table 2   *Ratio of female to male average admission rates 1972–76*

Age	All admissions	First admissions	Readmissions
0–	0.52	0.46	0.58
10–	0.99	1.00	0.95
15–	1.46	1.48	1.42
20–	1.15	1.26	1.09
25–	1.26	1.39	1.20
35–	1.32	1.27	1.34
45–	1.38	1.24	1.43
55–	1.45	1.23	1.50
65–	1.45	1.20	1.61
75+	1.17	1.07	1.27
All ages	1.38	1.35	1.40

Table 3   *Residents of psychiatric beds, average rates per 100,000 population, 1972–76, and female to male ratio of the average rates*

	Male	Female	Female: Male
0–9	4.8	1.8	0.38
10–14	12.2	8.8	0.72
15–19	32.8	38.0	1.16
20–24	71.8	65.2	0.91
25–34	103.4	80.4	0.78
35–44	157.4	119.2	0.76
45–54	278.0	201.6	0.73
55–64	364.6	303.6	0.83
65–74	448.8	541.2	1.21
75+	650.2	1100.0	1.69
All ages	173.8	218.2	1.26

Source: In-patient statistics from the Mental Health Enquiry, 1976, Table A5.

women at all ages up to sixty-five.[7] Only beyond sixty-five, and from fifteen to nineteen years old (see *Table 3*), do women have higher residence rates. However, since the over-sixty-fives contribute disproportionately to the resident population (they constituted some 49 per cent of all resident patients in England in 1976), the gender differential of this group is sufficient to dominate the aggregate picture (Department of Health and Social Security 1975).

The consultation and episode rates for conditions diagnosed by general practitioners as mental disorders similarly vary with age (see *Table 4*). Again, under fifteen years of age the differential is only small or shows a male excess, while among the over-fifteens, there is a female preponderance. What is striking, however, is that the female predominance is far greater than it was for the in-patient admissions. Although women's admission rates were some 39 per cent higher than men's, their consultation and episode rates were more than double. It appears that as we move from the more restricted group of those who become in-patients, to the far larger group of those who have some contact with their general practitioners for complaints diagnosed as mental disorders, the gender differential increases.

Some field studies attempt to cast their net very widely by using a broad measure of psychiatric morbidity; others attempt to measure the distribution of 'clinical' mental illnesses in the community and are more restrictive. As the measures of morbidity vary considerably it is not surprising that the results are less clear-cut than for patient statistics.

Table 4 *Episode and consultation rates for diagnosed mental disorders and ratio of female to male rates*

Age	Episode rates			Consultation rates		
	Male	Female	Ratio Female: Male	Male	Female	Ratio Female: Male
0–4	59.0	51.5	0.87	77.1	62.2	0.81
5–14	41.1	46.6	1.13	59.2	69.6	1.81
15–24	69.6	176.7	2.54	120.4	307.8	2.56
25–44	115.9	281.8	2.43	247.1	578.5	2.34
45–64	119.3	257.0	2.15	288.6	570.8	1.98
65–74	83.0	207.7	2.50	195.1	456.0	2.34
75+	92.8	162.7	1.75	197.8	366.8	1.85
All ages	89.1	195.2	2.19	186.2	400.5	2.15

Source: Morbidity Statistics from General Practice, 1970–71, Table 10.

Little systematic information of this type is available for this country and that for the USA is not entirely consistent. The 1950s Midtown Manhattan study of psychiatric symptomatology reported that although, overall, morbidity increased with age, 'in no age group is there a statistically significant sex difference' (Stole *et al.* 1975: 241). In contrast, a study by Gurin *et al.* assessing general adjustment, indicated that 'women expressed more worrying, more often felt they had experienced a nervous breakdown, and more often felt they had a personal problem that could have benefited from professional help' (Gurin *et al.* 1960: 41). Other studies have produced similar results, though generally the differences between men and women are not as large as they are in the general practitioner data presented above (see, for example, Leighton *et al.* 1963).

MARITAL STATUS

It has long been noted that marital status bears a marked relationship to the use of psychiatric facilities. Single people (and to a lesser extent those who are separated and divorced) have higher patient rates than those who are married. What is less frequently noted is that the gender differential reverses for the single and the married, with single men having higher rates than single women, while married women have higher rates than married men. Moreover, the gender differential is far greater for single people, than it is for the married (Gove 1972). This has been found in a range of data in both this country and the USA. Unfortunately there are no comprehensive data on psychiatric admissions by marital status for this country. However, the intermittent censuses of psychiatric beds show a similar pattern to that found in the USA, and in the more fragmentary data on admissions in England (see, for example, Lowe and Garratt 1959). Among single people, who contribute disproportionately to the patient group, men have higher residence rates than women. In contrast, among the married, a numerically more substantial group but with far lower patient rates, women have higher residence rates. The data for 1971, the most recent available, are presented in *Table 5*.

Community surveys of psychiatric symptoms also indicate the importance of marital status. The Midtown Manhattan study, for instance, found not only the usual higher scores for single people than for the married, but also considerably higher rates for single men than for single women. In contrast, the married women's scores were slightly higher than the married men's, although the differences were not statistically

Table 5 *Patients resident in mental illness hospitals and units by sex and marital status, England and Wales, 31 December, 1971 (rates per 100,000)*

Marital status	Male	Female
Single	704	685
Married[1]	91	127
Widowed	535	647
Divorced	835	780
All	272	322

[1] Includes 1,562 'separated' males, and 1,898 'separated' females.

Source: Census of Patients in Mental Illness Hospitals and Units in England and Wales at the end of 1971. Table 3.

significant (Stole *et al.* 1975). It should be noted that Gove (1972), in his discussion of gender differences in mental illness, focuses his analytic concern on the higher female rates among the married largely on the grounds that it is this differential that produces the aggregate female excess, and not on the equally interesting higher male rates among the single, given that single people are so heavily over represented among in-patients. In England and Wales at the end of 1971 almost 66 per cent of the male occupants of psychiatric beds aged fifteen years and over were single (Department of Health and Social Security 1975).

SOCIAL CLASS

No routine official statistics are collected for psychiatric patients in England that provide any measure of the class composition of the patient population, nor have there been any large-scale surveys to give us this information. However, the data that are available conform to the picture, given in many studies in the USA and elsewhere, of a negative association between social class and mental illness (Hollingshead and Redlich 1958). Moreover, there is some evidence that gender differentials vary between the social classes, though little attention has been paid to this issue.

Further calculation on the data provided by Hollingshead and Redlich (1958) in their well-known *Social Class and Mental Illness*, which studied all patients in psychiatric treatment in New Haven, Connecticut in six months in 1950, allows us to examine this issue. The data presented in *Table 6* show that although, overall, patient rates were slightly higher for men than for women, this aggregate picture hides significant variation. For social class V male patient rates were considerably higher than female, whereas in social class III female rates far exceeded the male rates; in social classes I, II, and IV there was little difference between male and female rates.

Table 6 *Gender differentials in patient rates per 100,000 population, by social class, New Haven Connecticut, May 31 to December 1, 1950*

Class	Male	Female	Female: Male
I and II	559.5	551.7	0.99
III	457.8	612.4	1.34
IV	647.7	636.6	0.98
V	2045.2	1309.5	0.64
All	849.3	750.7	0.88

Source: Hollingshead and Redlich (1958: supplementary tables).

HISTORICAL PERIOD

In England gender differentials in patient rates have changed considerably over the past century. During the nineteenth century men had marginally higher admission rates than women (see *Table 7*). By 1911 women's admission rates were marginally higher than men's; by the end of the 1930s the difference was more clear cut and, since then, the female excess has increased considerably.

In contrast, Gove and Tudor's (1972) analysis of data from field studies suggests that the female predominance of psychiatric morbidity on this type of measure is a post-war phenomenon. Patient data from the USA show enormous variation from sector to sector in gender differentials

Table 7 *Age and sex-specific admission rates to mental hospitals per 100,000 related population in England and Wales, 1884–1957*

	Male							Female						
Year	15	25	35	45	55	65+	All ages 15+	15	25	35	45	55	65+	All ages 15+
1884	46	91	115	111	107	107	87	44	88	111	107	98	90	83
1891	42	83	112	112	111	116	85	42	86	105	114	100	102	82
1901	45	88	118	122	128	149	93	42	84	111	125	116	130	89
1911	44	76	98	111	128	135	85	42	78	101	123	117	117	86
1921	39	70	87	94	111	128	79	41	74	96	115	107	106	82
1931	38	65	77	87	103	106	76	35	70	89	113	110	93	82
1939	64	86	90	97	111	115	91	46	85	108	136	137	110	100
1951	105	169	133	137	171	230	153	103	172	191	214	222	268	196

Source: Lowe and Garratt (1959).

and it is not easy to obtain a simple overall picture. However, male first admission rates to public state and county mental hospitals have been higher than those of women and by 1975 were approximately double (Milazzo-Sayre 1978).

DIAGNOSIS

One of the most consistent findings concerning the male/female distribution of psychiatric patients, which is manifest despite considerable variation and change in diagnostic categories and classifications, is that the gender differential varies markedly according to the type of mental illness. Women tend to have higher rates, both for in-patient and general practitioner contact, for neuroses, and affective disorders. The female excess is smaller, though still significant, for certain organic and psychotic conditions such as schizophrenia and senile dementia, but it is reversed for many of the personality and conduct disorders and the 'substance induced' psychotic conditions. Psychopathy, drug abuse, alcoholism, sexual deviation, drug- and alcohol-induced psychoses, and general paralysis (a condition resulting from syphilis) are all more common among male patients. Women, as has often been noted, predominate especially in the psychiatric disorders that are defined in relation to emotion, while men predominate in those that relate to behaviour (see, for example, Smith 1975 and Dohrenwend and Dohrenwend 1976). Or again, and equally significantly, the 'female' disorders are structured in relation to states that are essentially disturbing to the woman herself, whereas the 'male' disorders relate to what tends to be more disturbing to others than to the man himself. This suggests that where self-definition and self-recognition of 'symptomatic' problems are involved in the identification of a psychiatric disorder, women predominate; where behaviour that is considered offensive to others is the focus, men predominate (see Horowitz 1977).

The association between gender and type of mental illness is of obvious significance to any analysis of gender differentials in mental illness since the nature of any aggregate gender differential clearly depends on the types and distribution of mental illnesses that have been incorporated in the data. Gove and Tudor (1972), for instance, asserting confidently that mental illness is more common among women, purposely exclude both organic conditions and personality disorders from their definition and measure of mental illness, thereby excluding almost all the conditions in which males predominate. More important, the association between gender and type of mental illness can help explain some of the observed differentials in patient statistics. One reason why the gender differential is greater for general practitioner consultations than for in-patient admissions is that the distribution of the conditions handled by general practitioners differs from that dealt with by hospital psychiatrists on an in-patient basis. In general practice the problems largely fall into the categories of depression and neuroses, and, to a lesser extent, of personality or behaviour disorders. Psychoses, both organic and functional, account only for some 6 per cent of the mental illness episodes diagnosed by general practitioners; in contrast they constitute some 47 per cent of the diagnoses of those admitted as in-patients to psychiatric beds (Royal College of General Practitioners 1976). Similarly, there can be no doubt that the distribution of conditions warranting in-patient admission to psychiatric beds have changed considerably over time, and this is an important factor in the historical change in the gender differential in admission statistics. However, before further examining these changes and variations in the patient population, it is necessary to analyse the reasons for the association between gender and type of mental illness.

Gender and type of mental illness

Three particular factors contribute to the association between gender and type of mental illness: the constitution of the different categories of mental illness, which are differentially related to men's and women's normal behaviour; the impact of the psychiatric conceptualization of mental illnesses on societal and psychiatric assessments of men's and women's behaviour; and the differential visibility of, and opportunities for problematizing the experiences of men and women.

CATEGORY CONSTRUCTION

Categories of mental illness distinguish and identify as pathological certain forms of behaviour, thought, and emotion. These pathologies constitute exaggerations of, or deviations from, what is considered normal and appropriate thought and behaviour. However, since what is regarded as normal action and feeling is not the same for the two genders, the specification of some mental states as pathological creates categories of mental illness that are to a certain extent gender specific. For, in so far as particular types of mental illness are differentiated around emotions and behaviours whose normal expression is more common among one gender than another, then the pathological expression of these behaviours is likely to be more common among that gender. The argument here is not that different standards are applied to male and female behaviour when assessing whether it is pathological or not (this is considered below), but that pathologies are defined around thought and action that is, other things being equal, more likely to be manifested by one gender rather than another, since in its 'normal' form it is more acceptable for that gender.

The obvious examples of mental illnesses delineated around feelings and behaviour, which in a normal form are more acceptable in women than men, are the neurotic and affective disorders. These embrace pathologies of anxiety, fear, and depression, all feelings that are more permissible, and even encouraged, in women. Phobic neurosis or phobic anxiety illustrates the point. The General Register Office's *Glossary of Mental Disorders* defines it in terms of symptomatology:

'Under phobic disorders are to be included those conditions of abnormally intense dread in the presence of an object or situation often amounting to panic. Although the object may be individual and unique to the patient, certain forms are common e.g. dread of open or closed spaces, heights, water, etc.'

(General Register Office 1968: 14)

Although there is no suggestion here that this is an expected condition in people of a particular age or gender, or indeed with other social attributes, the apparently neutral description of symptoms is deceptive in so far as the disorder is differentiated in terms of characteristics that, when expressed in a normal way, are considered to be part of, or more common within, the feminine rather than the masculine character. The close relation to gender-specific behaviour is also apparent in the discussion of the syndrome in a standard English psychiatric textbook by Slater and Roth (1969). They elaborate a feature of phobic anxiety not mentioned in the *Glossary*:

'Traits of dependence on other individuals are conspicuous and the stresses which precede the onset of symptoms often appear to threaten some individual in the patient's personal environment with whom his sense of security is closely bound.' (Slater and Roth 1969: 923)

Yet, as we know, dependence is a part of desirable feminine behaviour. Nor is this example the most extreme in the way in which the pathological is more closely linked to the normal expectations for female behaviour than for male. At times the link is so close that it is even recognized as a problem in psychiatric texts. Slater and Roth, for example, question the status of hysteria as a distinctive syndrome, and at one point report what they describe as the penetrating and witty comment of two authors to the effect that 'the traditional description of the hysterical personality is a description of women in the words of men' (Slater and Roth 1969: 108).

Conversely, other mental illnesses are defined around pathologies of thought and action that in their normal form are more acceptable and more usual among men. Most obviously these include the disorders that relate to the use of illegal drugs and alcohol. Until recently, the use of such substances has been more normative, both ideally and statistically, for men than women. Hence it has not been surprising that the pathologies of drug and alcohol use have been more common in men, a point also emphasized in psychiatric texts. Slater and Roth say of alcoholism that 'the sex ratio which Parr estimated to be between 7:4 and 2:1 with males preponderating is close to figures derived from hospital admissions which show a ratio of approximately 3½:1' (Slater and Roth 1969: 389).

The claim that what constitutes normal healthy behaviour differs for men and women is given empirical support in the well-known study by Broverman et al. (1970). This study showed that clinicians' stereotypes of a mentally healthy woman differed from their stereotype of a mentally healthy man. It also found that the clinicians' stereotype of the latter was closer to that for the overall ideal of adult mental health, than that for a woman. This finding is difficult to interpret. For Gove and his colleagues (Tudor, Tudor, and Gove 1977), it provides evidence that the standards used to define men's behaviour as pathological are more stringent than those for women, since the male stereotype is closer to the overall ideal. Hence, other things being equal, we would expect men's behaviour to be more readily defined as pathological. The assumption here is of a dual standard of pathology for men and women. However, we could equally argue that the overall ideal is applied uniformly to both men and women in judging pathology. Therefore, in so far as women are expected to conform to the gender-specific stereotype of normality, then it is they who are more likely to fall short of the overall ideal. As it is, the significance of the study lies less in what it tells us about the relation between general ideals of mental health and gender-specific ones, or about the actual use of differing standards (which was not studied), and more in the evidence that it provides that expectations as to what constitutes normal behaviour differ for men and women. If we are to explore further the relation between the pathological and the normal for the two genders then we need to analyse the particular categories of mental illness themselves.

The contention that some categories of mental illness are to a certain extent gender specific assumes that, under pressure, individuals are more likely to manifest in an exaggerated or distorted form the thoughts, feelings, and actions that are typical of them when they are in a normal state. Hence women, who are allowed and even encouraged to express certain feelings (anxiety, misery, and elation), are more likely to manifest these behaviours in pathological form if disturbed, while men, who are socialized into other patterns of thought and feeling, will respond in different ways. This further assumes that mental pathology is a response to the problems and difficulties of everyday life. While there is sound empirical support for this view, it should not be taken to imply either that mental illnesses do not have any organic basis, or that social and psychological pressures ('stress', as it is fashionably called) play a causal role in all mental illnesses. All mental illnesses have, in my view, an organic basis, although the precise aetiological role of organic factors varies.[8] Moreover, the existence of a physical aetiology is not incompatible with a psychological or social one. Senile dementia, for instance, may well have psychological causes, and like physical illnesses it also has a social aetiology, though there has been little investigation of either.

Of course, my argument might seem to suggest that we all have more or less gender-typical pathological ways of responding to stresses, and that in consequence any observed variation in the levels of mental pathology indicates a real difference in the difficulties and stresses encountered by men and women. However, this is to ignore the selective way in which ways of thinking, feeling, and acting have come to be defined not merely as problematic (for the individual or others) but as problems to be embraced within the category of mental illness. The responses to stress are varied and only some fall into the category of mental illness; some may be regarded as forms of deviance, delinquency, and bad behaviour while others are seen as part of normal coping. We have only to think of some of the possibilities (anger and violence, a whole range of physical illnesses, delinquency, and crime, let alone mental disorder) to be aware of the dangers of making inferences about the levels of stress from data on the differential distribution of mental illness (see Cloward and Piven 1979).

Not all types of mental illness have built into them the sort of gender specificity I have indicated. While many of the neuroses are differentiated around pathologies of 'female' behaviour, and many of the behaviour disorders define pathologies of what is conventionally 'male' behaviour (the obvious exception here is anorexia nervosa, which is classified as a behaviour disorder and yet relates to female role expectations), many of the psychoses, whether organic or functional, are less obviously gender specific. With the majority of the psychoses the pathological is not an exaggeration of the normal but rather a disruption of it. Hence, even if we could show that the expected normality from which the pathological deviates differs for men and women, this would not in itself be evidence of any gender specificity in the category since the pathological is not an extension of the normal but stands in an oppositional relation to it.

EVALUATING BEHAVIOUR

Of particular importance here is the impact of the psychiatric conceptualizations of certain mental illnesses, emphasizing their gender specificity, which encourage presumptions as to the type of illness according to a person's gender. Although in theory mental illnesses are delineated in terms of symptoms and aetiology that are not gender specific, in practice the detailed elaboration of certain mental illnesses indicates very clearly the likely gender of patients, and, as a result, can have a marked impact on the identification and interpretation of the behaviour of men and women, strengthening the association between gender and type of mental illness. At certain times the assertions about the likely gender of patients in psychiatric tests are explicit while at other times they are more indirect. Slater and Roth, for instance, in their discussion of phobic anxiety, make the gender association clearly enough: 'the majority of patients in clinical practice are female and it is in women that the condition is seen in its most typical form' (Slater and Roth 1969: 92). Later they develop the link by considering why young married women in particular should be affected:

'It is of interest that the majority of patients are young married women. This may partly reflect the higher frequency of marriage among these patients, but it is probably related also to the fact that many of these subjects have been moved by marriage from a wide family circle to the relative isolation in which the young housewife often lives today.'   (Slater and Roth 1969: 93)

Such statements reinforce the idea that phobic anxiety is a female condition and so make it more likely that a woman's problems and experiences
will be identified in this way.

An even more striking example is anorexia nervosa, which is invariably presented as a distinctively female condition. The description of
anorexia nervosa in the same text almost excludes the possibility of
assigning the diagnosis to a man. It begins with a clear gender and age
restriction: 'This is a condition almost confined to women in the years of
adolescence and early adult life, although it also occurs rarely in young
men; it may occur as early as fourteen and is seldom seen after the age of
thirty' (Slater and Roth 1969: 124), and then continues with the very
clear assumption that the patient will be female (note the absence of the
customary male pronouns):

> 'In its most typical form it begins as an *attempt at dieting* for the sake
> of slimness by a healthy well-nourished girl, and in its earliest stages
> would probably be fairly easily reversed. The psychiatrist does not see
> the patient until she has lost some 15 kilograms, and by her refusal to
> take any more than a few bits of food a day is causing her relatives the
> greatest anxiety.'   (Slater and Roth 1969: 124)

Similar gender assumptions are made when characterizing some of the
'male' pathologies, both by explicit epidemiological assertions and by
comments about the likely aetiology. Discussing alcoholism, Slater and
Roth assert the male predominance among patients and then attempt to
account for it by suggesting an aetiology that clearly excludes most
women, thereby again reinforcing the association between men and
alcoholism.

> 'The large preponderance of male over female admissions in all
> countries probably owes something to occupational hazard in that
> alcohol consumption is a widely accepted and consistent feature of the
> social activities linked with professional and business life. The person
> who opts out of the conventional ceremonies of conviviality and their
> rounds of drinks is at some risk of being regarded as an outsider.'
>   (Slater and Roth 1969: 390)

The issue about assertions such as these does not concern their accuracy
(although not all of them have a sound empirical base) but rather the way
in which they affect the perception of an individual's condition by
generating conceptualizations of particular illnesses in which gender is

an integral component. As a result, the whole identification and processing of complaints is likely to be influenced by expectations about what are typical male and female problems. Women who feel miserable, discontented, and unhappy are more likely than men with similar experiences to feel that perhaps they are 'depressed' and should see a doctor, or are more likely to have others around them make such suggestions, simply because of the existence of the stereotyped imagery of depression as a typical female problem. Indeed, it is not only that when feelings of misery and malaise occur in a woman depression is more likely to be invoked as an appropriate description of the condition than under similar circumstances for men, even the initial categorization of the feelings as ones of misery and unhappiness is more likely, for a number of studies have shown that the very identification and recognition of basic emotions and feelings is learned (Schachter and Singer 1962).

Certainly there is evidence that the way in which people perceive their problems is affected by their social characteristics such as gender and social class, and, moreover, that the perception and diagnosis by psychiatrists is similarly affected. Women are, for instance, more likely than men to admit to psychological symptoms in situations of stress, and they are more likely to perceive themselves as having the less clear-cut symptoms of illness (Phillips and Segal 1969). David Mechanic, summarizing the differences between men's and women's experience of chronic illness, concludes that:

'Differences between men and women either disappear or become much smaller when objective measures are used, when the symptoms of illness are more tangible and visible, or when a greater degree of incapacity or impairment is evident. However women seem to report more subjective symptoms than men, particularly those symptoms that may be indicative of either physical disease or psychological distress.'
(Mechanic 1978: 188)

Other studies show that psychiatrists and other clinicians are affected by the social attributes of their patients both in terms of the identification and diagnosis of illness as well as the treatment decisions, and provide evidence of double standards in the treatment of patients (see Haase 1964; and Shader 1968). Women are, for instance, more likely than men to be prescribed psychotropic drugs; even for the same type of mental illness, they are also more likely to be referred to psychiatrists (Cooperstock 1971).

VISIBILITY

The visibility of an individual's problems is affected by a number of factors. Two are of especial importance. One is the extent to which a person is required to operate in the private or the public sphere. Because women tend to be more confined to the private sphere than men, the problems and difficulties they encounter and their responses to them are in general less visible to outsiders (Dahl and Snare 1978). In contrast, men's lives are enacted to a greater extent in a public milieu so that their problems and difficulties in coping tend to be more visible to others. This is of particular importance where the problematizing of experience and action is usually done by others, as with psychoses and behaviour disorders, rather than by self-definition and self-referral, as with the neuroses and affective disorders. As a result, when men show signs of psychotic or behavioural problems this is more likely to be publicly identified. In the case of the behaviour disorders, this further contributes to their association with men. On the other hand, with the neuroses and affective disorders, where visibility is less important in the identification process, women's greater tendency to identify psychiatric symptoms and seek help for them enhances the association of these conditions with women.

Another factor contributing to the visibility of people's problems is the level of demand that their role places upon them.[9] This varies over the life cycle. In old age, for instance, although the majority of men retire, women are usually expected to continue with their domestic labour. Hence deterioration in their role performance will be more visible than that of retired men, and their chances of being identified as a case of senile dementia are greater. Add to this the fact that proportionately fewer elderly women have surviving spouses, and the differential expectation to provide the daily domestic care of an increasingly senile spouse, and the high detection of senile dementia among women is not surprising.[10]

These three reasons for the association between gender and type of mental illness indicate that we cannot account for the existence of the association simply by positing a double standard of mental health for men and women, operating across all mental illnesses. Instead, they indicate that we need to consider a number of different features of the standards applied in judging behaviour as pathological. First, the relation of standards of pathology that delineate each mental illness to those of the relevant normality; second, whether for each mental illness the standards that define the pathology are in practice interpreted differently for men and women (the classic double standard); and third, whether the opportunities for judging the behaviour of men and women as pathological by the standards of particular mental illnesses also vary.

Changes and variations in the role of psychiatry

I want to turn now to the task of making sense of the observed variations in patient statistics. I shall start by looking at the historical change in psychiatry's relation to men and women.

Historically we can view the shift in psychiatry over the last century as a shift from a relatively restricted, largely custodial psychiatry based on asylums, to a much broader, more therapeutically oriented medical psychiatry involving both in-patient and out-patient care. In the second half of the nineteenth century psychiatry was still emerging as a distinctive specialism of medicine, alongside other specialisms. Its institutional basis was the asylums and private madhouses, many set up during the nineteenth century on a wave of humanitarian reform and moral enthusiasm (see Scull 1979 and Parry-Jones 1972). These institutions segregated and controlled the insane in the hope of moral reformation and with a view to restoring them to society and work. As the century progressed, the private madhouses became relatively and absolutely less important. The county and borough asylums increased both in size and number, and their segregative and custodial role became more dominant.[11] The public asylums had been established within the framework of the Poor Law and, like other Poor Law institutions, were places of last resort for those towards the bottom of the social scale. Anyone admitted to one of the public asylums had to be certified, and the dual stigma of both pauperization and certification helped to ensure that only the obviously insane, for whom little could be done, or those without any alternative means of support were admitted. Not surprisingly, the chances of recovery or discharge were not high (Scull 1979). Moreover, the size of the institutions and the staffing levels were such that there could be little possibility of active treatment programmes. Although admission rates to public asylums steadily increased throughout the nineteenth century, much of the overall increase in the resident population of the asylums resulted from the build-up of long-term inmates due to low levels of discharge. Between 1850 and 1900 the number of inmates in public asylums in England and Wales increased from 7,140 to 74,004 (Jones 1960: 210).

Inmates were assigned to one of four major diagnostic categories (in line with the categorization given in the Royal Commissioners in Lunacy Reports): mania, melancholia, ordinary dementia, and senile dementia. With the possible exception of melancholia, these were categories that were defined in relation to problems of reason and intellect, and would nowadays probably receive a diagnosis of psychosis, either organic or functional. Overall, although male admissions were marginally higher than female, gender differences were not large. However, the aggregate figures hide significant gender differentials for two of the four categories: melancholia, where women had higher rates (in line with existing data on psychotic depression, the category to which it bears most resemblance), and ordinary dementia, where men predominated.[12] The latter category would have included syphilitic patients with general paralysis, which was a condition more common among men. Improvements in the treatment of syphilis in the twentieth century have reduced the importance of this particular gender difference in the inmate population of the asylums. In England and Wales 'for the period 1908–12 acquired syphilis accounted for 19.4 per cent of male and 3.1 per cent of female admissions; for 1950–52 the corresponding proportions were 2.4 and 0.7 per cent' (Lowe and Garratt 1959: 88–102).

Medical involvement in mental disorders was not, however, entirely restricted to the newly established asylum psychiatry. Outside the public asylums physicians were called upon to deal with a number of complaints and problems by the affluent members of the middle and upper classes who could afford the services of a private physician and sought help on a voluntary basis (Rosenberg 1968). As a result, a number of physicians emerged as specialists in nervous diseases, building up a profitable office practice, alongside the role they played in the private madhouses and charitable asylums, as visiting physicians, proprietors, and superintendents. This was especially true in the USA where towards the end of the nineteenth century there was a rapid expansion in office psychiatry which differed in many respects from public asylum psychiatry. Patients were of higher social standing (the poor could not afford the fees of a physician), there was a higher proportion of women and of married people, and patients sought help on a voluntary basis.[13] Undoubtedly the problems and complaints they brought differed, too. They tended to be less severe, of shorter standing, to relate more to the intra-psychic conflicts and difficulties of the patients and less to publicly disruptive behaviour and, overall, to be less chronic in nature. Not surprisingly, in this context the specialists developed and amplified theoretical ideas and methods of treatment appropriate to the patients and their problems. They introduced new diagnostic categories and modified old ones (in the USA Beard (1880, 1881) introduced the term neurasthenia to describe a range of symptoms that he attributed to advances in civilization); and they introduced new treatment concepts (for example, Weir Mitchell's so-called rest-cure, though it was soon replaced by the far more influential psychoanalysis). And the new formulations, whether under old or new guises, reflected the social characteristics of the clientele. They were conceptualizations more acceptable to patients who were of higher social standing, and included a higher proportion of women and married people who sought help with their problems on a voluntary, out-patient basis.

While developments in private office psychiatry occurred later and were much less extensive in England than in the USA, the impact of the new American and European ideas was nonetheless significant. This was because of the changes that began to occur in public sector psychiatry in the twentieth century. A number of reformers, including the physicians specializing in nervous diseases, were anxious to bring about changes in asylum psychiatry. Their goal was to transform the asylums from custodial institutions that provided long-term care for chronic cases into medical establishments dealing with acute cases that could be offered a real chance of cure (see, for example, Maudsley 1867). The 1930 Mental Treatment Act introduced the first major changes directed to this end, with the introduction of voluntary admission, and new voluntary powers for local authorities to set up out-patient clinics. Both of these were intended to encourage patients to seek treatment early, a step which was considered the *sine qua non* of a more active therapeutic and, indeed, properly medical psychiatry.[14]

The result was both an expansion and a redirection of public sector psychiatry towards the sorts of patients and complaints around which office psychiatry had developed.[15] Office psychiatry could therefore supply the ideas, the concepts, and the treatments for the new public sector out-patient psychiatry, though there was need for some adaptations for the public sphere. Of course, not all the patients dealt with as out-patients or short-stay inmates in the newly labelled mental hospitals were middle- or upper-class married women. But office psychiatry had developed for them, and when imported into the public sector the psychiatric discourse of the office practitioners helped to shape and mould the new sphere in these directions (Blacker 1946).

In practice, therefore, the transformation from a custodial to a curative medical psychiatry, which has largely meant the addition of new areas of psychiatric practice alongside the old ones, has also meant a transformation in the social characteristics of the typical patients. Married women with neurotic and affective disorders now constitute a far more important group of patients than they did formerly.

A similar analysis can be applied and similar questions are also raised in respect to psychiatry's differential involvement with men and women over the life cycle. In childhood the psychiatric focus is on personality or conduct disorders (on visible behaviour problems that are disturbing to teachers or parents) or on intellectual deficit. It is only overt behavioural problems or mental subnormality that create sufficient concern to lead to psychiatric intervention, although there is some evidence that psychiatrists are being called upon to deal with a broader range of problems than formerly (see, for example, Box 1977, and Schrag and Divoky 1981). Admissions to psychiatric hospitals are relatively rare among the under-fifteens, but in the youngest age group especially it is behaviour or conduct disorders that are by far the most common diagnoses (see *Table 1*; and Royal College of General Practitioners 1976). Not surprisingly, boys have higher admission rates than girls (see *Table 1*). A similar pattern emerges in studies that attempt to make broader assessments of psychiatric morbidity among the young. The focus is largely on behavioural problems, and morbidity is found to be higher among boys than girls.[16] In adult life, when psychiatric ill health now covers a wider spectrum and includes a broad range of neurotic conditions and emotional disorders, women predominate, as we have seen. In old age, the focus changes once more. Intellectual performance and reason become the main concern, and for the reasons I have already suggested, women predominate in the patient population. There is, however, a marked contrast between Great Britain and the USA in provision for the elderly. While the old now constitute some 46 per cent of patients resident in psychiatric beds in this country, in the USA it is the elderly who have recently been de-institutionalized from the custodial asylums only to end up, it now emerges, in private sector nursing homes (Mendelson 1974).

We are left, therefore, with a number of important questions. Why at different times have particular aspects of men's and women's thoughts, feelings, and behaviour come to be regarded as problematic? Why at certain times and in certain cases have people looked to doctors for solutions to their problems? Why have doctors taken up the challenges provided by these problems in some cases and not others? Why, given the development of a medical conceptualization of a particular problem, does that problem become more prominent at certain times rather than others? We already have important clues to the answers to certain of these questions in the work of some writers.[17] All of them need further research

Conclusion

It is tempting to assume, as some authors have done, that because of their over-representation in patient statistics and their higher psychiatric morbidity assessed on the basis of what they say about themselves, women are less mentally healthy than men. However, given the way in which notions of mental illness are constructed and applied, it is clear that any conclusion of this nature, based on patient and 'morbidity' statistics is unwarranted. We cannot make inferences either about real difference in pathological behaviour between men and women, or about the stressfulness of the situations they encounter, from data that reflect the organizing and structuring of experience and behaviour by both patients themselves and professionals. Nevertheless, what we can say is that psychiatry has had a differential involvement in the problems of men and women at different points in its history and at different stages of the life cycle, and that the psychiatric conceptualizations of different mental illness are fashioned and created in ways that are often gender specific. The pressures, forces, and struggles that have led to this differential involvement must be the subject of further enquiry.

Notes

1 My concern here is with the concept of mental illness as it is used by psychiatrists. The term is, of course, a very controversial one, and there is now a lengthy literature on it.
2 For discussions of the evaluative nature of notions of illness and disease see King (1954) and Sedgwick (1972).
3 This literature is discussed in Kendell (1975b) and Mechanic (1978).
4 Some of the implicit assumptions made by talking of medicalization are discussed by Strong (1979).
5 Stafford-Clark, in his book *Psychiatry Today* (1963), describes the contrast as follows: 'The neuroses are those disorders of emotion or intellectual functioning which do not deprive the patient of contact with reality; the psychoses on the other hand, are characterised by a fundamental disturbance in the patient's appreciation of the nature of his environment and his response to it' (Stafford-Clark 1963: 92).
6 The limitations of official statistics of mental illness are discussed by Smith (1975).

7 In 1976 some 42 per cent of all female psychiatric residents had been in-patients for five years or more, whereas some 52 per cent of all male residents had stayed that length of time (see In-patient statistics from the Mental Health Enquiry).

8 In that respect the tendency to present organic and psychological accounts of mental illness as exclusive alternatives is, in my view, mistaken.

9 This issue has also been considered from a different point of view by Gove as part of his critique of the societal reaction view of mental illness. He contends that individuals with greater control over resources will be more likely to enter psychiatric treatment and to do so earlier (see Gove and Howell 1974; Gove and Tudor 1977).

10 Though there is still a differential among the elderly who are married (see Department of Health and Social Security 1975).

11 Between 1827 and 1930 the average number of patients per asylum increased from 116 to 1,221 (Jones 1960).

12 In 1879, for instance, of the male patients admitted to lunatic institutions of all types, 18.9 per cent received a diagnosis of melancholia, whereas 23.1 per cent of the female admissions were assigned to that category. The corresponding figures for ordinary dementia were 16.4 per cent of male admissions and 10 per cent of female (see Royal Commissioners on Lunacy 1880).

13 For some discussion of the situation of women seeking help see Smith-Rosenberg (1972) and Haller (1971).

14 The policy ideas underlying the legislation were put forward in the Report of the Royal Commission on Lunacy and Mental Disorder (1926).

15 The need for more out-patient services was set out in Blacker (1946).

16 I do not accept, therefore, the argument put forward by Gove and Herb (1974) that the higher levels of observed psychiatric morbidity among boys is a result of greater stress.

17 What we need is more detailed analysis of the application of particular diagnostic categories along the lines of Smith-Rosenberg's (1972) and Haller's (1971) studies.

References

American Psychiatric Association (1978) *Diagnostic and Statistical Manual of Mental Disorders*. Washington, DC.: American Psychiatric Association.

Armstrong, D. (1981) Pathological Life and Death: Medical Spatialisation and Geriatrics. *Social Science and Medicine* **15A**: 253–57.

—— (unpublished) 'Medical Knowledge and Modalities of Social Control.'

Beard, G. M. (1880) *Nervous Exhaustion (Neurasthenia): Its Nature, Symptoms and Treatment*. New York: Putnam.

—— (1881) *American Nervousness: Its Causes and Consequences*. New York: Putnam.

Blacker, C. P. (1946) *Neurosis and the Mental Health Services*. Oxford: Oxford University Press.

Blum, J. (1978) Changes in Psychiatric Diagnosis Over Time. *American Psychologist* **33**: 1017–031.

Box, S. (1977) Hyperactivity, The Scandalous Silence. *New Society* December 1: 458–60.

Broverman, I. K., Broverman, D. M., Clarkson, F. E., Rosenkrantz, P. S., and Vogel, S. R. (1970) Sex-role stereotypes and Clinical Judgements of Mental Health. *Journal of Consulting and Clinical Psychology* **34**: 1–7.

Cloward, R. A. and Piven, F. F. (1979) Hidden Protest: The Channelling of Female Innovation and Resistance. *Signs* **4**: 651–69.

Cooperstock, R. (1971) Sex Differences in the Use of Mood-modifying Drugs: An Explanatory Model. *Journal of Health and Social Behaviour* **12**: 238–44.

Dahl, T. S. and Snare, A. (1978) The Coercion of Privacy: A Feminist Perspective. In C. Smart and B. Smart (eds) *Women, Sexuality and Social Control.* London: Routledge & Kegan Paul.

Department of Health and Social Security (1975) *Census of Patients in Mental Illness Hospitals and Units in England and Wales at the End of 1971.* London: HMSO.

Dohrenwend, B. P. and Dohrenwend, B. S. (1976) Sex Differences and Psychiatric Disorders. *American Journal of Sociology* **6**: 1447: 454.

Foucault, M. (1971) *Madness and Civilization.* London: Tavistock.

—— (1978) *The History of Sexuality*, Vol. I. London: Allen Lane.

Freidson, E. (1970) *Profession of Medicine.* New York: Dodd, Mead.

General Register Office (1968) *A Glossary of Mental Disorders.* London: HMSO.

Gove, W. R. (1972) The Relationship Between Sex Roles, Marital Status and Mental Illness. *Social Forces* **51**: 34–44.

—— and Herb, T. R. (1974) Stress and Mental Illness Among the Young: A Comparison of the Sexes. *Social Forces* **53**: 256–65.

—— and Howell, P. (1974) Individual Resources and Mental Hospitalization. *American Sociological Review* **30**: 86–100.

—— and Tudor, J. F. (1972) Adult Sex Roles and Mental Illness. *American Journal of Sociology* **78**: 812–35.

Gurin, G., Veroff, J., and Field, S. (1960) *Americans View Their Mental Health.* New York: Basic Books.

Haase, W. (1964) The Role of Socio-Economic Class in Examiner Bias. In F. Riessman, J. Cohen, and A. Pearl (eds) *Mental Health of the Poor.* New York: Free Press.

Haller, J. S. (1971) Neurasthenia: The Medical Profession and the 'New Woman' of Late Nineteenth Century. *New York State Journal of Medicine* February **15**: 475–82.

Hare, E. H. and Wing, J. K. (eds) (1970) *Psychiatric Epidemiology.* Oxford: Oxford University Press.

Hollingshead, A. B. and Redlich, F. C. (1958) *Social Class and Mental Illness.* New York: John Wiley.

Horowitz, A. (1977) The Pathways into Psychiatric Treatment: Some Differences Between Men and Women. *Journal of Health and Social Behaviour* **18**: 169–70.

Jones, K. (1960) *Mental Health and Social Policy, 1845–1959.* London: Routledge & Kegan Paul.

Kendell, R. E. (1975a) The Concept of Disease and its Implications for Psychiatry. *British Journal of Psychiatry* **127**: 305–15.

—— (1975b) *The Role of Diagnosis in Psychiatry*. Oxford: Blackwell.

King, L. S. (1954) What Is Disease? *Philosophy of Science* **21**: 193–203.

Leighton, D., Harding, J. S., Macklin, D. M., Macmillan, A. M., and Leighton, A. H. (1963) *The Character of Danger*. New York: Basic Books.

Lowe, C. R. and Garratt, F. N. (1959) Sex Pattern of Admissions to Mental Hospitals in Relation to Social Circumstances. *British Journal of Preventive and Social Medicine* **13**: 88–102.

Luker, K. (1978) *Taking Chances: Abortion and the Decision Not to Contracept*. Berkeley, Calif.: University of California Press.

Maudsley, H. (1867) *The Physiology and Pathology of Mind*. London.

Mechanic, D. (1970) The Problems and Prospects in Psychiatric Epidemiology. In E. H. Hare and J. K. Wing (eds) *Psychiatry Epidemiology*. Oxford: Oxford University Press.

—— (1978) *Medical Sociology*. New York: Free Press.

Mendelson, M. A. (1974) *Tender Loving Greed*. New York: Random House.

Milazzo-Sayre, L. (1978) Changes in the Age and Sex Composition of First Admissions to State and County Mental Hospitals. United States, 1962–1975. *Mental Health Statistical Note 145*. National Institute of Mental Health.

Parry-Jones, W. (1972) *The Trade in Lunacy*. London: Routledge & Kegan Paul.

Parsons, T. (1951) *The Social System*. New York: Free Press.

Phillips, D. L. and Segal, B. F. (1969) Sexual Status and Psychiatric Symptoms. *American Sociological Review* **34**: 58–72.

Riessman, F., Cohen, J., and Pearl, A. (eds) (1964) *Mental Health of the Poor*. New York: Free Press.

Rosenberg, C. E. (1968) *The Trial of Assassin Guiteau: Psychiatry and Law in the Gilded Age*. Chicago: Chicago University Press.

Rosenhan, D. (1973) On Being Sane in Insane Places. *Science* **179**: 250–58.

Royal College of General Practitioners (1976) *Morbidity Statistics from General Practice 1970–71*. London: HMSO.

Royal Commission on Lunacy (1926) *Report of the Royal Commission on Lunacy and Mental Disorder*. London: HMSO.

Schachter, S. and Singer, J. E. (1962) Cognitive, Social and Physiological Determinants of Emotional State. *Psychological Review* **69**: 379–99.

Scheff, T. (1963) Decision Rules, Types of Error, and Their Consequences in Medical Diagnosis. *Behavioural Science* **8**: 97–107.

Schrag, P. and Divoky, D. (1981) *The Myth of the Hyperactive Child*. Harmondsworth: Penguin.

Scull, A. (1979) *Museums of Madness*. London: Allen Lane.

Sedgwick, P. (1972) Mental Illness *Is* Illness. *Salmagundi* Summer-Fall: 196–224.

Shader, R. J., Binstock, W. A., and Scott, D. (1968) Psychiatrists' Biases: Who Gets Drugs? *Social Science and Medicine* **2**: 213–16.

Slater, E. and Roth, M. (1969) *Clinical Psychiatry*. London: Balliere Tindall and Cassell.

Smith, D. E. (1975) The Statistics on Mental Illness: What They Will Not Tell us about Women and Why. In D. E. Smith and S. J. David (eds) *Women Look at Psychiatry*. Vancouver: Press Gang.

Smith-Rosenberg, C. (1972) The Hysterical Woman: Sex Roles and Role Conflict in 19th-Century America. *Social Research* **39**: 652–78.
Srole, L., Langner, T. S., Michael, S. T., Kirkpatrick, P., Opler, M. K., and Rennie, T. A. C. (1975) *Mental Health in the Metropolis*. New York: Harper & Row.
Spector, M. (1977) Legitimating Homosexuality. *Society* **14**: 52–6.
Stafford-Clark, D. (1963) *Psychiatry Today*. Harmondsworth: Penguin.
Tudor, W., Tudor, J. F., and Gove, W. R. (1977) The Effect of Sex Role Differences on the Social Control of Mental Illness. *Journal of Health and Social Behaviour* **18**: 98–112.

8

Rejoinder to Joan Busfield[1]

JENNIE WILLIAMS

During the last decade, considerable theoretical and research attention has been devoted to understanding why women have apparently higher rates of treated and untreated mental illness than men. One of the most prolific writers on the subject has been Walter Gove. He and his colleagues have consistently argued (for example, Gove and Tudor 1973; Gove and Geerken 1977; and Gove 1980) that the sex difference in the incidence and prevalence of mental illness is real, and is causally related to stressful and other psychogenic features of women's marital roles. On the whole, this analysis has been favourably received, perhaps partly because it provides an understandable and useful illustration of the high cost of being female in modern society. However, this thesis has been criticized by authors (for example, Dohrenwend and Dohrenwend 1975, 1977; Johnson 1980; and Smart 1977) who believe that the apparently higher incidence of mental illness in women is an artefact. There are various reasons for this conclusion, but it is commonly held that this artefact is created by the effect of sex roles and sex-role stereotypes on the likelihood that women will be included as treatment statistics or as a 'case' in community surveys. Reading Busfield's paper, it is evident that she subscribes to this latter view, and the processes that are highlighted by her analysis merit serious consideration.

Busfield begins with an indirect attack on the viability of comparing the incidence and prevalence of mental illness between the sexes. Attention is drawn to the problems and disagreements that surround attempts to define mental illness, both specifically and generally. This is then used to make the point that the concept of mental illness is mainly a social construct, and, therefore, is likely to be affected by certain biases. Busfield does not suggest that the concept of mental illness is a complete fabrication without any real basis, but she takes the view that the existence of these biases invalidates attempts to compare the incidence and prevalence of mental illness across different social groups. In short, whatever epidemiologists may think they are doing, Busfield believes they are not providing us with any useful information about the social demographic correlates of mental illness.

The essence of Busfield's argument seems to be that we do not have sufficient reliable information to start asking questions about the aetiology of mental illness. I think Busfield is correct in stressing that there is room for bias to operate in the definition and diagnosis of mental illness, but it is taking the argument to unnecessary extremes to suggest that therefore epidemiological studies tell us nothing about people and their problems but everything about the construction and use of social definitions. I agree that comparative data on treatment rates provide a dubious starting point for talking about the causes of mental illness, but the arguments presented by Busfield are not sufficient to dismiss all data collected in 'true prevalence' community surveys. Although well-designed studies of this type are at a premium, they can offer insight into the links between demographic variables and psychological well-being. One example of this is the work by George Brown and his colleagues on the relationship between social class and depression in women (Brown and Harris 1978).

Busfield moves on to challenge a number of popular interpretations of the observed patterning of mental illness in the sexes. She presents evidence that indicates that the association between sex and mental illness is also affected by other variables, which include age, marital status, social class, historical period, and type of diagnosis. How can we interpret these findings? At one level these patterns tend to mitigate against predominately biological explanations of the apparently higher incidence of mental illness in women. Several writers also argue that the effect on mental health of the interaction between sex and age (Gove and Herb 1974; Eme 1979), marital status (Gove 1972, 1980; Bernard 1972), and historical period (Chesler 1972; Gove 1972) are consistent with the sex role/stress/mental illness model. However, in two of the examples that Busfield considers in this section, the problem of interpreting the findings are secondary to the issue of the reliability of the data. For example, the problems of using historical data are well illustrated in the debate between Gove and Tudor (1977), and Dohrenwend and Dohrenwend (1975,

1977), where simultaneous claims are made that these data do and do not support a sex difference in mental illness. Similarly, it is also worth noting that only a small number of studies have examined both sex and marital status differences in untreated populations. Of these, the more recent studies (Warheit et al. 1976; Fox 1980) indicate that marital status effects are not as consistent and reliable as many people have assumed. However, diagnosis is perhaps the most interesting of the factors that Busfield considers and she spends some time discussing the association between sex and type of psychological disorder. Briefly stated, Busfield accepts that sex roles may affect the ways that men and women cope with difficulties in their lives. Her argument is that the sex bias inherent in the definition of mental illness and the diagnostic process lead people to believe (erroneously) that mental illness is more prevalent among women.

In support of this first point, there is now a growing literature on the ways that sex roles mediate mental health. For example, there is evidence to indicate that women's vulnerability to depression is mediated by the effect of sex roles on cognitive processes such as attributional style (Abramson et al. 1978; Radloff 1980), the structure and content of identity (Bart 1971; Spence et al. 1979; and Williams 1979) and, more generally, the decline of importance that is attached to relationships between women (Bernard 1976). However, I have reservations about Busfield's argument that psychiatry operates with a definition of mental illness that is biased towards symptoms and behaviour more common in women. This argument is based on the assumption that symptoms, behaviour, and disorder more common among women (depression, for example) are the functional equivalents of those more prevalent among men (for instance, alcoholism). I think this assumption is only achieved by over-simplification and the loss of valuable information about the causes, meaning, and implications of human behaviour.

What of the possibility that sex bias occurs in the diagnostic process? This is an issue that has stimulated considerable research interest, and several reviews of this work have appeared recently (Smith 1980; Whitley 1978; and Zeldow 1978). These authors reach the same particular conclusion that there is little evidence to support the operation of these types of bias, either among lay-people or professionals. Although, superficially, this seems to undermine Busfield's case, like other writers (for example, Davidson and Abramowitz 1980; Whitley 1978), I suspect that these null findings are primarily a function of the restricted research paradigm used in this area. However, it is important to remember that at the moment we do not have any real understanding of the strength, implications, or even direction of sex bias in clinical and lay judgements of mental illness.

In her final section, Busfield attempts to trace the historical origins of psychiatry's differential involvement with women and men. She argues that the realms of human behaviour and experience, which psychiatry has claimed as its own, have been, and still are, multiply determined. Following this, changes in the patterning of mental illness across and within the sexes are not suggested to provide us with any real information about the distribution or origins of psychopathology. Other writers (for example, Chesler 1972) take this position further by arguing that psychiatry's differential involvement, reflects the way that this institution colludes with other social institutions – and indeed women themselves – to control and limit women's behaviour. However, Busfield prefers not to comment on the origins of the situation she describes.

This historical analysis provides convincing reasons for a cautious approach to data on treated rates of mental illness. However, I do not think the same argument can be applied to the interpretation of data from community surveys. The majority of these studies do not operationalize formal psychiatric definitions in their data collection. Consequently, I do not think we have sufficient information to make pronouncements about sex differences in the prevalence of psychiatrically defined mental illness. As Dohrenwend and Dohrenwend (1977) point out, many of the recent studies rely on self-report inventories, which do not provide data on the occurrence of personality disorder, psychotic symptoms, and allied types of disorders. In addition, as Goldman and Ravid (1980) note, the studies also assess and quantify anxiety, maladjustment, and unhappiness, which have a tenuous relationship with formal psychiatric definitions of mental illness. However, there is little doubt that women have higher rates of symptoms in these studies, although their significance in terms of specific forms of mental illness is not very clear. I do not think it is possible simply to explain the sex-typing of these symptoms in terms of psychiatric bias, and it seems more appropriate to find out what it is about the lives and psychology of women that make them vulnerable to these sorts of distress.

To summarize, the issues raised by Busfield are important; they concern the definition of mental illness, the way sex-role related processes can affect both 'illness behaviour', and the social and professional reactions to mental illness in women and men. These problems are difficult to resolve and currently we are at the stage of having more theories than data to decide between them. However, this should not preclude from consideration the ways that sex-based social differentiation actually affects psychological well-being. Finally, it may be useful to reframe the issue. Given the well documented inequalities between the sexes, why should this not be reflected in the mental health of women?

Note

1 At the time of writing, the author was a Research Fellow at The Social Psychology Research Unit, the University of Kent at Canterbury.

References

Abramson, L. Y., Seligman, M. E. P., and Teasdale, J. D. (1978) Learned Helplessness in Humans: Critique and Reformulation. *Journal of Abnormal Behaviour* **87**: 49–74.

Bart, P. B. (1971) Depression in Middle-Aged Women. In V. Gornick and B. K. Moran (eds) *Woman in Sexist Society*. New York: Basic Books.

Bernard, J. (1972) The Paradox of the Happy Marriage. In V. Gornick and B. K. Moran (eds) *Woman in Sexist Society*. New York: Basic Books.

—— (1976) Homosociality and Female Depression. *Journal of Social Issues* **32**: 213–38.

Brown, G. W. and Harris, T. (1978) *Social Origins of Depression: A Study of Psychiatric Disorder in Women*. London: Tavistock.

Chesler, P. (1972) *Women and Madness*. New York: Doubleday.

Davidson, C. V. and Abramowitz, S. I. (1980) Sex Bias in Clinical Judgment: Later Empirical Returns. *Psychology of Women Quarterly* **4**: 377–95.

Dohrenwend, B. P. and Dohrenwend, B. S. (1975) Sex Differences and Psychiatric Disorder. *American Journal of Sociology* **80**: 1447–454.

—— (1977) Reply to Gove and Tudor's Comment on 'Sex Differences and Psychiatric Disorder'. *American Journal of Sociology* **82**: 1336–345.

Eme, R. F. (1979) Sex Differences in Childhood Psychopathology: A Review. *Psychological Bulletin* **86**: 574–95.

Fox, J. W. (1980) Gove's Specific Sex-role Theory of Mental Illness: A Research Note. *Journal of Health and Social Behaviour* **21**: 260–67.

Goldman, N. and Ravid, R. (1980) Community Surveys: Sex Differences in Mental Illness. In M. Guttentag, S. Salasin, and D. Belle (eds) *The Mental Health of Women*. London: Academic Press.

Gove, W. R. (1972) The Relationship Between Sex Roles, Marital Status, and Mental Illness. *Social Forces* **51**: 34–44.

—— (1980) Mental Illness and Psychiatric Treatment Among Women. *Psychology of Women Quarterly* **4**: 345–62.

—— and Geerken, M. R. (1977) The Effect of Children and Employment on the Mental Health of Married Men and Women. *Social Forces* **56**: 66–76.

—— and Herb, T. (1974) Stress and Mental Illness Among the Young: A Comparison of the Sexes. *Social Forces* **53**: 256–65.

—— and Tudor, J. F. (1973) Adult Sex Roles and Mental Illness. *American Journal of Sociology* **78**: 812–35.

—— (1977) Sex Differences in Mental Illness: A Comment on Dohrenwend and Dohrenwend. *American Journal of Sociology* **82**: 1327–336.

Johnson, M. (1980) Mental Illness and Psychiatric Treatment Among Women: A Response. *Psychology of Women Quarterly* **4**: 363–71.

Radloff, L. Sawyer (1980) Risk Factors for Depression: What Do We Learn From Them? In M. Guttentag, S. Salasin, and D. Belle (eds) *The Mental Health of Women*. London: Academic Press.

Smart, C. (1977) Women, Crime and Mental Illness. In C. Smart and B. Smart (eds) *Women, Sexuality and Social Control*. London: Routledge & Kegan Paul.

Smith, M. L. (1980) Sex Bias in Counselling and Psychotherapy. *Psychological Bulletin* **87**: 392–407.

Spence, J. T., Helmreich, R. L., and Holahan, C. K. (1979) Negative and Positive Components of Psychological Masculinity and Feminity and their Relationships to Self-reports of Neurotic and Acting-Out Behaviours. *Journal of Personality and Social Psychology* **37**: 1673–682.

Warheit, G. J., Holzer, C. E., Bell, R. A., and Arey, S. A. (1976) Sex, Marital Status, and Mental Health: A Reappraisal. *Social Forces* **55**: 459–70.

Whitley, B. E. (1978) Sex Roles and Psychotherapy: A Current Appraisal. *Psychological Bulletin* **86**: 1309–321.

Williams, J. A. (1979) Psychological Androgyny and Mental Health. In O. Hartnett, G. Boden, and M. Fuller (eds) *Sex-Role Stereotyping*. London: Tavistock.

Zeldow, R. (1978) Sex Differences in Psychiatric Education and Treatment. *Archives of General Psychiatry* **35**: 89–93.

9

City and home: urban housing and the sexual division of space

LINDA McDOWELL

For the majority of people, housing is one of the most important issues in their lives. A large proportion of time is spent at home. Admittedly a large part of this is spent sleeping, but about half our waking activities are carried out at home. For young children, the elderly, and particularly for housebound women, the proportion of time spent in the home is much higher. For women with small children the home is the location of both work and recreation; they eat, sleep, and 'rest' at the scene of their labour, and this labour is entirely solitary. A growing number of women now combine work in the home with participation in the labour market but it is still the widespread expectation, and practice (see Oakley 1974), that domestic labour is 'women's work'. Women clean, prepare food, mend clothes, and generally put things in order for their husbands and children, for whom the home is more normally regarded as a place of rest and respite from work. This assumption, combined with an almost passionate regard for the sanctity and privacy of the nuclear family, is embodied in state housing and planning policies. Most housing isolates each individual family unit while ensuring the minimum privacy for its members and thus maximizes the domestic work of individual women. Land use plans continue to segregate residential development to particular areas of the city, increasing the isolation of women who do not participate in the urban labour market and presenting problems for women who combine domestic and waged labour.

The structure and location of urban housing have been so taken for granted in Great Britain that until recently they have neither been adequately theorized nor challenged by political action. In this paper, following a critique of existing urban theory, I outline some of the ways in which sexual divisions are institutionalized in cities, and briefly consider the potential for women to organize locally to improve their own environments.

Urban theory

The public and the private, the city and the suburbs, work and home, men and women, these oppositions are found in much of the writing about contemporary capitalist cities. Indeed, the association of the sexes with particular spheres of urban activity, and hence different urban loca-tions, is so commonplace that it has only recently been subjected to critical examination. Men travel daily into the city centre for work while women stay at home in the suburbs. On this basis an edifice of urban theory has been erected, primarily by geographers, economists, and sociologists, purporting to explain the functional differentiation of urban space and the segregation of households into particular quarters of the city. Although the form and logic of the spatial division of different functions (housing, factories, offices, schools) is often difficult to see in large cities, urban space is not randomly divided but both actively structures and is structured by the particular set of social processes at work in one historical period and, because of its relative permanence, reflects the social relations of an earlier time.

Probably the most important feature of this division of cities has been the growing separation of home and work. During this century, the operation of the land market, both unregulated and regulated by state control, has resulted in the separation of what British planners have euphemistically termed 'non-conforming' uses − domestic and pro-ductive activities. This has been a gradual process, accelerated by capitalist urbanization. The rapid growth of towns and cities in the nine-teenth century, both by rural-urban migration and by natural increase, greatly increased the already developing shift from a predominantly rural subsistence economy where a high proportion of income was paid in kind to a reliance on wage relationships and employment outside the home. This was associated with a gradual segregation of women, par-ticularly in the middle classes, and the separation of home life from market forces. While for some time during the last century the import-ance of family 'outwork' blurred the division between home and work (that is unpaid and waged labour), its significance is now very limited (Hope et al. 1976; Hunt 1968). In the twentieth century, and particularly from the 1930s onwards, the separation of home and work has been accentuated by the rapid growth of suburban housing developments, areas that Raymond Williams (1960) regards as an arena of recreation from which the facts of production had been banished.

The theories of urban structure developed in the social sciences to explain this segregation have relied on a set or subset of the general economic relationships in capitalist societies. The models of the Chicago school, for example, developed in the 1920s, relied on an analogy to ecological processes in plant communities (competition, invasion, succession, and dominance) to explain the central location of productive activities and the positive relationship between income, social class, and increasing distance from the city centre in urban housing markets. Later critics demonstrated the historical specificity of this model to early capitalist industrial cities with an unregulated land market and private ownership of property where competition for land was entirely governed by the logic of profit. At about the same time, economists were developing models of urban structure based on neo-classical utility theory, explaining industrial and residential location as a result of competitive bidding between individuals with perfect information in an unregulated land market. The division of space reflects a trade-off between access to the city centre and space in peripheral locations. As accessibility is of greater significance for them, factories and offices locate on the most expensive central land. Affluent households choose spacious suburban living as they can afford the costs for the wage earner, presumably male, to travel to the centre while the urban poor are segregated into inner-area ghettoes. This division supposedly maximizes the utility or satisfaction of all concerned and represents an equilibrium spatial distribution. Criticisms of these models are legion (see, for example, Colenutt 1970 and Richardson 1971), and alternative analyses of residential differentiation have been developed.

Neo-Weberians influenced by Rex and Moore (1967) have studied the behaviour of the allocators or 'gatekeepers' of housing (building society managers, estate agents, and local housing officials for example), demonstrating that households can be ranked on the basis of their eligibility to meet the criteria of access established by these urban gatekeepers. Access to owner occupation is determined primarily by income and social class, to state housing by bureaucratic definitions of social need. Rex and Moore argued that if it can be accepted that there is a consensus in Great Britain about the desirability of different types of housing, headed by suburban owner occupation and followed as a close second by suburban public renting, then a hierarchical model of housing classes may be devised. Rather less convincingly, they have attempted to relate this social hierarchy of access to housing to a social division of space. The mechanisms by which a consensus about the value of particular types of tenure arises are not clear. The authors rely on reference to the 'status values of British society' suggesting that owner occupation is legitimated in terms of the ideal of 'a property owning democracy' and local authority tenancy in 'terms of the values of the welfare state' (Rex and Moore 1967: 275–76). The consensus about suburban location does not even merit this degree of explanation, but seems to be seen as a necessary corollary of tenure. The relationship between housing form, location, and access to other neighbourhood amenities and facilities is not considered. How does high-rise, high-density living, for example, score on the 'status values' scale?

Particularly noticeable in all three approaches is the total neglect of the significance of the home/work spatial separation for social relations between women and men. Indeed women are not even considered as a separate category; the unit of analysis is the household, typically assumed to be a nuclear family headed by a man, despite the increasingly small proportion of households that fall into this ideal category (Stapleton 1980). The trade-off models refer to the journey to work, implying only one waged worker, not recognizing that additional trade-offs may take place in dual-career families, or indeed between the location of work, schools, and other important centres for different household members. Admittedly more recent work in the managerial tradition has focused on the constraints on access to decent housing for those minorities that are neither deemed in need by local authorities nor creditworthy by financial institutions. Discrimination against unsupported wives, single parents, widows, and unmarried single women by the gatekeepers of the two major tenures has been documented. However, the implications of the separation of work in the productive sphere for wages, and work in the sphere of reproduction for 'love' (in both the romantic and colloquial sense), have not been seen as worth theorizing. These two types of labour characteristically take place in different parts of the city. Production based on waged labour in the marketplace is undertaken collectively in specialized locations, predominantly by men but also by women, whereas the household reproduction of this labour power, based on the unpaid labour of individual women, is undertaken in isolation in countless decentralized urban locations. This division not only influences the social relations between men and women but is embodied in the structure of the urban system and is given concrete expression in the built form of cities. While this arrangement is apparently beneficial for men, and necessary for the functioning of capitalist cities, it is inefficient for women and may eventually lead to urban protest movements based not on class but on sexual divisions, revealing the inherent contradictions in the sexual division of labour and space.

The physical embodiment of concepts of community – a major emphasis in the post-war British town planning movement – is based upon patriarchal assumptions about the role and life-style of women.[1] Similarly, intervention by the state into urban housing markets and the erection of large numbers of local authority-owned dwellings since the end of the First World War has been based on implicit assumptions about the segregation of women from areas of urban life other than those associated with running a home and child-care. The basis and consequences of these policies will be examined in the rest of this paper. In later sections the historical division of residential space in Great Britain is examined, albeit cursorily, in an attempt to illustrate how elements of the economic, political, and ideological structure of capitalist society result in a social division of residential space that is overlaid by a sexual division, based on the patriarchal structure of urban institutions. The strength of the anti-urban ideal in British social thought and policy, and the role of 'community' are considered first, followed by some discussion of the growth of state intervention and of home ownership, and public and private suburbanization. Rather than being the report of completed research, the sections that follow are based on a number of wide-ranging ideas and examples that are intended to stimulate further work and debate in the discipline. The implications of the changing structure of residential space for the social and spatial relations between men and women are currently undeservedly neglected in British urban studies.

Marxist and feminist theory: capitalism, domestic labour, and the division of space

Whereas the neglect of sexual differentiations in the city is virtually complete in the traditional theories outlined above, more recent work in a Marxist tradition has begun to analyse the relations of production and the role of ideology in capitalist societies, relating them to the division of space in cities in ways that have potentially fruitful implications for understanding sexual divisions. Work by Harvey in North America (1974, 1975, 1977) and Castells in France (1977, 1978), for example, has begun to show how the functional differentiation of urban space is related to the behaviour of financial and state institutions.

Housing *per se*, rather than the structure of urban space, has attracted the attention of other workers in a Marxist tradition (see Pickvance 1976). Unlike the predominant emphasis in earlier approaches on the consumption of housing by individuals or categories of households, the dual nature of the relationship of housing to a capitalist economy has been pointed out. In common with other economic goods, a large proportion of the housing stock in advanced industrial societies is produced for profit as well as being a consumer good. The significance of the dual relationship, however, rests on the fact that housing must be both produced and consumed for profits to be accumulated as its consumption is an essential prerequisite of the production process. Adequate housing is essential for the reproduction of labour power which provides the source of value and profits in the production process. As well as the need for existing labour power to be housed, future labour power (children) needs to be born and brought up as far as possible in healthy surroundings to ensure the maintenance of the labour force. It has been argued that this dual relationship is the primary reason for the introduction of legislation first, to improve the standards of working-class housing and, later, to provide state housing for workers when private capital failed to produce it at rents that the working class could afford. Such an analysis potentially places the role of women in reproducing labour power at the centre of interest but so far most workers in this tradition have failed to recognize its significance.

Feminists, on the other hand, have tended to concentrate on the organization and function of women's domestic work in capitalist societies. The growing literature on the sexual division of labour (see, for example, Gardiner 1976; Harrison 1973; Himmelweit and Mohun 1977; Molyneux 1979) has challenged the traditional distinctions between home and work in an attempt to demonstrate that domestic labour is productive. The majority of these studies, however, ignore the consequences of the *location* of the relations of production and reproduction. The spatial separation of wage labour and unpaid domestic labour (of the public and private domains of life) not only has implications for the social and patriarchal relations between men and women within the family, but also leads to conflicts and contradictions for women themselves in the organization of their daily lives as they use the city. These contradictions are now being experienced directly by an increasing number of women, a point that is illustrated by the growing number of married women who go out to work for a wage to increase the total family budget. The proportion of married women in the labour market has risen from 10 per cent in 1951 to 42 per cent in 1971. Many of these women work part-time to fit in with domestic responsibilities and child-care, and have to cope with an urban transport system that, in its routes and capacity, is based on conventional assumptions about full-time employment and the separation of work-related and domestic activities in everyday life. In addition, at the present time of high inflation and cuts in state intervention in the sphere of collective consumption (a decline in pre-school and day-care provision, rises in the costs associated with schooling such as meals and transport, and the reduction of social benefits and services generally), the contradictions are being exacerbated as many women struggle to provide at home services that were previously community-based. It is therefore argued that in order to provide a more complete explanation of the continued spatial separation of urban land uses, and insights into the changing structure of the housing market with the expansion of owner occupation and council housing in this century, any analysis must include not only consideration of the capitalist organization of wage labour, but also of the patriarchal organization of domestic labour or household production. Studies that neglect the sexual division of labour deny an important organizing principle of urban space.

Sexual differentiation, however, is not maintained solely by economic divisions. Residential space is also shaped by the political and ideological system. In these areas, too, there have been recent theoretical advances. Harvey (1978) has argued that the regulation of urban land uses, the practice of community planning, and the spatial separation of social classes can be understood as mechanisms of social control. In the sphere of housing, the encouragement of owner occupation has long been associated with its role in reducing social unrest. In 1927, Bellman, a former Building Society President, said, 'The man who has something to protect and improve – a stake of some sort in this country – naturally turns his thoughts to the direction of sane, ordered and perforce economical government. The thrifty man is seldom or never an extremist agitator' (1927: 54). Almost fifty years later, the Secretary-General of the Building Societies Association restated the same theme: 'even a small stake in the country does affect political attitudes. The greater the proportion of owner occupiers the less likely were extreme measures to prevail' (Secretary-General of the National BSA 1976: 2).

More recently, Boddy (1980) has traced, in building society statements and in government White Papers for example, the development of an ideology that portrays home ownership as a basic and natural desire. He quotes the 1971 White Paper, *Fair Deal for Housing*, as a representative example. Here it is asserted that:

'Home ownership is the most rewarding form of house tenure. It satisfies a deep and natural desire on the part of the householder to have independent control of the house that shelters him and his family. It gives him greatest possible security against the loss of his home . . . if the householder buys his house on a mortgage, he builds up by steady saving a capital asset for him and his dependents.'

(Department of Environment 1971: 4)

Less well recognized are the ideological assumptions about women's roles embodied in current housing policy and in the so-called natural desires for home ownership, although the assumptions about family structure in the quotation above are abundantly clear. However, the anti-urban ideal in British planning policies, and what might be called a domestic ethic emphasizing the importance of the home as a haven and as a woman's place, have also influenced land-use and housing policies, encouraging the segregation of housing, and consequently many women, to peripheral areas of the city. The domestic ethic has also been variously utilized to support both the entry and the withdrawal of women from the labour force and the rise of consumerism and domestic consumption associated with suburbanization.

The anti-urban ideal and the ideology of community

An anti-urban bias in British urban theory and planning practice, and indeed in British culture in general, has been documented in detail by a number of authors (Foley 1960; Glass 1968; Thorns 1972; Williams 1973). Connections between the romantic ideology glorifying nature, rural life, and changes in the built environment are clear. In the last century these include the building of rural estates by the bourgeoisie and the establishment of country houses and mansions, and, in this century, the flight from the industrial city, the 'garden city' movement, and the suburban compromise. However, it was not until an article by Davidoff *et al.* (1976) that the connection between the anti-urban ideal and the sexual division of labour was made explicit. Davidoff *et al.* show that with the development of industrial capitalism and rapid urbanization in the nineteenth century, the 'beau ideal' (an interlinking of the idealization of rural village communities and of home as a haven) found expression in British urban form in decentralization and segregation of the social classes and the sexes. An additional impetus was added by the fear of mob rule. As the century progressed, anti-urbanists became more vocal as problems of poverty, crime, vice, and ill health were directly, although not always correctly, attributed to the increases in city size. Thus, links can be traced between the ideology of home and garden and community, and the perceived threat to traditional authority posed by urban concentrations of the proletariat.

In the twentieth century, when it became clear that cities were here to stay, critics had to re-evaluate urban life. Their criticisms shifted to a concern to reduce what was seen as the isolation of the individual within a potentially anonymous urban structure where relationships were instrumental and impersonal. The physical solution was a city of communities where primary social relationships would predominate. British town planning, particularly after the Second World War, adopted these ideas uncritically and became identified with the garden city and community centre movement. Garden cities, garden suburbs, inter-war private suburbanization, local authority housing estates, and post-war new towns all explicitly relied on community planning, embodied in the neighbourhood unit, and implicitly enshrined the domestic ethic of family and home-centred activities. The majority of housing development was in self-contained new towns or on peripheral greenfield sites. Work-centred production activities and home-centred domestic labour (men's and women's lives) were spatially distinct. In Becontree, for example, an enormous 'cottage' estate (the very name, design, and layout enshrining a rural and domestic idyll) for 112,000 people begun in 1921 and completed in 1934, there was virtually no local employment until Fords moved to nearby Dagenham in 1931.

An important corollary of the neighbourhood principle (a self-contained group of several hundred houses with associated local facilities of shops, parks, primary school, and health care facilities, benevolently interpreted as reducing travel time and costs for women and children, less benevolently as minimizing choice) was the aim of social balance. This was a part of the early twentieth-century garden city movement and was resuscitated in the post-war new town era, partly in reaction to the divisive social segregation of the classes in inter-war suburban developments. Social balance has been variously interpreted as a further mechanism of social control, a bourgeois invention to increase the diffusion of middle-class values of domestic privacy and individualized consumption, and reduce the possibility of working-class unification in struggles over distribution as well as production. On the other hand, Fabians supported social balance as a way of improving the opportunities of the less fortunate, particularly advocating its supposed advantages for schooling.

However, another interpretation of 'community' is possible. The notion is not solely a bourgeois or patriarchal invention. It has a long history as an authentic working-class counterpart, as a defensive weapon in the class struggle, and also as a vehicle for neighbouring solidarity and self-help. The more idealistic views of working-class communities and mutual support, particularly between women, as popularized by Young and Willmott (1962) in Bethnal Green, for example, have, however, been challenged. In a study of family relations and urban structure in nineteenth-century Lancashire, Anderson (1974) has argued that although the separation of conjugal roles leads to the key importance of neighbourhood in women's lives, these local relationships were not automatically supportive but based on a functional and calculative orientation to kinship and neighbourhood interaction. Anderson argues that the traditional community solidarity portrayed in Bethnal Green only became possible in the inter-war and immediately post-war years when local aid was no longer extremely costly in cash terms, adding in parentheses 'though still costly in time, which was not scarce, *at least for women*' (Anderson 1974: 178; my emphasis).

Community solidarity has also been seen as the basis for political organization. Harvey has referred to working-class struggles based on area of residence as 'a defensive and even offensive weapon in the class struggle' (Harvey 1978: 128), and Castells (1977) has attributed equal significance to what he labels 'urban social movements' in uniting political struggles in the spheres of production and consumption. However, both commentators seem to have failed to recognize the potential of community organization as a weapon in women's struggle to challenge the patriarchal assumptions behind the apparently liberal aspects of the local state's control of collective consumption. Struggles in the community sometimes cut across class boundaries and are based on women's oppression in consumption, in their everyday life, as women. Marjorie Mayo (1977) has begun to document the influence of women's involvement in community organization. However, the question must be raised (if not answered) of the extent to which the division of space by class, and by life cycle stage, undermines the potential for women to organize on issues of distribution and consumption. There are marked variations in local access to goods and services in different parts of the city and these have implications for the distribution of life chances between social classes. One example of this is the importance of school catchment areas to middle-class households deciding where to live (St John-Brooks 1980).

State housing and the domestic ideal

To my knowledge there is no specific work linking the origins of state housing and the form of its provision to the ideology of home and community, although recent studies (see especially Merrett 1979) have located the reasons for state intervention in the housing market in the conflict between falling rates of profit from private investment in domestic property and the need for improved standards of working-class housing to ensure the adequate reproduction of labour power and the conditions of social reproduction. For this reason, and to ensure the perceived legitimacy of the social order, state housing has been supported by both major parties in Britain, although with different degrees of political commitment. For the labour movement, municipal housing is also a means of advancing the material interests of a class.

Although the proportion of households living in local authority accommodation has continued to rise during this century, at least until recently, the impetus to large-scale intervention has twice resulted from the aftermath of war: destruction and low building rates during the war, rising marriage and birth rates afterwards, and fears of social disorder (the squatting movement, for example, after the Second World War). This has been accompanied by a withdrawal of women from the labour force and a reinforcement of the domestic ethic of home as a haven against the uncertainty of a changing world. The type of property built after both wars was predominantly houses for single families, on green-field peripheral sites. Under the 1919 (Addison) Act, the 1923 (Wheatley) Act, and the 1924 (Chamberlain) Act, 700,000 houses were built, mainly with two and three bedrooms, laid out on cottage estates. From 1931 to 1939, general purpose building declined and slum clearance took precedence. Two hundred and sixty-five thousand local authority houses were built in these years, only 23 per cent greater than the annual output of the private sector, whereas owner occupation in the suburbs was becoming increasingly popular for households lower down the social scale. Both types of development exacerbated the separation of home and work, thereby increasing the isolation of women. Peripheral locations combined with single family dwellings confirmed the wish not only to preserve the integrity of the nuclear family, but also to keep it as separate as possible from other families and any outside intrusion. During the 1930s flats were popularly regarded, in England and Wales at least, as violating individual privacy. In a debate in the House of Commons in 1938 the member for Argyleshire argued that 'flats are an abomination ... never meant for human beings ... flats make Communists while cottages make individuals, and incidentally make good Conservatives' (see Spring-Rice 1939: 16), thus nicely combining the desire for privacy with the recognition of the links between housing policy and social quiescence.

Although the erection of state-owned dwellings probably improved physical housing conditions for less affluent households, in real terms living standards often declined. Travel costs frequently rose, inadequate public transport, especially for shift workers, was a severe problem, and meagre provision of communal facilities, lack of choice of shops, and rising housing costs all contributed to more difficult living conditions. In a study of the lives of working-class women in the 1930s, Spring-Rice recorded the financial costs entailed by a move to better housing. For Mrs W, for example, who was about to move into a new corporation housing estate in Brighton, the 'higher rent will necessitate a terrible pinching in the food budget' (Spring-Rice 1939: 130); and for an unmarried woman in Preston the higher rents in local authority accommodation presented her with a dilemma: 'I have been offered a better home but the rent was double this one and as the family is in and out of work I feel I don't know what to do' (Spring-Rice 1939: 130). Other problems of the new estates were recorded, including distance from the wage-earner's work. Two women in Birmingham, living on one of the corporation estates on the outskirts of the city, complained of the train and bus fares for their husbands and sons. But perhaps the most serious consequence was for the children of these working-class mothers. Spring-Rice noted that:

> 'the fact that school medical officers have remarked upon the deterioration in physical fitness of children who have moved from bad to good housing conditions, is a proof that the lower standard of diet necessitated by a higher rent is not off-set by the healthier home environment, better conditions of rest, better ventilation, more open space around the home, etc., etc.'   (Spring-Rice 1939: 153)

The same pattern of a large post-war programme of local authority building, accompanied by a decline in the proportion of women in paid employment, and followed by the gradual withdrawal to concentrate on slum clearance, was repeated after the Second World War. Again, the implicit acceptance of the domestic ideal appears to have been virtually complete. Although Beveridge perceptively linked housing conditions and women's oppression; commenting that:

> 'The housewife's job with a large family is frankly impossible and will remain so, unless some of what now has to be done separately in every home – washing all clothes, cooking every meal, being in charge of every child every moment when it is not in school – can be done com- munally outside the home.'   (Beveridge 1942: 264)

and

> 'Nothing short of a revolution in housing would give the working housewife the equivalent of the two hours of additional leisure a day on five days a week that has come to the wage earner in the past seventy years.'   (Beveridge 1942: 275)

This does not seem to have sparked off a similar awareness among housing policy makers. (A complete search of White Papers and other documents from the period remains to be undertaken.) Houses with two and three bedrooms and a garden remained the dominant form. Between the Wars, only 12 per cent of all local authority dwellings were built as flats. The proportion increased in the public sector in the 1960s but remained very low among property built for sale. The present size distribution and type of the stock in the two main tenure categories is outlined in *Table 1*.

The majority of women, particularly those who do not engage in any form of wage labour, remain isolated within their own homes. The fol- lowing passage from Spring-Rice's study of women's lives is almost as applicable today as when she wrote it in 1939.

Table 1 *Size distribution of dwellings in England and Wales*

	Owner-occupied dwellings (1971) %	Local authority dwellings (1976) %
1 bedroom	2	17
2 bedrooms	28	29
3 bedrooms	58	51
4 or more bedrooms	12	3

Table 2   *Type of dwellings in England and Wales*

	Owner-occupied dwellings (1971) %	Local-authority dwellings (1976) %
Detached house	27	1
Semi-detached house	39	36
Terraced house	28	30
Purpose-built flat or maisonette	2	30
Other	4	3

Source: Department of Environment (1977).

'Their task [that of mothers] is more unremitting than that of any man. . . . The last thing that can be expected of them is quiet thought and any action other than the minimum demanded by the immediate job in hand. They lead private and often very solitary lives; their work is unpaid and unorganised. Its inevitability is taken for granted not only by themselves but also by the other half of the public, who themselves have grown up and thrived on it. Members of Parliament . . . do not see what is going on in the small dark unorganised workshop of the home. Men and young people who work in large communities and in the political lively bit of the factory, the railway or the mine, have time and energy and opportunity to make their voices heard. And though the better economic conditions which are the basis of most of their dividends would benefit their wives and families most of all, there is none the less a primitive acceptance by the men, as well as by the women themselves, of the general conditions of a housewife's life.'

(Spring-Rice 1939: 18)

Despite some progress in community organization and campaigns to improve the conditions of domestic labour and, of course, a wider variety of labour-saving devices in the home, for most women domestic labour remains a primarily private, unorganized, and unpaid task.

The management and allocation of state housing also reflects the patriarchal assumptions of local state policy. Great emphasis in allocation is placed on domestic virtues, such as housekeeping standards and cleanliness. Prospective tenants are inspected by housing visitors (Ungerson 1971), who may arrive unannounced, and families are graded according to their suitability for particular types of property. Various minority groups, including 'problem' families, single parents, and ethnic minorities, among whom many families are headed by un-supported women, frequently receive the poorest dwellings in the lowest status areas. In the early post-war years, explicit advice on the standards expected in the new house was handed out, presumably to women. In the 1950s, one housing manager advised:

'Keep your home clean and tidy. Endeavour to have some method of cleaning as you go along; do not try to clean the whole house in one day. Regular bedtimes for children and adults except on special occasions. Sit down properly at table. Hang up your pots and pans or put them on a shelf. . . .' (see Ward 1974: 12)

Such patronizing advice is no longer usual although, as Tucker makes clear, local housing authorities

'prize above all a good (i.e. solvent, tractable, clean and quiet) tenant and tend to favour *him*, as any private landlord would. Because *he* is deemed likely to treat it carefully, *he* is generally given one of the authority's newest and best homes.' (Tucker 1966: 11; my emphasis)

Domestic labour is not the sole task for many women, who combine their unwaged work at home with waged work in the labour market. The proportion of women in the labour force has increased steadily since the 1930s with the exception of the peak and decline in numbers during and immediately after the Second World War. Work remains to be done in pointing up the links between the peripheral location of housing and women's role as a reserve army of labour. It was surely no coincidence that the vast programme of peripherally-located single family state housing was related to women's post-war withdrawal from the labour market. Yet in later years, as the economy expanded, the pool of married women on these suburban estates has proved an attractive and flexible source of labour for the light assembly industries that also began to decentralize and expand into the suburbs. In the next section, I indicate certain links between suburbanization and the consumer boom that was generated to consume the products of these new suburban industries.

Suburban privatization and the glorification of domesticity: the rise of consumer industries

While the separation of home and work and the sexual division of labour help to ensure the reproduction of labour power at relatively low costs for capitalist economies, the anti-urban ideal and the ideology of community are used by the state to ensure and reinforce the legitimacy of this sexual division of space and labour. It has also been argued that suburbanization and the withdrawal from local kinship networks to highly individualized family units based on age and class-segregated housing estates have been used directly to counter the tendency to over-accumulation and falling rates of profit in the North American economy (Harvey 1975, 1978).

Home ownership and state suburbanization have opened up a new life-style based on family possession of consumer durables, thereby support-ing the rise of vast new industries. The domestic ethic has been manipulated since the Second World War to encourage the consumption of a new range of products by both sexes, but particularly women. The disjunction between the reality of suburban isolation and idealized images of wives and mothers as creative managers of modern homes was probably greatest in the USA in the 1950s. Betty Friedan's *The Feminine Mystique* (1963) vividly documents the implications: the 1950s baby boom; the decline in the percentage of girls going on to college (from 47 per cent in 1920, to 35 per cent in 1958); the rise of the home sewing industry as a multi-million-dollar business; the growing recogni-tion by advertisers that women who were freed from domestic drudgery by appliances, who were healthy, reasonably educated, and relatively affluent, were 'free' to choose clothes, cars, and innumerable domestic appliances. The boast that women wielded 75 per cent of the purchasing power in America was not taken lightly. Professionalization and special-ization of domestic products followed: women were presented by adver-tisers as experts choosing between different products to run an efficient home.

Similar stages can be documented in Great Britain: the immediate post-war rush into the 'security' of home and children; the post-war baby boom, followed by another in the late 1950s; the closure of day nurseries; the spectre of latch-key kids and pseudo-scientific theories of maternal deprivation; the rise of commercial television and other forms of adver-tising presenting images of domestic life; and the phenomenal boom of building societies into big business, hiding behind a smokescreen of helping the small saver and the family (think of the well-known logo that Abbey National has used since the Second World War of a couple strid-ing arm in arm into the future under an umbrella fashioned from the roof of a house).

Owner occupation has now risen to 53 per cent of the total housing stock and although its importance varies by social class, it is no longer restricted to a privileged minority. Appreciating house values have become an integral part of the domestic economy of many households: hundreds of thousands of suburban owner-occupiers rely upon the rising capital value of their house for increased purchasing power. Freehold home ownership is often used as security against the credit purchase of large-scale consumer durables. Thus, manufacturers, importers, and retailers of cars, freezers, washing machines, colour TV sets, sound systems, furniture, and garden accessories, for example, rely on the continued demand for, and appreciating value of, the traditional suburban home to maintain demand for their products. In their turn they support the conservative strategy of building societies that results in the majority of mortgages going to young married men.

Table 3 *Post-war rises in the possession of selected consumer durables in Great Britain (percentage of all households)*

	1956[1]	*1975*[2]
Washing machine	19	71
Refrigerator	7	85
Vacuum cleaner	51	91
Television	40	95

Sources: 1 Young and Willmott (1975; 23).
        2 Office of Population Censuses and Surveys (1975).

Changes in the form of houses have increased women's involvement in conspicuous domestic consumption. Picture windows make the interior visible to all, open-plan layouts have removed the division between work (kitchen) and leisure (living rooms) in the home and made it virtually impossible for a woman to have a room of her own. To pay for this domestic ideal, many women have been forced into the labour market, frequently into part-time jobs, without security, and so into suffering the double oppression of capitalist exploitation at work and patriarchal domination at home.

Inner area, high-rise council estates

In the face of the dominance of the anti-urban ideal, community ideology, and post-war suburban domesticity, the temporary phenomenon of inner-city high-rise developments that have proved so inimical to the traditional family life demands explanation. During the late 1950s and early 1960s the building of high-rise blocks of flats was encouraged both by state policy and private industry. Ironically, part of the explanation lies in the very same anti-urban ideal that was so influential in the garden city and new town movement. Fear of the physical spread of cities led to post-war legislation to restrict growth by designating urban green belts round the major cities. In the late 1950s and 1960, as housing redevelopment programmes gathered momentum, a coalition of interests led to a swing from peripheral green-site development to inner area high-rise housing for the displaced residents of redevelopment areas. Urban authorities were restricted by the green belt and often unable to purchase land or extend their boundaries beyond it. In addition, they feared that the loss of rate revenues and subsidies would outweigh the costs of rebuilding in the city. On the other hand, the combination of the vested interests of shire landowners, disguised as a desire to conserve the value of rural living, and suburban fears of an influx of proletarian (and labour-voting) households proved an immovable obstacle for those city authorities who wished to expand their population beyond the green belt. Added to this was a central government subsidy system encouraging high-rise development, the growth of non-traditional building methods by large construction companies often with local or national political influence, and a growing number of local authority architects imbued with poorly digested ideas from the modern movement (especially Gropius and Le Corbusier) with their designs for 'vertical garden cities' and 'communities in the air' packaged to appeal to the garden-loving, anti-urban British. Unfortunately, the omission of key facilities such as communal laundries, shops, and day-care and play spaces, which were recommended by Le Corbusier and Gropius to make high-rise living tolerable, largely accounts for their adverse reception by housebound women and women with children. Fortunately the rapid escalation of the proportion of local authority dwellings built as high-rise flats between 1961 and 1965 fell just as dramatically in the late 1960s. However, the proportion of dwellings that were flats did not begin to fall until 1972. It is difficult to evaluate the importance of women's struggles in the community on housing issues, but there is no doubt that they have been important in particular local issues. However, the patent absurdity of 'vertical garden cities' makes it clear what a strong grip the anti-urban, domestic ideal has in Great Britain and how small a voice women have in the design of their environment.

Conclusions

The majority of women today live in nuclear families; on marriage they leave the so-called protection of one man (their father) for another, although a small but growing percentage of women have a few years of independent living, often as a corollary of higher education, or, later, because of separation or divorce. However, at the present time 66 per cent of British women aged sixteen and over are married. Divorce figures are rising but so are figures for remarriage and *Table 4* clearly demonstrates the overwhelming predominance of a patriarchal family structure in this country.

Table 4 *Family structure in Great Britain*

Traditional male-headed family unit (80% of all people)	51% of people live in a family unit headed by a married couple and dependent children; 9% of people live in a family unit headed by a married couple and independent children; 20% of people live in a family unit headed by a married couple.
Single-parent families (8% of all people)	Almost half single parents with dependent children live alone; most of the rest live with their parents. The majority are women.
Others (12% of all people)	2% of people live in multi-family units; 8% of people live alone; 2% of people live with one or more unrelated people.

Source: Central Statistical Office (1980).

In Great Britain there are few opportunities for satisfactory independent living. Housing policy is based on unquestioned assumptions of male-dominated family forms and relationships, and a sexual division of labour. The structure of urban housing markets legitimates the ideological significance of privatized family life and domesticity, and institutions in both the public and private sectors operate on these assumptions in the production, allocation, and location of housing. Thus the division of space reflects and influences the social relations between men and women in cities. The sexual division of labour is mirrored by a sexual division of space where 'non-conforming' uses (that is wage labour and domestic labour) are segregated by the operation of the urban housing and land markets and by state regulation and control of them.

The functioning of capitalist cities relies on the unpaid labour of women. I searched the indexes of the classic texts in urban studies for some recognition of this fact but found little, apart from a passing, although incisive, comment from Castells in *City, Class and Power*:

'The feminist movement is threatening the very logic of the urban structure, for it is the subordinate role of women which enables the minimal "maintenance" of its housing, transport and public facilities. In the end, if the system still "works" it is because women guarantee unpaid transportation (movement of people and merchandise), because they repair their homes, because they make meals when there are no canteens, because they spend more time shopping around, because they look after others' children when there are no nurseries, and because they offer "free entertainment" to the producers when there is a social vacuum and an absence of cultural creativity. If these women who "do nothing" ever stopped to do "only that", the urban structure as we know it would become completely incapable of maintaining its functions. The contemporary city also rests on the subordination of "women consumers" to "men producers".'

(Castells 1978: 177–78)

For those women who are both producers and consumers, the present structure of urban land use presents severe problems. Whether the contradictions that arise from the organization of space on both capitalist and patriarchal principles will ever lead to women challenging existing divisions remains to be seen. However, the present division of space along class lines undermines the potential for women to organize themselves on issues of distribution and consumption. It seems more likely that the class-based nature of most local action will continue.

Notes

1 While not wishing to debate the utility of the concept of patriarchy and its relationship to particular modes of production (see Beechey 1979), it is important to define the specific use of the term in this paper. It is used here to refer to the general system of male power over women that exists in all areas of life in Great Britain today. Thus it is used in a historically specific sense, and is a descriptive, rather than explanatory, concept. I have not attempted to explain the basis of sexual divisions in cities, nor to explore why there is such a division at all.

References

Anderson, M. (1974) *Family Structure in Nineteenth-Century Lancashire.* London: Cambridge University Press.
Beechey, V. (1979) On Patriarchy. *Feminist Review* **3**: 66–82.
Beveridge, W. (1942) *Social Insurance and Allied Services.* Cmnd 6404. London: HMSO.
Boddy, M. (1980) *The Building Societies.* London: Macmillan.
Castells, M. (1977) *The Urban Question.* London. Edward Arnold.

—— (1978) *City, Class and Power*. London: Macmillan.

Central Statistical Office (1980) *Social Trends*. London: HMSO.

Colenutt, R. (1970) Urban Land Use Models. In C. Board, R. J. Chorley, P. Hoggett, and D. R. Stoddart (eds) *Progress in Geography*. London: Edward Arnold.

Davidoff, L., L'Esperance, J., and Newby, H. (1976) Landscape with Figures. In J. Mitchell and A. Oakley (eds) *The Rights and Wrongs of Women*. Harmondsworth: Penguin.

Department of Environment (1971) *Fair Deal for Housing*. Cmnd 4728. London: HMSO.

—— (1977) *Housing Policy Technical Volumes*, Parts 1, 2, and 3. Cmnd 6851. London: HMSO.

Foley, D. (1960) British Town Planning: One Ideology or Three? *British Journal of Sociology* 2: 211–31.

Friedan, B. (1963) *The Feminine Mystique*. London: Gollancz.

Gardiner, J. (1976) Political Economy of Domestic Labour in Capitalist Society. In D. Barker and S. Allen (eds) *Dependence and Exploitation in Work and Marriage*. Harlow: Longman.

Glass, R. (1968) Urban Sociology in Great Britain. In R. Pahl (ed.) *Readings in Urban Sociology*. Oxford: Pergamon.

Harrison, J. (1973) *The Political Economy of Housework*. London: Bulletin of the Conference of Socialist Economists.

Harvey, D. (1974) Class Monopoly Rent, Finance Capital and the Urban Revolution. *Regional Studies* 8: 239–55.

—— (1975) Class Structure in Capitalist Society and the Theory of Residential Differentiation. In R. Peel, P. Haggett, and M. Chisholm (eds) *Process in Physical and Human Geography: Bristol Essays*. London: Heinemann.

—— (1977) Government Policies, Financial Institutions and Neighbourhood Change in United States Cities. In M. Harloe (ed.) *Captive Cities*. London: John Wiley.

—— (1978) The Urban Process under Capitalism: A Framework for Analysis. *International Journal of Urban and Regional Studies* II: 101–31.

Harvey, D. and Chatterjee, L. (1974) Absolute Rent and the Structuring of Space by Government and Financial Institutions. *Antipode* 6: 22–36.

Himmelweit, S. and Mohun, S. (1977) Domestic Labour and Capital. *Cambridge Journal of Economics* 1: 15–31.

Hope, E., Kennedy, M., and De Winter, A. (1976) Homeworkers in North London. In D. Barker and S. Allen (eds) *Dependence and Exploitation in Work and Marriage*. Harlow: Longman.

Hunt, A. (1968) *A Survey of Women's Employment*. London: HMSO.

Mayo, M. (ed.) (1977) *Women in the Community*. London: Routledge & Kegan Paul.

Merrett, S. (1979) *State Housing in Britain*. London: Routledge & Kegan Paul.

Molyneux, M. (1979) Beyond the Housework Debate. *New Left Review* 116: 3–28.

Oakley, A. (1974) *The Sociology of Housework*. London: Martin Robertson.

Office of Population Censuses and Surveys (1975) *General Household Survey*. London: HMSO.

Pickvance, C. (ed.) (1976) *Urban Sociology: Critical Essays.* London: Tavistock.

Rex, J. and Moore, R. (1967) *Race, Community and Conflict.* London: OUP.

Richardson, H. W. (1971) *Urban Economics.* Harmondsworth: Penguin.

St. John-Brooks, C. (1980) Playing the School System. *New Society* 16 October: 112–13.

Secretary-General of the National BSA (1976) Report on an Address by N. Briggs. *Building Societies Gazette.*

Spring-Rice, M. (1939) *Working-Class Wives.* Harmondsworth: Penguin.

Stapleton, C. (1980) Reformulation of the Family Life-Cycle Concept. *Environment and Planning A* **12**: 1103–118.

Thorns, D. (1972) *Suburbia.* London: MacGibbon & Kee.

Tucker, J. (1966) *Honorable Estates.* London: Gollancz.

Ungerson, C. (1971) *Moving Home.* London: Bell.

Ward, C. (1974) *Tenants Take Over.* London: Architectural Press.

Williams, R. (1960) Conversation (with R. Hoggart). *New Left Review* **1**.

—— (1973) *The Country and the City.* London: Chatto & Windus.

Young, M., and Willmott, P. (1962) *Family and Kinship in East London.* Harmondsworth: Penguin.

—— (1975) *The Symmetrical Family.* Harmondsworth: Penguin.

10

Rejoinder to
Linda McDowell

ELIZABETH LEBAS

In considering this rejoinder to Linda McDowell's proposals, one particular issue became evident. It was not simply a question posed in terms of what urban studies can contribute to feminism, but something more complex, concerning the situation in urban studies and the ways in which academic approaches both define their subject and their obstacles. The separation of home from work is a basic example. Perceived by anthropologists and sociologists as a major indicator of modern sexual divisions, it is also ignored by them as an essential feature of modern urbanization. Feminists engaged in urban studies would contend that sexual divisions and urbanization are integral, though it is reasonable to add that they have yet to demonstrate precisely how. In this new domain of feminist urban studies, there are two obstacles that remain.

First, the post-war competition in urban studies between sociology and geography. With the possibility of a feminist perspective, each discipline has claimed a concept for itself; for geography this has been 'space', while for sociology this has been 'gender'. Articulated together these seem inevitably to produce an immutability that defies any dynamic explanation. In order for feminist urban explanations to progress, these concepts will need radical redefinition.

The second obstacle lies precisely in the profound but recent influence of neo-Marxist urban explanations. Hailed as the rejuvenators of an ailing field, their conceptualizations have been inimical to a feminist approach. It is important that readers recognize that a feminist urban studies must struggle with a short and yet powerful legacy of thought that neglected the place of relations of work in urbanization and constructed a notion of social reproduction that could not entertain the existence of sexual divisions.

I hope that this rejoinder will show how a shared feminist intent also reveals points of contact and disparity between two disciplines within urban studies. My intention is also to outline the relevance of urban research and analysis to feminist discussions, and to point up analogous omissions and problems of explanation.

Eva Gamarnikow (1978), in 'Women and the City', pointed to a basic problem of neo-Marxist urban theory that a conceptualization of the city as a unit of collective consumption inevitably engendered. The capitalist city *per se* is seen as embodying the process of reproduction, thereby denying the role of other agencies and structures such as the family and patriarchy. Although I recognize the considerable advances made by neo-Marxist urban theory in explaining the economic and political mechanisms that affect the everyday life of ordinary people and their subordination to a capitalist urban system, I am more pessimistic than McDowell about its potential for feminist analysis. However, it should be said that the field is in a dynamic state, and to counter my pessimism I could point to a growing interest in urbanistic ideologies as they are articulated to those of domesticity (Wright 1975, 1980) and could mention a move away from massive theorizations of the state towards an understanding of the disciplines exercised in maintaining and structuring relations between work and home (see Bleitrach and Chenu 1979), as well as other areas that are being rediscovered and researched. But these emerging interests do not necessarily mean that a second revolution is at hand in urban studies that will announce the end of current urban theories. I will concede, however, that they do suggest that a coherent analysis of sexual divisions in urban studies will necessarily and positively threaten its present frameworks and academic mode of interchange.

In fact there are signs in this country and elsewhere that urban and architectural research on sexual divisions is being carried out, but often with extremely modest means, and often appearing as unpublished papers and student theses (see *Casabella*; *Blod By*; and *Heresies*). Susan Francis's (1980) critique of building design, and Helen Austerberry's and Sophie Watson's (1981) research on female homelessness represent an expanding interest in this area, characteristically being expressed in day meetings, short courses, and informal seminars.[1] But at this stage the general viewpoint is more empirical and, as I do not question this emphasis, I would like to consider here the more questionable areas of urban analysis, that is those that arise once description is complete. As there are many such areas, I intend to focus on two: first the theme of reproduction in neo-Marxist and French urban theory, and second the recent American feminist and geographical analyses of sexual and spatial segregation. If there is one factor that unites these rather disparate approaches, it is that feminist analyses cannot simply be grafted onto old (or even new) sociologies and geographies for to do this inevitably means the unintended acceptance of the sexist premises that underlie these disciplines.

In examining the question of reproduction in neo-Marxist urban theory I was provoked by the quotation from Castells's latest English publication, *City, Class and Power*, in McDowell's paper (see pp. 160–61), and by issues raised by women students and colleagues during seminars. As translator of the original French text, I remember my annoyance at this concessionary passage in the concluding section of a collection of articles, because there was little in Castells's previous writings to suggest any recognition of either the role of women or sexual divisions. There is no need to seek textual legitimation from a favoured theorist to realize that without the work of women the urban system would fall apart. However, if we look more closely at the theoretical underpinnings of the work of Castells and others we can understand why and in what ways their problematics *preclude* the analysis of sexual divisions.

Inscribed within a periodized and strategic theory of advanced capitalism resting on a notion of overaccumulation (see Boccara 1974; Marx 1971), these theorists put forward a conception of reproduction based on waged labour as a commodity at the centre of the contradiction between development of productive forces and relations of production. This commodity of waged labour is unlike any other commodity because it alone produces value. In this economic system the state intervenes both to guarantee the 'communal and general conditions of social production' (Marx 1973: 533), and to counter the tendency for the rate of profit to fall. This intervention is both economic and political. For labour it is represented as the provision of goods and services that are wholly or partly de-commodified (and is analogous to the devalorization of selected capital) so that their consumption is not reflected in the cost of labour to capital.

Many contradictions are encountered in this process of intervention that, at the level of consumption, are expressed by two fundamental factors. The provision of de-commodified goods and services by the state entails a redistribution of surplus value that is subject to class struggle, among powerful economic interest groups, and between working and capitalist classes. Within advanced capitalism where finance capital dominates, it is the latter class that will dictate to the state the modes of redistribution of surplus value. But, in addition, at the level of consumption, another contradiction also exists. This rests on the fact that under different economic and political circumstances goods and services can have both use and commodity value. This is most clearly expressed in housing.

Within this framework the city takes on a variety of theorized entities that are specified according to the role that is suggested for it at different moments in the cycle of capital accumulation. For Castells (1977), the distinguishing feature of the capitalist city is its function in reproducing labour power, a function that is conditional on the fact that the city is a system of de-commodified goods and services. As such it is a unit of collective consumption; collective because it is a collection of households consuming, and because these goods and services are provided collectively. It is the city as a whole rather than the household that reproduces. The object of urban analysis is to understand how this reproduction is orchestrated by the state, and how this in turn gives rise to conflicts and contradictions.

What problems does this pose for a feminist analysis? First, as Christopher Pickvance (1974) has pointed out, this model of the city is essentially demographic, made up of a collection of individuals (in this case waged workers), and there is little sense of the city as a social structure. Susanna Magri (1972) has also noted that throughout this research the understanding of the household is essentially statistical, having no hierarchy or power relations. But these critics do not consider the effects of omitting an analysis of the relations of reproduction between theorized city and quantified household. The model assumes the centrality of reproduction and socialization of waged labour, but there is no perception of the supply of labour as a factor of its costs and socialization, and this omission is surprising given that this model comes from a country that has exercised strong pro-natal policies and where family allowances are an essential income for poorer families. That women have a role in the physical supply of labour power, and that they make it available to the market is ignored. (The Victorians seem to have had a clearer perception of the relations between demographic growth, urban conditions, and class power (Stedman-Jones 1971).) Thus in this model, in part because it focuses on the unassailable and exclusive reality of the wage relation, we have no means of understanding the relations of the provision of means of collective consumption to non-waged labour, nor of how these contribute to the non-commodification of domestic labour.

More recently, Pickvance (1980) has pointed out that in this model the state appears as the only agent of socialization. We have to go outside the French literature for analyses of the articulation of urban and domestic ideologies (see Wright 1975, 1980), but as soon as we realize that there are very important connections between urbanism, anti-urbanism, and domesticity, many questions arise for feminists. Dolores Hayden (1980) has recently commented that feminists, in their search for socialized domestic labour, have been of all political shades, and that as a result of their position in the family women have contributed to the ideological acceptance of the wage relation. Moreover, the family is not a self-enclosed oppressive institution on its own. The state also constructs the family through urbanistic ideologies, the provision of collective means of consumption, which are geared to the rearing of children (see Davin 1978) and to the leisure activities of an idealized family; and at times it can be shown to be a construction that is not exclusively ideological, but that bears a very direct relationship to crises in capital accumulation.

For example, the promotion of council house sales and home ownership are not policies that aim only at valorizing privatization for its own sake. They relate to quite identifiable stages of accumulation, political negotiations, and to crises in the construction industry and the circulation of property capital (see, for example, Ball 1976; O'Donnell 1978; and Harloe 1981). But we must be careful not to analyse the state and the family via urban policies simply in terms of their congruence; we must also remember that those policies that are 'good' for capital are not good for all capital and that they may be 'bad' for the capitalist family they wish to maintain. It is unfortunate that this area of work is largely neglected, for this kind of urban economic research could help to project the family into the political economy, something that I feel is often lacking in feminist analyses.

This over-interpretation of the state as agency of reproduction with the city as executor suffers from a problem that is also evident in feminist theories of reproduction. This is the problem of functionality and teleological necessity of reproduction (Barrett 1980). The applied research surrounding this theoretical model of the city is useful in showing the difficulties of proving the efficacy of agencies of reproduction and socialization. Labour processes and labour markets are so complex, their turnover so rapid, and the movement of capital so geographically dispersed, that it is questionable whether only the most punctual of state policies can ensure the effective maintenance of skills and the means of their reproduction when and where they are needed (Bleitrach and Chenu 1979).

In addition, this theoretical trinity of waged labour, state, and consumption not only denies an account of the role of women in unwaged labour, but also omits any account of their productive role in the production of collective means of consumption. It is not only the women who stay at home who maintain the urban system, but also the women who work, paid or unpaid, for the state in the production of its services. In these studies there are no accounts of the role of state employees as the producers of the urban system and as those who are seriously affected by reductions in social state expenditure.

Many critics have emphasized the overdetermination of the state in this theoretical model and rather than repeat their observations I will turn instead to its implications for a political theory of urban protest. Castells's (1974, 1978) undoubted contribution to urban analysis was its politicization. The myth of the benevolent state was finally put to rest in urban studies. By placing the state centre stage, its precise role in diffusing, veiling, and also creating new bases of conflict was recognized. The increasingly social nature of advanced capitalism, its inscription in the urban environment, led Castells to attempt to identify the social bases of struggle other than those immediately centred in the workplace but related to it. Just as there were workplace struggles, there were urban struggles centred on the quality or absence of publicly provided use-values. These were recognized as having different modes of organization and ideologies, but Castells focused on organization rather than counter ideologies. As Hilary Rose (1978) has mentioned in an article on Women's Aid, more attention to ideologies could have been a possible point of entry into examining the connections between feminist and urbanistic demands.

Feminists have already remarked that Castells's studies of urban social movements have no female participants even though housing is the main object of contention, and in literally hundreds of cases studied, there is, despite a meticulous attention to the composition and genesis of these movements, no perception that women are the object of a sexual dynamic and struggle. Cynthia Cockburn (1977) has directed attention to this in her study of Lambeth, *The Local State*. But this problematic on urban social movements is weak not simply because there is no palpable presence of women, but also because there is no analytical place for them. As the urban system is the only referent, there can be no analysis of what lies underneath. In short, Castells depoliticizes the domestic sphere (however unintentionally) in order precisely to politicize the urban system.

I have mentioned Castells's model because it is the only one available in translation. However, I have implied that other neo-Marxist urban explanations exist that have also failed to make connections between the nature of the provision of means of collective consumption and the domestic creation of use-values. I have briefly tried to indicate some problems inherent in neo-Marxist urban theory. Other problems can also be found in feminist analyses, particularly in notions of the domestic realm as being the 'sphere of reproduction' (see, for example, Ehrenreich and English 1975). This approach over-privatizes the function of domestic organization and makes it difficult to see the relations between the production and consumption of use and commodity values. In the United States this approach has characterized a new corpus of research that attempts, quite literally, to locate women on the urban territory (see *Signs* 1980).

Here again I am ambivalent. First, I am uncertain about the assumptions of the frameworks that underpin this research. A neo-classical approach to residential location is juxtaposed with a conception of urban development reflecting the processes of privatization of the domestic sphere. More specifically, these location theories assume that the location of individuals in urban space is essentially a reflection of individual preference subject to market constraints, and, in turn, the privatization of the domestic sphere is illustrated by the growth of the suburbs and their dislocation from the economic activities of the central city. In this way women are located in the domestic sphere, geographically found at the edges of the central city, while men, selling their labour on the market, can be found at its centre.

This is a simplification of the model, but its explanatory outcomes are more complex. It implies that because women are in the suburbs and engage in domestic labour, then the suburbs are subordinate to the central city. This would suggest a conventional separation of consumption from production, and as Ann Markusen (1976) has shown, the suburbs are politically and in fiscal terms dominant over the central city. Moreover, as Markusen relates elsewhere (1980), instead of an increased suburbanization, what is occurring is the growth of small towns and the flight from the metropolis. In locating women almost exclusively in the suburban domestic sphere, a double segregation appears to take place. The home appears as a middle-class ghetto, having few relations to the outside except for the constraints, urban in nature, that are exercised upon it. These are seen as constraints on reproduction, and it is easy to interpret them as preventing women from exercising what in the end is considered their unquestioned and true calling, the reproduction of others. There are other ways whereby urban constraints (absence of infrastructures, radial transportation networks, etc.) could be interpreted — for example, in terms of their expressing the contradictions between domestic and commodity production, but this is not explored.

Perhaps the most unsatisfactory feature of this model is that it rests on an uncritical application of conventional urban analysis. How can the principle of individual choice be applied to women who are subordinate in domestic organization? For example, an analysis of the power dynamics of moving house would give us an interesting insight into the relations between work and domestic interests. It might also reveal what conventional sociological studies have shown, that households (however defined) have little choice as to where they locate. Class remains the major determinant of access to housing and there is hardly a perception of class in these studies.

Have these studies managed to acquire the two bugbears of both feminist and urban analyses, that is biologism and environmental determinism? Have they also contributed to the perpetuation of a simplistic understanding of the separation between home and work? When looking at changes in relations of production and their reflections in urban development, we can notice that fundamental changes are occurring. Particularly in the dense inner city we have the survival and reorganization of super-exploitative forms of domestic commodity production that relate to both formal and informal economies (see, for example, Hurstfield 1978). We also have a growth of use-value production by means of domestic capital, and as Pahl (1981) suggests, this implies new forms of domestic sexual divisions. Electronic office equipment in the home may also mean that for certain categories of employees their home may become a satellite of their workplace. Flexi-time, a shorter working week, as well as outright unemployment, are also recreating the relations between home and work (Duclos 1981). It would do well to examine these trends.

I hope that McDowell and I have begun to make a little clearer what we as urbanists can offer feminism. We may ask what feminists can offer to an understanding of urban change. Recently I read an article by Farge (1979) on women in eighteenth-century Paris. In a few lines I had a sense of Paris as it was, how women related to men and their children, how they lived and worked, the meaning of the house for them, and their movements in the city and their appropriation of it. That is what I expect from feminist analysis because that is what I want to know.

Note

1 For example, the course organized by Helen Austerberry and Sophie Watson on Women and Housing at the City Literary Institute, the day workshop organized at Kent University in May 1981 on Women and Housing Policy, and the requests by my own students at the Graduate School of the Architectural Association to have a special workshop on The House and Sexual Divisions.

References

Austerberry, H. and Watson, S. (1981) A Woman's Place: A Feminist Approach to Housing in Britain. *Feminist Review* **8**: 49–62.

Ball, M. (1976) Owner-occupation. In Political Economy of Housing Workshop of the Conference of Socialist Economists *Housing and Class*, Vol. II. London: CSE.

Barrett, M. (1980) *Women's Oppression Today – Problems in Marxist Feminist Analyses*. London: Verso Editions.

Bleitrach, D. and Chenu, A. (1979) *Discipline d'Usine et Vie Quotidienne*. Paris: Maspéro.

Blod By (1981) Kvinder. Special issue February **11**.

Boccara, P. (1974) *Etude sur le Capitalisme Monopoliste d'Etat: Sa Crise et son Issue*. Paris: Editions Sociales.

Casabella (1981) Condizione Femminile e Condizione Abitativa. Special issue with English abstracts March **XLV**.

Castells, M. (1977) *The Urban Question*. London: Edward Arnold.

—— (1978) *City, Class and Power*. London: Macmillan.

—— Cherki, E., Godard, F., and Mehl, D. (1974) *Sociologie des Mouvements Sociaux Urbains: Enquete sur la Region Parisienne*. Paris: Ecole des Hautes Etudes en Sciences Sociales.

Cockburn, C. (1977) *The Local State: The Management of Cities and People*. London: Pluto.

Davin, A. (1978) Imperialism and Motherhood. *History Workshop* **5**: 9–65.

Duclos, D. (1981) Capitalist State and the Administration of Time. In M. Harloe and E. Lebas (eds) *City, Class and Capital – The Political Economy of Cities and Regions*. London: Edward Arnold.

Ehrenreich, B. and English, D. (1975) The Manufacture of Housework. *Socialist Revolution* **5**(4): 5–40.

Farge, A. (1979) L'Histoire Ebruitée des Femmes dans la Société Pré-révolutionnaire Parisienne. In C. Dufrancastel, A. Farge, C. Fauré, G. Fraisse, M. Perrot, E. Salvaresi, and P. Werner (eds) *L'Histoire sans Qualités*. Paris: Galilée.

Francis, S. (1980) 'New Women, New Space: Towards a Feminist Critique of Building Design.' MA thesis. Department of General Studies, Royal College of Art.

Gamarnikow, E. (1978) Women and the City. *International Journal of Urban and Regional Research* **2**(3): 390–403.

Harloe, M. (ed.) (1977) *Captive Cities: Studies in the Political Economy of Cities and Regions*. London: John Wiley.

—— (1981) The Recommodification of Housing. In M. Harloe and E. Lebas (eds) *City, Class and Capital – The Political Economy of Cities and Regions*. London: Edward Arnold.

Hayden, D. (1980) *The Grand Domestic Revolution: A History of Feminist Designs for American Homes, Neighborhoods and Cities*. Cambridge, Mass.: MIT Press.

Hurstfield, J. (1978) *The Part-time Trap*. London: Low Pay Unit.

Magri, S. (1972) *Politique du Looement et Besoins en Main d'Oeuvre*. Paris: Centre de Sociologie Urbaine.

Markusen, A. (1976) Class and Urban Social Expenditures: A Local Theory of the State. *Kapitalistate* **4–5**: 50–65.

—— (1980) City Spatial Structure, Women's Household Work and National Urban Policy. *Signs* **5**(4): 23–44.

Marx, K. (1971) *Capital*, Vol. III. London: Lawrence & Wishart.

—— (1973) *Grundrisse*. Harmondsworth: Penguin.

O'Donnell, P. (1978) *The Beginnings of the Modern Home in the 1920s*. Childhood and Government Project, University of California, Berkeley. Working Paper 19.

Pahl, R. E. (1981) Employment, Work and the Domestic Division of Labour. In M. Harloe and E. Lebas (eds) *City, Class and Capital – The Political Economy of Cities and Regions*. London: Edward Arnold.

Pickvance, C. G. (1974) From Social Base to Social Force: Some Analytical Issues in the Study of Urban Protest. Paper given at the Eighth World Congress of the International Sociological Association, Toronto. Also in M. Harloe (ed.) (1977) *Captive Cities: Studies in the Political Economy of Cities and Regions*. London: John Wiley.

—— (1980) The Role of Housing in the Reproduction of Labour Power and the Analysis of State Intervention in Housing. In Political Economy of Housing Workshop of the Conference of Socialist Economists *Housing and Class*, Vol. III. London: CSE.

Quennell, P. (ed.) (1969) *Mayhew's London – Being Selections from 'London Labour and the London Poor' by Henry Mayhew*. London: Spring Books.

Rose, H. (1978) In Practice Supported, in Theory Denied: An Account of an Invisible Urban Movement. *International Journal of Urban and Regional Research* **2**(3): 521–37.

Signs (1980) Women and the American City. Special issue supplement **5**(3).

Stedman-Jones, G. (1971) *Outcast London*. Oxford: Clarendon Press.

Wright, G. (1975) Sweet and Clean: The Domestic Landscape in the Progressive Era. *Landscape* **20**(1): 38–43.

—— (1980) *Moralism and the Model Home: Domestic Architecture and Cultural Conflict in Chicago 1873–1913*. Chicago: Chicago University Press.

11

Patriarchal relations and law: an examination of family law and sexual equality in the 1950s[1]

CAROL SMART

The concept of patriarchy has become controversial within feminist discourse. Its meaning is frequently unclear and its relationship to capitalism has posed apparently intractable theoretical problems. For these reasons this paper does not actually use the concept, although terms such as 'patriarchal relations' or 'patriarchal structures' are obviously derived in some way from the concept of patriarchy. However, such terms do not necessarily invoke a concrete base, a particular mode of production, or a rigid system of male domination. They imply a more fluid system, containing numerous contradictions and employing varying and various mechanisms and strategies in the exercise of power. Yet they still take patriarchy as a referent and so it is important, in the current climate, to justify their use through a brief discussion of the debate on patriarchy.

The debate on patriarchy

Central to the debate is the problem of definition.[2] As Beechey (1979) has shown, the meaning of patriarchy varies considerably according to the particular discourse within which it is located (for example, psychoanalysis, materialist feminism, and revolutionary feminism). Consequently, the debate is not purely semantic but also involves fundamental differences in approach to, and analysis of, sexual oppression. The concept of patriarchy poses the most severe problems for socialist or Marxist feminists precisely because the use of such a term is taken as involving the integration of marxian theories with concepts derived from opposing, or simply different discourses. There are two facets to this problem. One is that for socialist feminists 'patriarchy' implies a concept that is usually constructed as trans-historical rather than historically specific. Moreover, it is a term that usually implies the prioritizing of sexual oppression over class oppression while at the same time containing elements of a biological determinism or essentialism. All of these features are rejected or at least problematized by socialist feminists and in consequence there is a tendency to reject the term patriarchy altogether. Sheila Rowbotham's critique is one example of this rejection. She maintains that

> 'the word "patriarchy" presents problems of its own. It implies a universal and historical form of oppression which returns us to biology. . . . By focusing upon the bearing and rearing of children . . . it suggests there is a single determining cause of women's subordination.'
> (Rowbotham 1979: 970)

The second facet of the problem is of a different order. Patriarchy is not rejected just because it has become associated with particular analyses but also because it is constituted *within* specific discourses and cannot be isolated and used in conjunction with concepts derived from elsewhere. The most critical attack on feminists who attempt this marriage of concepts comes from Cousins who argues that

> 'it is frequently the case that there is an impossible recourse to two "materialisms": on the one hand, the concept of patriarchy with its corresponding causality of cause as origin and on the other hand, a Marxist concept of social totality with its corresponding causality of determination in the last instance by the economic. In so far as they locate a different "material basis" and do so through a different concept of determination, they cannot be coherently sustained as being complementary.'
> (Cousins 1979: 65)

Michèle Barrett has similarly been critical of such an enterprise, pointing out that although the concept of patriarchy is consistent within certain discourses, it becomes problematic within an analysis of sexual oppression under capitalism:

> 'It seems admissable in some contexts to refer to patriarchal ideology, describing specific aspects of male-female relations in capitalism, but

as a noun the term "patriarchy" presents insuperable difficulties to an analysis that attempts to relate women's oppression to the relations of production of capitalism.'   (Barrett 1980: 19)

Of course, this formulation is itself problematic in that it posits ideology as something that can cross discursive divides while the material is so differently constituted that it necessarily must remain within the discourse in which it was originally formulated. This aside, however, both Cousins and Barrett have identified a problem inherent within the rules of formal theory. I shall return to this point later, but first I want to look at one of the 'insuperable' difficulties encountered in attempting to integrate feminist concepts into marxian discourse.

The most common theoretical problem encountered by socialist feminism is the relationship between class and sexual oppression or, in other words, the relationship between the mode of production and relations of reproduction. Having rejected the primacy of gender relations, the problem has become one of how to formulate an analysis that either gives equal weighting to both, or more usually, to theorize the way in which patriarchal relations are ultimately subordinate to the mode of production, or to determination by the economic in the last instance. An example of the latter approach is McDonough and Harrison's (1978) paper 'Patriarchy and Relations of Production'. They posit two separate structures of oppression in which sexual oppression is subordinated to class oppression:

'Though women are placed simultaneously in two separate but linked structures, those of class and patriarchy, it is their class position which limits the conditions of the forms of patriarchy they will be objectively subjected to.'   (McDonough and Harrison 1978: 36)

Moreover, McDonough and Harrison further subordinate relations of reproduction to the relations of capitalist production by arguing that the former operates to sustain the latter.

'Thus the natural and material function of women to procreate for social use is transformed into two economic functions necessary to perpetuate the social relations of capitalist production.'
                                (McDonough and Harrison 1978: 34)

This element of a functionalist argument, in which relations of reproduction are seen to react to the needs of capital, is evident elsewhere in the work of socialist feminists. For example, Mary McIntosh (1978), while rejecting the concept of patriarchy as such, reproduces the same problem inherent in understanding the relationship between gender relations and capitalist relations in her analysis of the state. She argues that 'the state can initiate or guide changes in the family household system in relation to capital's need for the labour power of married women as well as in relation to the reproduction of the class in general' (McIntosh 1978: 279). Patriarchal relations are thereby theorized as changing according to modifications in the requirements of a separate or determining economic formation while women's experiences of patriarchal relations are mediated by their position in this alternative material structure. This adherence to a determination by the economic in the last instance has meant that patriarchy, or gender relations, are always depicted as somehow contingent upon another essentially economic structure, and that relations of reproduction are afforded virtually no autonomy other than those characteristics that are derived historically from a period prior to capitalist development.

Having raised these problems and pointed to the difficulties of referring to a concept of patriarchy, I do not want to suggest that these feminists are 'incorrect' in subsuming patriarchal relations to the mode of production. Nor is it my intention to develop a 'correct' position. Rather, I want to shift the debate away from the extremely formal terms in which it tends to be expressed. It is the way that correctness and incorrectness are at issue that is part of the problem that socialist feminists face. It might be useful to take an analogy to clarify this point. During the 1970s the domestic labour debate traversed similar ground. Feminists became preoccupied with the correct definitions of productive and unproductive labour, and use and exchange value. Undoubtedly, as Kaluzynska (1980) argues, part of this process was an attempt to make feminist theory respectable by showing that it could be integrated into Marxist theory. It is also probable that the debate was entirely necessary in order for feminist theory to progress. But in retrospect it was a sterile debate that could not be solved. The fact that housework was a valuable and unwaged activity was not ultimately affected by whether that value was synonymous with the concept of value as employed in Marxist analyses. Similarly, in discussing concepts like patriarchy or patriarchal relations there seems little point in attempting to justify their use by fitting them into an alternate discourse. But neither is the rejection of such concepts justified because they simply fail to fit.

The evaluation of these terms must be grounded on criteria other than whether or not they can be encompassed by Marxist theory. Moreover, if the criteria by which we evaluate the existence, relative influence, autonomy, or the ideological versus material content of patriarchy are founded upon rigid rules of formal theory rather than on concrete analysis, then feminist analysis will become increasingly academic and removed from feminist politics. The theoretical problems that 'patriarchy' has posed for so many feminists might be more revealing of the inadequacy and inflexibility of dominant schools of thought rather than an inherent incorrectness in the range of ideas and experiences embraced by the concept. If it were abandoned, as some feminists suggest, then feminist theory could be deprived of its major instrument of criticism against social, political, and economic theories that exclude the category of women and ignore the special nature of their oppression. It would also remove a symbolic concept that has provoked major developments in theorizing and understanding women's oppression and that reflects the necessary autonomy of the Women's Movement in the political sphere. As Alexander and Taylor (1980) have argued

'[Patriarchy] has helped us to think about sexual division – which cannot be understood simply as a by-product of economic class relations or of biology, but which has an independent dynamic that will only be overcome by an independent feminist politics.'

(Alexander and Taylor 1980: 161)

If patriarchy does come to constitute an obstacle to understanding the oppression of women then it should be modified. However, its inadequacy as an explanatory concept should not be judged in terms of its failure to reside within a Marxist discourse nor because it has most usually been constructed in terms of a biological essentialism or a universalism.

To understand more adequately the specificity of women's oppression it might be useful to turn away from trying to integrate the monolithic structures of capitalism and patriarchy and instead concentrate on specific instances of gender domination and its interrelation with factors of race and class. (It is for this reason that this paper does not refer to patriarchy as such but uses the concept of patriarchal relations, which is derived from the term patriarchy but which deliberately avoids constructing an alternate general theory to compete with existing formulations.) Although with this approach we may risk losing sight of the totality, this is by no means inevitable and it avoids the overwhelming problem of striving to produce a general theory grounded in the epistemological foundations of entirely separate discourses (Marxism and psychoanalysis, for example). Moreover, it is more likely to produce analysis of direct relevance to political action and strategy by the Women's Movement. In consequence, the way in which patriarchal relations are actually mediated or determined by, or are even determining of, features of a given mode of production can be analysed in their historical specificity rather than in terms of a generality that has no room for 'subtleties' (Rowbotham 1979) or contradictions.

Patriarchal relations and law

I now want to turn to the relationship between patriarchal relations and law. This relationship has traditionally been a focus of feminist interest although it has usually been expressed differently, for example in terms of law and sexual inequality or discrimination. Despite these differences, the role of law in reproducing, creating, or obscuring sexual inequality, and the potential of law to relieve women's oppression, has occupied feminists and social reformers for decades. For example, in *The Subjection of Women*, published in 1869, John Stuart Mill and Harriet Taylor placed considerable emphasis on the need for full legal equality for women. They argued that women should have the same formal legal rights as men in order to remove artificial obstacles to social equality. They also maintained that the legal subordination of women to men in marriage helped to create a situation in which 'each individual of the subject-class is in a chronic state of bribery and intimidation combined' (Gardiner 1976: 41). For Mill and Taylor, women's legal disabilities regarding property ownership and divorce led to conditions of virtual slavery that could only be relieved by granting women equal legal rights. Engels (1972), however, who has provided a more radical resource for feminists, argued that legal inequalities were a reflection of social inequalities and that consequently the law could not constitute a solution to oppression. Engels maintained that formal legal equality could not bring an end to patriarchal (or class) relations and that paper equality could do little to eradicate inequalities that were embedded in social and economic conditions. Nevertheless, he still treated the achievement of legal equality as a valid political strategy:

> 'the peculiar character of man's domination over woman in the modern family, and the necessity, as well as the manner, of establishing real social equality between the two, will be brought out into full relief only when both are completely equal before the law.'
>
> (Engels 1972: 82)

In other words, for Engels it was necessary to demonstrate that legal reform would not eliminate the structures of dominance that exist outside or beyond the law, but it was nonetheless important to lay bare both the error of the liberal position and the real basis of sexual domination by showing the ineffectiveness of legal reforms in transforming the social order. Engels, however, did not go on to substantially develop his ideas on women's oppression and the law, and most of the Marxist or radical analyses that have been produced over the last decade have been more concerned with the law and the state debate in connection with crime, wage-labour, or class relations than with patriarchal relations. However, feminists have maintained their interest in law, although most of the feminist literature in this area has concentrated on the social implications of legislation (for example, see Land 1976), or on the roles that law traditionally allocates to women (see, for example, O'Donovan 1979). As yet there is little material available on the relationship between law, the state, and the specific reproduction of patriarchal relations in ideological and material terms. The work that addresses itself to the nature of law as such has tended to depict it and its enforcement as sexist. The recognition that the judiciary tends to be a predominantly male group, the identification of laws (such as those on rape and prostitution) that are particularly oppressive to women, and the observation of statutes that exclude women or concede to them lesser rights, have led many feminists and sympathizers to perceive the law as biased or prejudiced against women. For example, Karen DeCrow (1975) argues that 'then as now, the rights of women were interpreted in the courts by men, and usually by men who had been raised in the male supremacist tradition' (DeCrow 1975: 187). The problem with this type of analysis is that it presumes that the courts operate fairly and in an unbiased way towards other litigants. It presumes the possibility of a juridical structure uncontaminated by other social institutions. Moreover, bias is seen to operate through the agency of individuals who implement or draft the law. This is not to say that individuals are insignificant to the process of law, nor to exclude the influence of the political and social views of individual judges and other legal personnel; rather this level of analysis is insufficient on its own. In Marxist theories of law this position (see, for example, Griffiths 1977), which tends to explain the class nature of the law in terms of the class background of the judiciary, has been consistently criticized (see Hall *et al.* 1978). As Picciotto argues

'While obviously factors such as the cultural and ideological background of judges are very relevant, it is inadequate to attribute the class character of a social institution simply to the social origins of those who control it. Most Marxists would agree that revolutionary change entails the transformation of the very character of social institutions such as the state and the legal system, and not simply the replacement of the personnel which operates them.'

(Picciotto 1979: 166)

Unfortunately there has been a tendency for the work of feminists or their sympathizers to analyse the law in this way. For example, Sachs and Wilson (1978) treat the all-male character of the judiciary, in combination with their class background, as the explanation for the operations of the law in relation to women. In particular they concentrate on the refusal of the judiciary at the turn of the century to allow women to be defined as 'persons', which in turn denied women access to the professions. This, they argue, was due to the judiciary's desire to protect the material interests of men against the threat of women leaving the home and securing well-paid employment.

'In the case of beliefs related to male domination, the argument would be that upper-middle-class men in diverse occupations shared an interest in keeping women as head servants at home and keeping them out of the ranks of competitors at work. In other words, men had and still have a material stake in resisting the emancipation of women.'

(Sachs and Wilson 1978: 11)

The judiciary as men are therefore understood as subscribing to sexist attitudes to protect their material interests. These views, which are specific to their gender and class and are not biologically determined, are reflected in their adjudications and in turn, according to Sachs and Wilson, render the law as a whole sexist. This raises problems for understanding legal change. For example, did masculine material interest change suddenly in 1919 prior to the introduction of the Sex Disqualification (Removal) Act? Moreover, is male interest a homogeneous concept that is so easily identified? It is in fact impossible to fully explain the way in which the law and the legal system serve to reproduce patriarchal relations by reference to the specific interests of its masculine members. As I argue below, some developments benefited some men at certain times, but other developments operated to undermine patriarchal authority within the family. Nevertheless, legal reforms have not managed to eradicate gender oppression and many legal practices still disadvantage women. This is the basis for another feminist position on law to which I now turn.

The failure of law to improve the social and economic position of women, even where it is expressly designed to do so (for example, the Equal Pay Act 1970 and Sex Discrimination Act 1975), and the outrage that many feminists feel over the outcome of rape trials, and the apparent unwillingness of law to protect women against domestic violence, have led to a situation in which law as a whole is implicitly taken to be an instrument of patriarchal oppression. Indeed it may seem difficult to avoid this conclusion particularly when considering issues such as rape, prostitution, and domestic violence. Moreover, there are similarities between this approach and certain Marxist analyses of class oppression in which the law is depicted, historically and currently, as a means of controlling the working classes through restrictions on unions and strikes, and through the biased interpretation of law by the judiciary. But this conspiracy thesis does not only rest on evidence of overt forms of oppression, such as legislation which permits a man to rape his wife, but also on legislation or legal practice that on the surface is non-sexist but in reality oppresses women. For example, DeCrow argues that

'Women have fared miserably under the law, not only in the decisions which went against us, but even in the cases that went "for" us; and we are deluding ourselves if we think that women can get justice in the courts. The record of court decisions, statutes, state constitutions, and legislative interpretations – all of these were written by men. And until they begin to be written by feminist women and feminist men, women will never achieve equity in our legal system.'

(DeCrow 1975: 3)

The idea that law simply favours the interests of men, and that legislation and legal practice are constantly guided by these principles, does not stand up to closer examination. There are three main problems with this approach. First, it ignores the historical process that can modify the consequences of legislation and is outside the control of the legal profession. For example, the Married Women's Property Act (1882) was hailed at the time by feminists as a very significant improvement in women's rights as it meant that a wife's property was not automatically vested in her husband. However, the 'separation of property' principle on which this was based, and the emphasis on strict legal ownership, became a source of injustice to wives with the post-war increases in divorce because so few jointly owned their matrimonial homes. Consequently, more husbands, who were sole legal owners, could turn their wives out of the matrimonial home on divorce because more couples were divorcing.

The legislators in 1882 could not have predicted that divorce would increase so dramatically and so the consequences of the Act some seventy years later cannot be simply attributed to them.

Second, the conspiracy thesis presumes a readily identifiable set of male interests that can be unambiguously served. Yet the issue of the custody of children on separation or divorce is an indication of how inaccurate this is. On the one hand the courts appear to favour the mother over the father in principle[3] because although the primary consideration must be the 'best interests of the child', those interests are usually identified with having a mother to look after the child's daily needs. In this way the courts reinforce the mothering role, although in the majority of cases they simply give judicial sanction to a *de facto* custody, as most children stay with their mothers when there is a breakdown (see Barrington Baker *et al.* 1977). The reinforcement of this role needs to be considered in the context of the considerable power it can give women within the politics of personal relationships. Prior to the 1925 Guardianship of Infants Act, women did not even have the same formal rights to custody as men, and until the post-war period it was common for adulterous mothers to be punished by being deprived of their children entirely.[4] In fact, the courts now distinguish between the 'bad wife' and the 'bad mother' and it is unusual for them to give custody to a father unless the mother neglects or abuses her children.[5] In consequence, while the law is reinforcing the ideology of motherhood, it has increased the power of mothers within the family.

Third, to assert that the law serves the interests of men ignores the impact of the class structure that mediates the consequences of legislation. For example, in awarding maintenance the courts can, and do, reduce a husband's income below subsistence level even in the knowledge that the Supplementary Benefits Commission will not raise his income because benefits cannot be used to pay a court order.[6] The interests of poor or low-income men are therefore not served at all by the enforcement of maintenance. Moreover, although the proportionate financial burden of maintenance payments may be less for middle- and upper-class men due to tax relief and wider margins of disposable income, they do not interpret the duty to maintain ex-wives as in their interests either. Indeed, pressure groups like Justice on Divorce argue that maintenance payments for ex-spouses are entirely unjust to men. It would seem therefore that in this area at least the law is serving the interests of the state in protecting the public purse, rather than operating to protect the interests of men as a category.

One major problem in analysing law has been the tendency to generalize from specific instances or cases. This process has disallowed evidence of contradictions or has treated them as examples of repressive tolerance rather than as potential critiques of the theoretical position that is espoused. There is therefore a need to return to the concrete and to re-examine legislation legal practice in specific, historical contexts. This is already occurring, especially in the area of labour and welfare law, but there is little work concentrating on family law. This is particularly problematic for feminism as the family, or the household, has been identified as central to an analysis of women's oppression. What follows is therefore an attempt to partially fill that gap by examining the development of family law, and in particular divorce law, in Great Britain during the 1950s.

Family law in the 1950s

The 1950s was a decade of particular significance for women as it represented a period in which ideologies of motherhood and a re-affirmation of women's domestic role became increasingly pronounced (see Wilson 1980; Birmingham Feminist History Group 1979). The War had a profound effect on Great Britain, and the immediate post-war years witnessed drastically increasing divorce and illegitimacy rates. At the same time there were fears about whether the population was adequately reproducing itself because the birth rate, despite the baby boom of 1947, was displaying a downward trend. The family became identified as a potential source of national stability, a buffer against rapid social change, and a mainstay of the social fabric. The Royal Commission on Marriage and Divorce, which sat between 1951 and 1955, consistently reflected this view. For example it stated:

> 'The Western world has recognised that it is in the best interests of all concerned — the community, the parties to a marriage and their children — that marriage should be monogamous and that it should last for life.' (Royal Commission on Marriage and Divorce 1956: 7)

The Royal Commission ultimately recommended that there should be no changes in the law on divorce and separation as the majority of its members were convinced that the harm done to social stability as a consequence of easier divorce would outweigh the misery experienced by individuals who were unable to divorce and remarry. The state, having identified the family as a key institution, operated at this time in a very direct fashion to maintain its stability. Attempts to liberalize the divorce law or to reduce the stigma of illegitimacy through parliamentary measures were all resisted or diverted by the Conservative Government during the 1950s, on the grounds that they would weaken the bonds of marriage and consequently the family, resulting in dire social consequences.

State policies that reflected the renewed importance of family stability had their parallels in psychological, psychoanalytical, and sociological theories that expressed in scientific terms the overwhelming social necessity of 'normal' nuclear family units. Moreover, such views could be disseminated to the general population through welfare agencies, such as health visitors and social workers, which were developing as professions in the post-war period. The family was the central focus for these professions, and their favoured neo-Freudian casework approach, coupled with the dominant functionalist view of the family, meant that 'modern' theories on child-care, interpersonal roles and relations, and child-development (particularly the significance of the mother's role) were brought into play and impinged on the lives of people who would never read Bowlby or Freud.

At a time when ideologies of motherhood and family life were at their height (see White 1970) and women still had a particularly weak status in the labour market in spite of the increasing numbers of working wives, the government postponed any developments in family law in an attempt to recreate a pre-war family structure. It was an attempt to use legislation to prevent social changes that were an outcome of fundamental economic transformations in post-war Britain. In so doing, a particular form of patriarchal relations was imposed on the family that was increasingly incompatible with the economic and social reality of family life and the needs of the economy. For example, divorced or deserted wives were not granted any rights to remain in the matrimonial home; they were not entitled to keep money they had saved out of their housekeeping, and their indirect contribution to the acquisition of family assets through domestic labour was not recognized at all. This failure to legislate in the 1950s consequently provides a clear example of the way in which the law was utilized to try to reproduce a family form in which women were maintained in a position of dependence upon male breadwinners during a period when the alternative of waged work was not a reality for many women, especially when they had children.

However, legislation, or the failure to introduce legislative reforms during this period, does not provide an adequate basis on which to analyse the law and its role in reproducing patriarchal relations within the family. It is equally, if not more, important to examine developments in case law that were not infrequently at odds with the legislation at this time. Unfortunately, the evidence of case law is also fairly partial and selection is not at all random. They are selected by lawyers for their legal rather than social significance, and consequently we do not have access to many cases that might have been more interesting to feminist research. Moreover, when using historical material it is very hard to assess how much the reported cases, especially those in the Court of Appeal, influenced the practice of lower courts that dealt with many more people. However, it seems likely that the restrictions on the courts that were able to exercise jurisdiction over divorce, and the relatively small numbers of judges who could preside over divorce cases at this time, meant that there would be a much greater control from the Court of Appeal, and the Divorce, Chancery and Probate Division than there is today from the Family Division of the High Court. Nevertheless it is important to be cautious about drawing too many conclusions from the evidence of case law.

Case law

The key cases that occurred during the 1950s can be broadly categorized into those concerned mainly with sexuality and the consequences of non-marital sex or homosexual behaviour, and those dealing with the division of property and property rights

SEXUALITY

Until the 1969 Divorce Reform Act was introduced in 1971, the most usual ground for divorce had been adultery. Indeed, the 1857 Matrimonial Causes Act, which first gave secular courts the jurisdiction to dissolve marriages, only allowed the ground of adultery or aggravated adultery as a basis of divorce. The history of secular divorce is therefore tied to evaluations of sexual or moral behaviour. New grounds were introduced in the 1937 Matrimonial Causes Act, namely wilful desertion, cruelty, and incurable insanity, but adultery remained the most common matrimonial 'offence'. In addition, the ground of cruelty often involved explicitly sexual elements such as homosexuality – or the refusal to have intercourse. Wives could also divorce their husbands on the grounds of rape, sodomy, or bestiality.

Much of the law on divorce was therefore concerned with establishing

'facts' about spouses' sexual behaviour and, although statutory provisions on the grounds of divorce were similar for men and women, in
practice the courts treated husbands and wives differently, and there
were different consequences to a finding of 'guilt' for the spouses. For
example, in the 1950s a wife's lover was routinely compelled by the
court to appear as co-respondent in the case. The husband could then sue
him for damages and could often recover any maintenance or the value of
property given to his wife as alimony by extracting it from her lover.
However, a husband's lover could only be made a respondent in unusual
circumstances and a wife could not sue her for damages. This particular
inequity, which could make a divorce on the grounds of adultery far
more threatening to a woman, was not fully removed until 1970 when
the Law Reform (Miscellaneous Provisions) Act was introduced. In the
1950s adultery by a woman was therefore still treated in terms of a
'property' offence by another man from whom damages could be
claimed.

Other aspects of sexual oppression involved questions of maintenance
and custody of children. Until the 1970 Matrimonial Proceedings and
Property Act, the law did not oblige a wife to pay maintenance to a
husband except where he was classified as insane and kept in hospital.
This lack of reciprocity, which was an inevitable reflection of the
economic dependence of wives, nonetheless focused judicial attention on
the behaviour of the wife as she had to 'earn' her maintenance (it was not
hers by right). The adulterous wife was rarely awarded maintenance
(Eekelaar 1978; McGregor 1970) even though the High Court was
entitled to award her some kind of subsistence. The magistrates' courts,
however, never awarded maintenance to an adulterous wife. Even if she
committed the adultery years after a deserting husband had left her this
was sufficient grounds for the court to revoke an order. Until 1960 this
practice was based on common law but the Matrimonial Proceedings
(Magistrates' Courts) Act introduced the principle into statute law. In
this way the courts operated a sanction over the sexual behaviour of
women during marriage but also extended this control beyond the *de
facto* marital relationship.[7] As a consequence, the separated wife had to
remain 'chaste' for life or she risked losing her right to maintenance.
Although many women probably did remain celibate when they were
legally separated, the effect of this legal practice was to make all
separated women into potential economic pariahs. As soon as they had a
sexual or an implied sexual relationship with another man they could be
forced into an economic dependence on him and the patriarchal marital

relationship was reconstituted. (Similar points have been made concerning the cohabitation rule.) It also encouraged a surveillance of women's sexual behaviour by separated husbands who had much to gain from discovering whether their wives had sexual liaisons.

However, the courts were quite capable of acting punitively towards husbands as well as wives and in consequence the operation of the law cannot simply be reduced to a notion of treating women unfairly. In fact, during the 1950s the courts were eager to enforce the husband's marital duty to maintain his wife or ex-wife if she was the blameless party. Moreover, the judiciary were not inclined to require a wife to go out to work to reduce a husband's maintenance order if he had been 'at fault' during the marriage.[8] In Rose v Rose, for example, Lord Denning actually stated 'it did not as a rule lie in the mouth of a wrongdoing husband to say that she ought to go out to work simply in order to relieve him from paying maintenance' (Rose v Rose [1951]: 29). In some cases, therefore, the courts recognized the economically vulnerable position of the wife and were not prepared to make her give up her 'wifely' role simply to suit her husband. But judicial perception of these issues varied considerably, and the most important feature of decisions in the 1950s appears to have been the question of morality and fault, and not the material situation of the woman involved.

Decisions concerning custody also provided occasion for the courts to exercise sanctions over behaviour identified as harmful to the family structure or the moral order (the two often being taken as synonymous). By the 1950s automatic father-right had been abolished but adultery and desertion could still lead to a mother losing custody of her children. However, by the 1950s the higher courts were reflecting the growing ideology of motherhood and began to assume that children, particularly young children, were almost always better cared for by their mothers.[9] It is interesting that this development did not constitute a replacement of father-right by mother-right but was rather a judicial recognition of the social significance of maternal socialization.[10] The focus of the change was therefore the child; it was not an equalization of men's and women's rights *vis-à-vis* the custody of children.

Judicial response to sexual incompatibility between couples also provides several instances in which legal practice can be seen as reproducing the patriarchal order within the family. Although there was no such thing as divorce on the grounds of incompatibility, in reality the grounds of cruelty was consistently stretched to cover these situations. It is therefore particularly revealing to note under which particular circumstances the judiciary were prepared to define behaviour as cruelty, and whether it varied according to the sex of the petitioner.

A refusal to have children nearly always constituted cruelty as far as the courts were concerned, even though it was then usually necessary to show that the behaviour was both deliberate and 'aimed at' the other spouse. The courts were therefore ready to define any thwarting of the 'natural instinct' to have children, whether it was due to the husband or the wife, as a form of deliberate cruelty. In one exceptional case Lord Denning maintained that a wife's 'unnatural' fear of childbirth did not amount to cruelty to her husband, but this case was out of step with usual practice at that time.[11] However, the courts were keen to point out that while granting wives divorce on the grounds that their husbands would not give them children, they would not do so if their husbands simply refused to have intercourse with them. In Walsham v Walsham the judge remarked 'mere abstention by the husband from intercourse could not amount to cruelty or give the wife any remedy even though it might injure her health' (Walsham v Walsham [1949] 1 All E.R.: 774). The courts were therefore only concerned with the fulfilment of a supposedly natural instinct and not with the issue of sexual satisfaction, at least where women were concerned.

During the 1960s the explicit question of sexual incompatibility started to come before the courts. In the 1950s the main issue had been reproduction and not sex *per se*. Unfortunately, it is difficult to determine whether this development reflects a change in the major concerns of married couples or simply a recognition by divorce lawyers of what the courts would tolerate. However, the shift from reproduction to sexual satisfaction reveals very different judicial responses to men and women. Essentially the courts were more ready to interpret a refusal to have intercourse on the part of a wife as cruelty, and therefore sufficient grounds for divorce, than they were to define a refusal by the husband as a cruel act.[12] In P v P the judge refused to accept that a refusal to have sex was of the same significance for men and women because of the essential difference in the roles the sexes were supposed to play during sexual intercourse. 'It cannot be said, I think, that a husband who refrains from intercourse "refuses to permit it". He is the positive partner in the act and, unlike a wife, more is required of him physically than mere permission' (P v P [1964] 3 All E.R.: 919). The judiciary apparently took the position that a wife could, and should, tolerate sex even if she did not want to, while for a husband it would be much more stressful to give his wife satisfaction unwillingly because he was the active, rather than passive, partner.

The extent to which the judiciary celebrated an ideology that treated sex as natural, and naturally different for men and women, as well as applying different standards to different people according to their gender, is also apparent in cases involving extra-marital sex or homosexuality. For example, where it was shown that a wife was a lesbian, or at least had a close relationship with another woman,[13] the courts readily interpreted this as cruelty, while a husband's rejection of heterosexual relations would not automatically lead to the granting of a divorce.[14] Similarly, where adultery or extra-marital liaisons were concerned, the courts were more permissive of men's behaviour than women's,[15] treating male sexuality as naturally less repressible while condemning women who moved outside their marital relationship for sexual satisfaction. It becomes apparent that the judiciary did not apply the various tests of, or the precise legal definition of, cruelty in every case. Indeed the extent to which the criteria of 'intention' or 'behaviour aimed at' were utilized seems to have depended on a prior moral evaluation of the specific case which in turn was based on dominant ideologies of female and male sexual and reproductive needs. But in addition women were seen as bearing an extra responsibility, and hence culpability, as far as the moral standards of the community were concerned. In 1950, in a warning about the dangers of sex equality addressed to the National Marriage Guidance Council, Lord Justice Denning maintained that 'the morality of the race depends on the morality of the womenfolk' (Denning 1950: 3). Women, therefore, were placed in an entirely different position to men by the courts as far as sexual behaviour was concerned.

PROPERTY

Until the end of the 1950s the development of the law on matrimonial property in this century was based on the principle of 'separate property', derived from the Married Women's Property Act 1882. Essentially this meant that a wife was allowed to own her own property, but the ownership was established according to the name in which assets were held. Consequently, the predominant practice of conveyancing matrimonial homes into the sole name of the husband, even though it was intended as a shared asset, rendered the man the sole legal owner. Unless a wife could prove that she had paid part of the deposit or mortgage repayments she had no strict legal rights at all. If she had paid for items of consumption (such as food or clothing) from her wage, thereby freeing a husband's wage to pay for the mortgage or items of furniture, the courts would not necessarily treat these as contributions to be weighed against each other because they would mainly be concerned with who actually paid for the remaining assets. A wife who had not earned a wage at all during her marriage was in an even weaker position as the courts took no account of domestic labour as an economic contribution. Indeed it was not until the 1964 Married Women's Property Act that wives were even allowed a share of the money they may have saved out of their housekeeping allowance. Prior to this all of the allowance was deemed to belong to the husband because it came out of his wage and was not treated by the courts as a family income. In effect, the wife who was not earning a living by waged work and who had no previous savings or inherited wealth, had no access to money of her own. She was only permitted to use her husband's money for the duration of their marriage. In addition, the husband had no statutory duty to maintain his wife while cohabiting with her; maintenance became a requirement only after cohabitation ceased.

Until the 1958 Matrimonial Causes (Property and Maintenance) Act was passed, it was legally possible for a husband to desert his wife and children, to sell the matrimonial home (if it was conveyanced into his name) and thereby render them homeless, while pocketing all the proceeds of the sale himself.[16] In fact even after this Act was passed husbands still managed to virtually evict wives and children by raising loans on the matrimonial home and becoming bankrupt or by selling to an 'innocent' third party.[17] In the house-owning sector wives therefore had very little security, even though in practice the courts (especially Lord Justice Denning) attempted to mitigate against the injustice experienced by wives with dependent children.[18] The rented sector was, however, no better as the majority of tenancies then, as now, (see Todd and Jones 1972) were held in the husband's name only, and the courts had no powers to order the transference of tenancies. The non-working wife was therefore exceptionally vulnerable, and divorce or separation could be disastrous for her if she had no alternative source of income or shelter.

Ironically the situation regarding matrimonial property was a consequence of matrimonial legislation that treated men and women as if they were 'equal'; the law presumed women and men were equally 'free' to work or stay at home, to own property individually or jointly, and to acquire assets. Yet, as the Rt. Hon. Sir Jocelyn Simon, who was President of the Probate, Divorce and Admiralty Division, maintained, 'any law of matrimonial property which does not recognise and make allowances for the difference in general economic function of husband

and wife is likely to operate with great unfairness on married women' (Simon 1964: 18). While the law in the 1950s apparently treated men and women as equal, in practice it disadvantaged wives who were in a structurally different position to husbands. In spite of recognizing the economic dependence of wives as far as maintenance issues were concerned, the law at this time refused to provide any legal security or adequate property rights to wives. In so doing it reinforced the husband's duty to maintain his dependants, preventing them from becoming burdens on the welfare state, and simultaneously reinforced women's economic vulnerability outside the family structure. But it did not allow women any legal remedy to the situation by recognizing their contribution to the economic structure of the family in the form of domestic labour. In the 1950s, therefore, the divorced or separated woman's economic security was largely to be achieved by remarriage or, in other words, re-entry into the patriarchal family structure that had in part created her insecurity. Unless she had a strict legal claim to property, her rights on divorce were entirely contingent upon the courts' moral evaluation of her behaviour. Although the courts spoke of a woman's right to be housed and maintained by her husband, it was a right that was vested in a legally constructed moral evaluation of whether she was a 'deserving' wife. The court therefore had tremendous powers in this respect and it was this power which meant that individual judges, depending on their moral values, could act more or less punitively towards women who failed to fulfil their 'marital duties'.

Conclusion

Matrimonial law in the 1950s represents a structure in which judges were given maximum discretion to decide cases on their individual merits. This structuring of the judicial process had particular consequences for women and wives who had few formal legal rights, because it rendered them open to a moral evaluation before they could achieve any economic security on divorce or separation. Thus, during the fifties, there was a conflict between those courts that followed the principle of formal legal rights only (and were thereby very harsh on women) and other, usually higher, courts that tempered this harshness with a moral dimension. The latter would go against the 'letter of the law' to provide justice to the 'deserving' wife, and she was usually the woman who had conformed most closely to the 1950s' ideal of wife and mother.

This gradual improvement in the judicial treatment of wives was therefore grounded in an appreciation and celebration of a patriarchal family structure where the wife carried out domestic labour and child-care for love. However, this performance of her duties merely gave a moral claim, and not a legal right, to claim an interest in matrimonial assets.

As with many other areas of law reform the developments in family law in the 1950s present contradictions. The recognition that principles of 'strict legal ownership' and 'separation of property' disadvantaged women because of their material position in the domestic economy did not, as a consequence, provide women with rights based on that specific position. Neither were women in a position to demand those rights (for example, the right that domestic labour should be treated as an economic contribution to the family economy) precisely because they were pre-dominantly situated within the domestic sphere with a weak involve-ment in the waged economy. The law in the 1950s, while improving marginally the economic position of some women on breakdown, essen-tially operated to reproduce this social organization, providing legiti-mation for ideologies of motherhood and dual moral standards, and recreating the economic dependence of women. It was able to sustain a family form that was oppressive of women, particularly working-class women,[19] because ideological developments in post-war Britain stressed the role of women within the domestic sphere. It was only with the major changes in women's employment pattern in the 1960s (along with significant ideological changes) that a new wave of legislation on family law became possible. In the 1950s, however, the law, coinciding with state policies, attempted to stabilize a family structure that had its origins in pre-war Britain and which was predicated upon a specifically patriarchal division of labour between the sexes.

Notes

1 At the time of writing this paper, the author was a Research Fellow at the Centre for Criminological and Socio-Legal Studies at the University of Shef-field. The research was funded by the SSRC.
2 I cannot go into this debate in as much detail as is really required as that would involve writing another paper. However, I think it is useful to select certain points for discussion.
3 The exception to this are those cases where the mother is a lesbian. This issue is further complicated by judical reaction to homosexuality. For case law on recent custody decision (not involving lesbians) see W v W (1976) *The Times* November 26; D v D (1976) Fam. L. 6, 149; Re K (Minors) [1977] 2 W.L.R. 33.

4 This is extremely rare now although in one case in 1975 (B v B (1975) *The Times* May 15) Lawton L J gave custody to the father, who was a clergyman, because the mother's adultery would affect their moral upbringing. He stated that if women who left their husbands took the view that romantic love would triumph over all and there was no danger of losing their children, it was right that it should be brought home to them that there was a grave danger of their doing so. This case is, however, considered 'bad law' and is not followed.

5 In Willoughby v Willoughby [1950] P184 CA Singleton L J stated, 'I have yet to learn that the fact a woman commits adultery prevents her in all circumstances from being a good mother' (P184).

6 The courts increasingly recognize that such punitive orders are pointless as men fail to pay or give up working. The tendency now is for the man to pay an amount that he can manage and will not object to paying, and to supplement the wife's income from the SBC. In this way the state avoids creating more 'burdens' for itself by maintaining the man's incentive to work.

7 In one case (Chorlton v Chorlton [1952] 1 All E.R. 611) a husband attempted to have his maintenance order discharged when his divorced wife had sexual intercourse with another man. Although he did not succeed, the reason for his failure is interesting. The court ruled that it was not adultery because the man concerned was not married at the material time. The fact that the woman was herself no longer legally married did not enter into discussion. In this way the courts left it open for future husbands to try to exercise similar control over their ex-wives.

8 Rose v Rose [1951] P29; LeRoy Lewis v LeRoy Lewis [1954] 3 W.L.R. 549.

9 Willoughby v Willoughby [1950] P184 CA.

10 This is reflected in the sociological and psychological literature of the decade that emphasized not only the importance of socialization but also the centrality of the mother's role in the process.

11 Fowler v Fowler [1952] 2 TLR 143.

12 Compare P v P [1964] 3 All E.R. 919, and B(L) v B(R) [1965] 3 All E.R. 263 with P(D) v P(J) [1965] 2 All E.R. 456, and Evans v Evans [1965] 2 All E.R. 789.

13 Gardner v Gardner [1947] 1 All E.R. 630; Spicer v Spicer [1954] 1 W.L.R. 1051.

14 Bohnel v Bohnel [1960] 1 W.L.R. 590 CA.

15 Compare Cox v Cox (1952) 2 TLR 141, with Sapsford v Sapsford and Furtado [1954] 3 WLR 34.

16 Stewart v Stewart [1948] 1 KB; Roberts v Roberts [1953] CPL 23.

17 National Provincial Bank v Ainsworth [1965] AC 1175.

18 In fact Lord Denning and the Court of Appeal stretched statutory enactments to provide some protection for wives. His generous interpretations of the law, which recognized the plight of a number of wives, were eventually overruled by the House of Lords in 1965. The Court of Appeal was therefore acting in an independent fashion.

19 This was because the magistrates' courts, which were used predominantly by working-class women, operated a more rigorous moral standard, particularly with regard to adultery, than the higher courts.

References

Alexander, S. and Taylor, B. (1980) In Defence of 'Patriarchy'. *New Statesman* February 1: 161.

Barrett, M. (1980) *Women's Oppression Today*. London: Verso.

Barrington Baker, J., Eekelaar, J., Gibson, C., and Raikes, S. (1977) *The Matrimonial Jurisdiction of Registrars*. London: SSRC.

Beechey, V. (1979) On Patriarchy. *Feminist Review* **3**: 66–82.

Birmingham Women's History Group (1979) Feminism as Femininity in the Nineteen-Fifties? *Feminist Review* **3**: 48–65.

Cousins, M. (1979) Material Arguments and Feminism. *m/f* **2**: 62–70.

DeCrow, K. (1975) *Sexist Justice*. New York: Vintage.

Denning, Lord Justice (1950) *The Times*. May 13: 3.

Eekelaar, J. (1978) *Family Law and Social Policy*. London: Weidenfeld & Nicolson.

Engels, F. (1972) *The Origins of the Family, Private Property and the State*. New York: Pathfinder.

Gardiner, J. (1976) A Case Study in Social Change. In *Patterns of Inequality*. Open University Unit 32: D302. Milton Keynes: Open University Press.

Griffiths, J. A. C. (1977) *The Politics of the Judiciary*. London: Fontana.

Hall, S., Critcher, C., Jefferson, T., Clarke, J., and Roberts, B. (1978) *Policing the Crisis*. London: Macmillan.

Kaluzynska, E. (1980) Wiping the Floor with Theory – A Survey of Writings on Housework. *Feminist Review* **6**: 27–54.

Kuhn, A. and Wolpe, A. M. (1978) *Feminism and Materialism*. London: Routledge & Kegan Paul.

Land, H. (1976) Women: Supporters or Supported. In D. Leonard Barker and S. Allen (eds) *Sexual Divisions in Society: Process and Change*. London: Tavistock.

McDonough, R. and Harrison, R. (1978) Patriarchy and Relations of Production. In A. Kuhn and A. M. Wolpe (eds) *Feminism and Materialism*. London: Routledge & Kegan Paul.

McGregor, O. R., Blom-Cooper, L., and Gibson, C. (1970) *Separated Spouses*. London: Duckworth.

McIntosh, M. (1978) The State and the Oppression of Women. In A. Kuhn and A. M. Wolpe (eds) *Feminism and Materialism*. London: Routledge & Kegan Paul.

Mitchell, J. (1975) *Psychoanalysis and Feminism*. Harmondsworth: Penguin.

O'Donovan, K. (1979) The Male Appendage – Legal Definitions of Women. In S. Burman (ed.) *Fit Work for Women*. London: Croom Helm.

Picciotto, S. (1979) The Theory of the State, Class Struggle and the Rule of Law. In B. Fine, R. Kinsey, J. Lea, S. Picciotto, and J. Young (eds) *Capitalism and the Rule of Law*. London: Hutchinson.

Rowbotham, S. (1979) The Trouble with Patriarchy. *New Statesman* 21 December: 971–72.

Royal Commission on Marriage and Divorce 1951–1955 Report (1956) Cmnd 9678. London. HMSO.

Sachs, A. and Wilson, J. H. (1978) *Sexism and the Law*. Oxford: Martin Robertson.

Simon, J. (1964) *'With All My Worldly Goods. . . .'* Holdsworth Club Presidential Address. University of Birmingham.

Todd, J. E. and Jones, L. M. (1972) *Matrimonial Property*. London: HMSO.

White, C. (1970) *Women's Magazines*. London: Michael Joseph.

Wilson, E. (1980) *Only Halfway to Paradise*. London: Tavistock.

12

Rejoinder to Carol Smart

ERIKA SZYSZCZAK

The feminism that developed in the 1960s in the form of the Women's Movement believed that recourse to the law could achieve a degree of liberation for women from the traditional roles allocated by society. It became apparent, however, that token and piecemeal legislation was inadequate to secure any major change in womens' position in society and this has resulted in a lack of direction for the Women's Movement. In the late 1970s and 1980s, therefore, the feminist movement has sought a clarification of the particular role that law plays in defining and maintaining a certain status for women within contemporary capitalist society.

As Carol Smart points out, both law and the family have been central to feminist politics and represent a major concern and focus for struggle. The theme of her research can be seen as legitimate for several reasons. Historically the 1950s was a reactionary period for women. They were the formative years of the Welfare State, the implementation of the Beveridge proposals, and, implicit in them, the ideology of women's dependency in the family. The decade also saw the reluctant return to the home for many women who had been drawn into the labour market out of necessity during the war years and who had shown they were capable of undertaking jobs traditionally allocated to men.[1]

The subject-matter is of interest in that the family has been traditionally viewed as a primary place of socialization. The family situates women in a contradictory position; they are given security and play a powerful role in reproducing and maintaining social relations while being subject to the implicit notion of dependency and its concomitant restrictions. It is these inherent complexities within the present family structure, maintained in law and through both its legal and quasi-legal agents such as social workers, that the Women's Movement itself has not theoretically analysed.

The approach taken by Smart has several advantages. While she recognizes that the relationship of law to the family is complex in itself, the relationship of law to patriarchal relations is even more diffuse. Thus in the same way that it is not possible to apply adequately the straight functionalist argument that the family form is beneficial to capital, so analysis that posits law as a tool of patriarchal oppression is too simplistic. Smart concentrates on an analysis of ways in which law represents a specific ideology that can result in oppression for women while at the same time giving them a particular and venerated status within society. To pin-point specific discrimination is a first step towards questioning and then restructuring women's traditional roles.

The relative dearth of socio-legal research in this area has been reflected in the types of literature that have emerged since the recent revival of feminism in the 1960s. There has been an emphasis on and around practical rights books such as Gill's and Coote's (1972) *Women's Rights*, leading to more informal self-guides on a localized level by women's groups. The other resort has been to rhetoric such as 'the law discriminates against women' and linked to emotional terms such as 'biased' or 'sexist'. This is not to say that work such as that of Sachs and Wilson is worthless. Clearly, judicial bias needs to be identified. Smart alludes to the fact that since 1945 family law has been shrouded in judicial discretion and that this allows for highly individualized rulings. The personal prejudices and assumptions of the law agents should be acknowledged especially since the peculiar nature of English law allows the judiciary to be specialists in virtually all branches and prejudices will permeate throughout the law (see Griffith 1981). A notorious example is Lord Denning, who is seen in family law as the champion of deserted wives. However, if one looks at pronouncements in a case from the family law arena with one from a recent application for equal pay, one sees how prejudices work both ways because of assumptions made of women's role in society. In a case concerning maintenance after divorce, Lord Denning assumed that

'When a marriage breaks up there will thence-forward be two households instead of one. The husband will have to go out to work all day and must get some woman to look after the house — either a wife if he remarries or a housekeeper if he does not. He will also have to provide maintenance for the children. The wife will not normally have so much expense. She may go out to work herself but she will not usually employ a housekeeper. She will do most of the housework herself perhaps with some help. Or she may remarry in which case her new husband will provide for her. In any case when there are two households the greater expense will, in most cases, fall on the husband than the wife.'[2]

These fundamental assumptions of women's role can also be seen in the more recent case of Worringham and Humphries v Lloyds Bank.[3] This case was brought by two female employees claiming that the pension scheme operated by Lloyds Bank was discriminatory in that it was not obligatory for female employees under the age of twenty-five but was obligatory for all male employees. To equalize salaries, Lloyds Bank paid male employees under the age of twenty-five an extra 5 per cent on their gross salary which was immediately deducted and paid to the trustees of the pension fund. While there may be some economic credence to his points we again see Lord Denning engaging in a neat role of sex-stereotyping: 'The young women under twenty-five are often birds of passage. They come for a short time and then fly off to get married and bring up their children. The men are usually long-stayers. They make their careers at the bank until they retire', Smart has produced a much deeper analytical piece of research than has been undertaken previously of a specific role allocation developed in law. Clearly, constructive approaches to research such as the move towards gender-neutral legislation suggested by O'Donovan (1979) can only be successfully implemented if one starts with Smart's premise, that is, to explain in an historical context the gender role allocation of law and its consequences.

Elizabeth Kingdom (1981) has supported the approach adopted by Smart in other areas of her work in that it disseminates the effects of law and gives an indicator as to which of the present-day struggles for particular rights are worth pursuing. Although I think a more constructive strategy is required than merely exposing the effects of law in a static, descriptive way, Kingdom argues to the contrary. She sees a dynamic in that the approach points the way to measures that may be necessary to overcome past and present discrimination against women.

Smart's use of the analytic tool of patriarchy is, however, weakened by her own exposition that today there is a divergence of opinion as to what the term means. Given this central definitional problem I feel she could have defined her approach more rigidly and explained more distinctly what patriarchal relations are being reproduced and the consequences, and why they are a significant focus of attention for research on women. This is particularly important since the patriarchy thesis has been challenged by Adlam (1979) and, more recently, by Donzelot (1980).

By moving from a notion of universal and transhistorical patriarchy to a specific historical analysis, Smart has gone some distance in mitigating the Marxist disquiet with a patriarchal approach. However, in her paper there is no theoretical explanation as to why law is chosen as a focus of attention. I think it is necessary to have more analysis of the role of law itself given its interrelationship with the present-day Women's Movement. The present disquiet with the effectiveness of law to achieve parity of treatment between men and women has led some members to question the usefulness of law in eradicating the private and ideological oppression of women within the material and cultural values of society.

Law has been the traditional focus of attention for groups within capitalist society who wish to assert rights. The choice of law in itself is political in that it is both a primary and final arbiter for society. One of the values of looking at law to explain how it maintains and institutionalizes sex differences is that it tends to reflect in some kind of synchronism, albeit not always directly, other social and institutional assumptions. However, it tends to have a coercive force not equalled by other institutional arrangements, not simply in the sanctions it imposes but also in the expectations it inculcates and demands from society. Thus in family law we see the perception of the 'good' wife who is able to obtain maintenance on divorce, and the 'good' mother who is allowed custody of her children. Even more far-reaching are ideals of the standards of behaviour required from marriage seen, for example, in the judicial responses to divorce petitions. An additional constraint is imposed in that we ourselves then measure our behaviour and other people's in terms of these expectations. I feel that a clearer analysis of the role of law and its effects for society, and in particular its relationship to the capitalist mode of production, is necessary if any adequate thesis for political strategy for the Women's Movement is to be advanced.

Furthermore, it is useful to look at the relationship between law and the state, in particular the role law plays in individualizing claims. The 'rights' within the family must surely be the greatest form of fragmentation (see Holloway and Picciotto 1978). The ideology of 'divide and rule' inherent within the capitalist system puts the onus upon the individual to pursue his or her claims and this distracts from collective political action. The ineffectiveness of the present Sex Discrimination and Equal Pay Acts (see Snell 1979; Coussins 1980) serves to reinforce the point that if the Women's Movement is to have a constructive political strategy then a wider analysis and appraisal of law and the state are necessary. This is especially relevant for present discussions on how the Alternative Economic Strategy (AES) can be modified to meet women's particular needs (Gardiner 1981). Without this the practice of adding on feminist demands to the AES can at best only result in fragmentary reforms.

While the institutionalization of sex differences and its impact for women is of great importance, by concentrating on these effects the Women's Movement must be aware of the accusation of political irrelevance. Taking the category of women out of the totality of social relations may lead to a distorted analysis of the legal process in which, for instance, the oppressive nature of family law for women is given greater weight than its treatment of minority groups such as homosexuals and members of ethnic groups not professing the Christian commitment to monogamy. Nor can it be assumed that the variety of struggles against forms of legal oppression can all be assimilated under one banner, particularly when the nature of that oppression differs even for one particular law, when the potential gains for changing the law differ for the various groups, and where different groups have different bargaining strengths in changing the law.

Notes

1 This paper is part of a larger project looking at family law since 1945 and therefore the question of whether decade divisions are justified is not discussed.
2 *Wachtel v Wachtel* [1973] Fam. 72 and 94.
3 *Worringham and Humphries v Lloyds Bank* [1980] 1 C.M.L.R. 292.

References

Adlam, D. (1979) The Case Against Capitalist Patriarchy. *m/f* **3**: 83–102.
Coussins, J. (1980) Equality for Women, Have the Laws Worked? *Marxism Today* January: 6–11.
Donzelot, J. (1980) *The Policing of Families*. London: Hutchinson.
Gardiner, J. (1981) Feminism and the Alternative Economic Strategy. *Marxism Today* October: 24–30.
Gill, T. and Coote, A. (1972) *Women's Rights*. Harmondsworth: Penguin.

Griffith, J. A. G. (1981) *The Politics of the Judiciary*. London: Fontana.

Holloway, J. and Picciotto, S. (1978) Towards a Materialist Theory of the State. In J. Holloway and S. Picciotto (eds) *State and Capital, A Marxist Debate*. London: Edward Arnold.

Humphries, J. (1979) Class Struggle and the Persistence of the Working Class Family. *Cambridge Journal of Economics* **I**: 241–58.

Kingdom, E. (1981) Sexist Bias and Law. *Politics and Power* **3**: 97–114.

O'Donovan, K. (1979) The Male Appendage – Legal Definitions of Women. In S. Burman (ed.) *Fit Work for Women*. London: Croom Helm.

Sachs, A. and Wilson, J. H. (1978) *Sexism and the Law*. London: Martin Robertson.

Snell, M. (1979) The Equal Pay and Sex Discrimination Acts: Their Impact at the Work Place. *Feminist Review* **1**: 37–57.

Name index

Subject index